TO THE RAMPARTS

TO THE RAMPARTS

*How Bush and Obama Paved the Way
for the Trump Presidency, and Why It
Isn't Too Late to Reverse Course*

RALPH NADER

edited by Jim Feast

SEVEN STORIES PRESS
New York • Oakland • London

Seven Stories Press
140 Watts Street
New York, NY 10013
sevenstories.com

College professors and high school and middle school teachers may order free examination copies of Seven Stories Press titles. To order, visit www.sevenstories.com or send a fax on school letterhead to (212) 226-1411.

Library of Congress Cataloging in Publication Control Number: 2017061017
ISBN 978-1-60980-847-1 (hardcover); ISBN 978-1-60980-848-8 (ebook)

Printed in the USA.

9 8 7 6 5 4 3 2 1

Contents

Opening Orientation

You don't get more old school than me. I still type on an Underwood typewriter, not a computer. Moreover, I still read print newspapers and keep files of clippings from them to glance through when I'm thinking of past events. Taken aback when Trump was elected, like many who barely believe such a walking illustration of ignorance and arrogance could step into the White House, I pulled out my clippings and began paging through them. First I looked at the campaign, how Clinton fumbled and how Trump managed to finesse every revelation of his lack of civility, truth, and common sense. Then I leafed back further to examine the primaries, noting how much Sanders was ignored by the media and shut out by the Democratic National Committee apparatus, how the Republican field was filled with tired retreads, and how Trump managed to shift his TV persona of being a winner into the political field. But trying to fathom the unfathomable—why voters, with the key help of the Electoral College, voted for such a manifestly phony, dissembling character to sit in the Oval Office—I found I had to pull out older volumes of clippings and consider the Obama regime. Could it be that the Democrats and Obama laid the groundwork, at least indirectly, for the triumph of reality TV over reality?

As I glanced over the clippings, I began to conceive of a project for this book. I have already spoken and written about the dismaying change in American newscasting, whereby only the most recent, flashy events are covered and, worse, are explained by *superficial* reference to other *recent* events. Trump's success in his presidential run is ascribed to stupefied voters or Hillary's lackluster performance or the economic malaise of the working class. *No digging beyond the topsoil!*

Folks, it's below the topsoil that the real causes lurk. It's there that the groundwater percolates. In this book, I will examine some profound causes that brought us Trump. Sure, he got quite a few voters to believe his hype. But was that because they were desperate, or was it because they didn't see Hillary as representing their interests? And if the latter was the case, was that because Hillary was an unsympathetic person, who didn't project a caring, "I feel your pain" attitude in the manner of her husband, or was it because she was not putting herself behind a people's agenda? And if the latter, was this a recent phenomenon or was it presaged by an equally mandarin, albeit better concealed, viewpoint held by Obama?

One thing that elected Trump, as everyone agrees, was the voters' sense of *total disillusionment with Washington politicians.* But the faces on TV make it sound like this disillusionment is as perennial as complaints about the weather. Not so.

My reading of the past few years is that this disenchantment is neither ever-present nor without cause. Sure, Trump profited big-time from it, but he hardly caused it. Sure, the Republicans, holding their noses, got in line behind Trump, but, again, I don't cite them for the voters' discouragement. No, *the voters' sense of abandonment rests solidly on the shoulders of the Democrats who let them down—big time.*

I say this because the Democrats are the ones to whom the public has *historically* looked for progressive change. It was they, not the Republicans, who promised to be in their corner. It was a Democrat, Roosevelt, who ushered in the New Deal, with public works programs to help with massive unemployment, and who established regulations over the banks, brokers, and other industries. It was a Democrat, Johnson, who fought for and signed major civil rights law to counter the disenfranchisement of black people. It was the Democrats who had the people's back and at least tolerated trade unions from the 1940s on.

Historically, the Republicans were the hard-bitten apostles of the so-called free market and the handmaidens of wealth. The poor woman and man pinned few hopes on the Republicans. It was the Democrats to whom the voting public turned when hankering for fairness, compassion, or progressive change. And when the Democratic Party *fell away* from pushing hard for reform, the public *fell hard*. It fell into disillusionment with politicians, and this generalized into such despair that they were willing to elect as president a reassuring charlatan wrapped in an American flag.

This book will show how Barack Obama, Hillary Clinton, Eric Holder, and other Democratic leaders in the Obama years turned a deaf ear to many of the cries of the people. This was shown most graphically in that, in his eight years as president, Obama jetted around nearly five hundred times to fat-cat political fund-raisers where he could glad-hand the wealthy, but paid nary a visit to the grass roots to spend learning and galvanizing time with ordinary people or their national civic groups nearby in Washington, DC.

But here is what I'm *not* saying. *I'm not equating Democratic Party policies with those of the Republicans.* We have to make a distinction here, which will be outlined in this book. Take the areas in which there is continuity between the previous Democratic regime and the new Trump administration, such as foreign policy and the Democrats' unwillingness to nail or punish corporate criminals. Set that against where there is a clear difference between parties, as in the Democrats' signing of the Paris climate accords and Trump's repudiation of them, or the two administrations' views of civil rights, with the Democrats pushing to extend their protection and Trump rolling it back.

Even with their espousal of environmental and consumer protection, civil rights, Social Security, and elderly Medicare, the Democrats hardly went vigorously on in favor of these progressive values when they were in power; Obama's failure to raise the frozen $7.25 per hour minimum wage is just one of the more egregious examples. To put this more graphically, I would say that if I were grading the parties on their ability to deliver on laws that would change the lives of the vast populace for the better, I would flunk them both. The Democrats would get a D+ and the Republicans an F. Neither could be proud of their record.

Now Trump, although he had no intention of helping a public whipsawed by lost jobs, diminished access to justice, and broken infrastructure and services, did sense their cries. But *it was the Democrats' dereliction of duty that made them cry out.* And not only did the Democrats refuse to bring about changes the voters were hungering for, such as reining in corporate crime and power, but they seemed to *have nothing to offer.* Even now, with Trump sitting in the Oval Office or puttering about on the golf links, Democrats are bashing him and also not championing a positive agenda.

Let me say it plainly: For success, *policy must precede message.* You can't win with "Vote for me." You can only win with "Here are my policies and my record, vote for me." Come up with authentically backed policies that improve the lives of the people, and the public will vote you into power. A lesson seemingly lost on most current Democrats, including their lax leaders.

To be in the parlous state we are in, with a predatory, cunning, unstable ignoramus in the White House, there must be deep-rooted causes, not just "topsoil" ones. The two points I will stress are that, as mentioned, the Democrats failed to fully push for a people's agenda, and, also of great importance, Obama and the Democratic Party failed to keep the party itself up to fighting strength, so it lacked the grassroots organization and brain trust needed to resist the Republican onslaught.

Let's look at how this happened step by step over the years, but *not* as a historical exercise. Not at all. My hope is that by writing this book I will open Democrats' and other progressives' eyes to the many values shared by the Left and Right, values like the desire to end corporate welfare and convert to a renewable energy (solar) economy. I will show that the way to defeat Trump going forward is to embrace (not marginalize) issues such as raising the minimum wage. These are the real-life policies that win big in elections and the voters' hearts. Democrats, as well as some third-party candidates, have to get behind these policies. It's a question of do or just further fade away.

PART I

THE DEMOCRATS SQUANDER THEIR OBAMA VICTORY

Let's look back at how the Democrats failed year after year to deliver the goods to the people. Without forgetting that the Democrats are superior to the Republicans in some key policy areas, here I will highlight their repeated fumbling of the ball on significant issues. Surrounding the deepening corporate state, for example, they largely let Credit Suisse off the hook for its willful lawbreaking, which defrauded the IRS. I will describe policies in which the Democrats' activities and corporate funding were largely in line with the Republicans', such as Obama's willingness to ignore the Constitution and federal laws when it came to conducting armed forays into other countries.

Let's begin with an overview, in which I will look back at the first sobering setback the Democrats faced after Obama's triumph in 2008. By the 2010 elections, the first held after Obama became president, the Republicans were already turning the tide. There were large election losses in 2010, following a Republican gerrymandering coup, with the loss of the House of Representatives to John Boehner and Eric Cantor. This could hardly all be blamed on Obama's lackluster campaign support for Democratic candidates. The real culprit was that the two parties were vigorously dialing for the same commercial dollars to finance their campaigns. The resultant inhibitions and self-censorships brought the parties' real agendas closer together.

It seems to me the only way for the Democrats to win would have been to *fundamentally* separate themselves from Republicans by shifting their sights from big donors to the less well-off general public. Directions that would have saved them then might be prescribed right now as an agenda to battle back against Trump. These are eight initiatives that would allow the Democrats to landslide the Republicans in any election.

In 2010 *none* of these initiatives, which many who speak for the public were advocating, were embraced by the Democrats. To begin immediately on my central theme, it was the failure to pick up on populist measures that led to a defanged Democratic Party being run over by Trump's pseudo-populist rhetoric. Here's what I think should be the central platforms of a recharged Democratic Party, apart from facilitative electoral reforms, discussed later.

First, resurrect the old Democratic Party's historic role in safeguarding the federal minimum wage and labor laws from Republican dissolution. It is astonishing that, since the passing of Senator Ted Kennedy, there have been so few lawmakers campaigning to raise the minimum wage or even restore it to its previous levels. If the minimum wage of fifty years ago—$1.60 per hour—were adjusted for inflation, today it would amount to about $11 per hour. A long-overdue minimum wage hike would pour tens of billions of dollars into job-producing consumer demand during this recession. It would end a decades-long windfall for employers who have been increasing prices and their own salaries while receiving many tax breaks and subsidies. To objections from the curled-lip House Republican Eric Cantor, before his primary defeat in 2014, I would say, "You don't believe workers in your district should make as much as workers made fifty years ago when their productivity was half what it is today, Eric?"

Second, announce the filing of legislation that declares immediate drafting of all able-bodied and age-qualified children and grandchildren of all members of Congress any time that branch or the president plunges us into another war. Besides forcing Congress to pay attention to its constitutional war-declaring and -funding responsibilities, this legislation would hold our humble public servants accountable by making them share the risk presently foisted on a few million, mostly low-income, families.

Third, cut the huge, bloated, wasteful military budget, really end the endless boomeranging wars with astute diplomacy, and channel the expected savings into repairing and renovating America through a national public works program with good-paying, non-exportable jobs.

Fourth, among other popular tax reforms, shift much of the tax burden onto activities that Americans do not like, such as pollution, huge Wall Street speculation, corporate crime waves, and profits from systemic product waste. Even ExxonMobil supports the idea of a carbon tax, which would help the environment. The motto: tax what you burn before you tax what you earn.

Fifth, announce a national energy conversion campaign based on efficiency and renewables. The only true energy independence comes from the sun in its many manifestations. Shifting America's energy policy will create more local employment and small businesses down to the community-neighborhood levels. Goodbye to the planet-destroying toxic fossil fuel and fearful atomic energy cartels.

Sixth, crack down on corporate and governmental violations of our Constitution and laws. No more no-fault government and no more no-fault big business. If the law is to be observed in the streets, then it must be observed in the suites. People are being pushed around, disrespected, defrauded, injured, and given the runaround by arrogant corporate bureaucrats using nameless, robotic, and tyrannical "fine print" contract barricades. There have to be accountabilities that the abused citizens can invoke in addition to directives through tort law civil actions.

Seventh is a proposal to establish a public national complaint-handling system using the Internet to help consumers, taxpayers, and workers, for a change. You've got a beef with your incommunicado insurance company, bank, energy company, pension fund, cable company, hospital, telephone/gas/water/electricity provider, or some government agency you can't even get through to file your complaint, then refer to the national system. Think of the reductions in dread and anxiety levels for millions of families.

A complaint-handling system will save billions of hours from being wasted on just trying to get through, much less get your complaint heard. It will also be a good way for policy makers to detect patterns. Patterns lead to deterrence, fewer complaints, and fewer dollars lost. What a way to show sensitivity to the daily irritations and frustrations of the American people!

Eighth, create a democracy movement based on simple facilities for people who choose to band together in various roles. In return for what you, the taxpayers and consumers, have had to spend to bail out and otherwise pay these large companies, the Democratic Party should press for inserts in their billing systems and those of corporate carriers inviting you to voluntarily join and contribute dues to a nonprofit of your choosing, staffed with full-time champions who are directly accountable to you. No results, then no dues next time, and no taxpayer subsidies. These facilities would shift some institutional power from the haves to the have-nots. This idea is working in Illinois for residential utility consumers through their nonprofit group, Citizens Utility Board (CUB).

I bring up these proposals to open the book because, as we'll see, it was Obama's and the Democrats' failure to push forward such proposals, empowering the general populace and giving them more of a voice in their own government, that contributed to many voters' indifference to this party's later attempts to get out the anti-Trump votes.

1.

Upgrading Minimum Wage of Minimal Interest to the Democratic Party

Foremost among these demands is that the Democrats get on the stick about boosting the minimum wage. A telling story will make clear both my advocacy for this long-overdue initiative and the sad ripple effect the Democrats' inaction has had.

With two colleagues, I was meeting with Richard Trumka, head of the AFL-CIO, in his office, which is within sight of the White House. This must have been in about 2012, after some years under Obama's presidency. My remarks were something on this order:

"I know you say great things about raising the minimum wage on your websites and in the literature you hand out. But can't you see that's not enough? Why doesn't your federation *take major action on this?* You could devote money and put a lot of union muscle into this campaign. Of course, this would especially benefit non-union workers, but you claim your organization represents all workers. Moreover, as you know, lifting the minimum wage does help all workers, even those who are not directly affected."

Trumka's reply was candid, if devastating. He moved a little in his chair, making a gesture toward the White House. "Why should I flail away [on this issue] before he takes the lead?"

This was hardly a valid excuse on his part, but it does underline how Democrats' lack of enthusiasm for increasing the minimum wage has played the pivotal role of a damper here, drawing down the fire of others (in unions and grassroots advocacy groups) who might have gotten into the fight more heavily if they saw the Democrats on the hustings.

Of course, it was not Obama alone who defaulted here; though Trumka may have pointed to him—it was the whole Democratic Party that was blameworthy. Riding in on a progressive wave, the Democrats seemed primed to boost the wage minimum wage after Obama's election. The minimum wage did rise in 2009, but this was no thanks to the people in power—it was part of a previous graduated increase that had started in 2007, led by the late senator Ted Kennedy. Since that time no movement has been seen, although Obama had eight years to fight for it.

Talking to Democrats should serve as a reminder of why the wage needs to be raised and what a no-brainer it is to fight for this increase if you want to pick up a landslide victory over Republicans.

Historically speaking, it was the way this winning issue with voters was sidetracked and ignored that helped pave the way for Trump. It's not as if the arguments in favor of a minimum wage hike were lacking. Just consider these points:

1. A wage increase represents pure fairness for millions of hard-pressed American workers and their families. Over 70 percent of Americans in national polls (which includes conservative voters) support a minimum wage that keeps up with inflation.
2. There has been a drumbeat of local politicians embracing a wage increase. In 2012 eighteen states raised minimum wages, to $11 an hour—to reach $13.50 by 2020.
3. Since at least 1968, businesses and their executives have been raising prices and their salaries (note: Walmart's CEO makes

over $11,000 an hour, plus lavish benefits!), but they have not increased the wages of their increasingly more productive workers, whose federal minimum wage is lower in purchasing power than it was fifty years ago.

4. The tens of billions of dollars that an adjusted minimum wage will provide to consumers' buying power will create more sales and more jobs. Aren't economists always saying the most important way out of the recession and the investment stall is to increase consumer spending?

5. Most independent studies collected by the Economic Policy Institute show no overall decrease in employment due to a minimum wage increase. Most studies show that job numbers overall go up. The landmark study rebutting claims of lost jobs was conducted by professors David Card and Alan Krueger in 1994.

6. Many organizations with millions of members are on the record as favoring an inflation-adjusted increase in the federal minimum wage. They include the AFL-CIO and member unions, the NAACP and La Raza, and hundreds of nonprofit social service and religious organizations. They need to move from being on the record to being on the ramparts.

7. With some Republicans supporting a higher minimum wage, even under Trump, a push in Congress would split the iron unity of the Republicans. This issue may also encourage Trump voters to vote for Democrats. A Republican worker in McDonald's or Walmart or a cleaning company still wants a living wage to support his or her family.

Looking back, calls by grassroots organizations and others for a raise in the minimum wage during the Obama years left Democrats unmoved. However, to his credit, Rep. Jesse Jackson Jr. (D-IL) in June 2012 did introduce the "Catching Up to 1968 Act of 2012" (H.R. 5901)—legislation to raise the federal minimum wage to $10 per hour.

While a few true congressional champions of the people such as Jackson got behind the issue—it's also something I was involved with advancing at the time—the majority of Democrats kept reveling in the "swamp."

When Jackson introduced the measure, the minimum wage was $7.25, way below the unrealistically low federal poverty definition of $18,123 per year for a family of three. Adjusted for inflation, the 1968 minimum wage today would be about $11.00 per hour.

Together with Rep. John Conyers (D-MI), Rep. Dennis Kucinich (D-OH), and Robert Weissman, president of Public Citizen, at that time I was pleased to be with Rep. Jackson at a news conference to explain this long-overdue necessity for millions of hard-pressed, working Americans of all political persuasions.

The purpose of the minimum wage, first enacted in 1938 under President Franklin Roosevelt, was to provide a minimally livable salary. This implied at least keeping up with inflation, if not with new living expenses not yet envisioned seventy-five years ago. While businesses like Walmart and McDonald's have been raising their prices and executive compensation since 1968, these companies have received a windfall from a diminishing real minimum wage paid to their workers.

Since the minimum wage has not been raised, these arguments are still totally valid today. The economics behind the Jackson bill are strongly supportive of moral and equitable arguments. Most economists agree that what our ailing economy needs is more consumer demand for goods and services, which will create jobs. Tens of billions of dollars flowing from a higher minimum wage will be spent by poor families and workers almost immediately.

At the time Jackson's bill was introduced, I said, "Were the Democrats in Congress to make this a banner objective for election year 2012, their adversaries, Speaker John Boehner (R-OH) and Senator Mitch McConnell (R-KY), would not be able to hold one hundred percent of their Republicans on this popular issue. That means the bill's backers could override these two rigid ideologues—so-called public servants—who make over $100 per hour off the taxpayers, plus generous pension, health insurance, life insurance, and other benefits."

But the bill was defeated, another nail in the Democrats' platform.

If Trump is to be defeated, the Democrats have to get out of bed with the fat cats. While these big-bucks characters are upping their obscene pay every year, they often seem to be more circus proprietors than businesspeople because they pay their workers so little.

This whole debate over the minimum wage also casts a spotlight on the big corporate bosses who pay themselves $11,000 to $20,000 per hour and the harm such avarice causes their own companies' workers and shareholders, as Steven Clifford has so brilliantly documented in his new book, *The CEO Pay Machine.*

If the Democrats want intellectual heft to rebut the carping, craven objections of the corporatist think tanks and trade associations (headed by bosses making big-time pay themselves), they cannot do better than to refer to the work done by the Economic Policy Institute in Washington, DC.

More income for the poor means less child and family poverty, which means less reliance on federal outlays for the poor to survive. The big companies—for example, Walmart—take advantage of federal aid, steering some of their employees to food stamps, Medicaid, and housing and energy assistance programs. As Terrance Heath noted in an op-ed in Nation of Change: "So all of us are subsidizing the wealthy owners and executives of Wal-Mart, McDonald's, and Target."

A 2012 report by the respected National Employment Law Project (NELP) titled "Big Business, Corporate Profits, and the Minimum Wage" said that "the majority (66 percent) of low-wage workers are not employed by small businesses, but rather by large corporations with over 100 employees." The fifty largest employers of low-wage workers are mostly "in strong financial positions." And note this finding by NELP: "The top executive compensation averaged $9.4 million [in 2011] at these firms." This means that the bosses, before taking a lunch on January 2, made more money than a minimum wage worker makes in a year. Talk about the corrosive effects of inequality: the top 1 percent took 93 percent of the nation's income growth in 2010, according to Holly Sklar of Business for a Fair Minimum Wage.

Enlightened business leaders are ready to support the Democrats on this minimum wage increase initiative. Years ago in 2012 Jeff Long, a senior vice president of Costco, gave the obvious reasons that the retrograde corporatists ignore: "At Costco, we know good wages are good business. We keep our overhead low while still paying a starting wage of $11 an hour. Our employees are a big reason why our sales per square foot is almost double that of our nearest competitor. Instead of minimizing wages, we know it's a lot more profitable for the long term to minimize employee turnover and maximize employee productivity and commitment, product value, customer service and company reputation." The starting wage at Costco in 2017 was $13.

Those in the corporate oligarchy who oppose a higher minimum wage have no moral standing whatsoever. Many of the nation's corporate giants pay no income tax or very little, far less than a cab driver. Between 2008 and 2013, GE's effective tax rate was 9 percent, despite earning over $34 billion. GE paid *no* federal income tax for several years prior to 2008. It is hard for companies making record profits, paying executives record pay, and spending trillions of dollars on unproductive stock buybacks to enhance their own compensation packages to have any credibility on this subject. The Democrats should have enacted legislation for a higher minimum wage during Obama's eight years. Instead, startling as this may seem to readers wearing rosy spectacles, Obama kept regressively lowering his estimate of the dollar amount needed for an eventual minimum wage boost.

In his 2013 State of the Union speech, Obama said, "Let's declare that in the wealthiest nation on Earth, no one who works full-time should have to live in poverty, and raise the federal minimum wage to nine dollars an hour."

Wait a minute. In 2008, Obama campaigned to have a $9.50 per hour minimum wage by 2011. In 2013, he said he would settle for $9.00 by 2015! Going backward into the future.

Apparently, it didn't matter to Obama that at that time the US had the lowest minimum wage of any major Western country (Australia's was nearly $15.00, France's was over $13.00, and the Canadian province of Ontario's was $10.25—all of these countries also have health insurance for all).

It didn't matter, as I mentioned, that two-thirds of low-wage workers in our country work for large corporations such as Walmart and McDonald's, whose top CEOs make an average of $10 million a year plus benefits. Nor did it matter that corporations like Walmart have had to pay workers much more in places like Western Europe than in the United States (where these companies got their start), and that they've still made good profits where the minimum wage is higher.

Haven't you noticed how few workers there are now in the "big box" chain stores compared to years ago? Well, one Walmart worker today does the work of two Walmart workers in 1968. That is called a doubling of worker productivity. Yet many of today's

Walmart workers, earning less than $11 an hour, are making significantly less than their counterparts made in 1968.

My collaborators and I got out on the picket lines around the time of Obama's insufficient minimum wage proposal, and we demonstrated at shopping malls where Walmart had established giant stores. We noted that one million Walmart workers were making far less, in inflation-adjusted dollars, than what Walmart workers made in 1968.

In 1968 Walmart was run by its founder, the legendary Sam Walton, who started with one store in Rogers, Arkansas. Sam had to pay his workers wages that were worth much more than wages today because the law required him to do so.

The clenched-jaw opposition to raising the minimum wage continues, led by a punishing US Chamber of Commerce and a consortium of CEOs. Low wages paid by stores that service poorer people eventually translate into less money spent in those stores, since the consumers are strapped. Internal emails leaked from Walmart in 2013 indicated the company's awareness of this vicious circle, and executives expressed concern about the spending level of the low- to middle-income shoppers the company depends upon most.

"Where are all the customers? And where's their money?" bewailed Cameron Geiger, a Walmart senior vice president. What Walmart's bosses themselves are coming to realize is that raising their workers' wages would lift the income of millions of workers, who in turn would spend some of that extra cash at Walmart stores.

Even H. Lee Scott, who was once Walmart's CEO, told company executives that "the US minimum wage of $5.15 an hour has not been raised in nearly a decade ... it is out of date with the times. ... Our customers simply don't have the money to buy basic necessities between paychecks."

A few years ago, feeling the heat from environmentalists, high-level Walmart managers visited the late Ray Anderson, the pioneering CEO of Interface Corporation in Atlanta, the largest carpet tile manufacturer in the country. Mr. Anderson was the corporate leader in taking recycling and reduction in pollution to unsurpassed levels, while regularly cutting costs. Doing well by doing good!

The cutting costs part attracted their attention. These managers are now among the executives running Walmart, and the changes they have made—reducing excessive packaging materials, saving on water and energy, and increasing recycling—have brought Walmart lower costs and public praise.

Yet when it comes to their workers—euphemistically called "associates"—Walmart bosses can't seem to absorb the evidence that paying them $15 an hour would reduce the company's notoriously high worker turnover and improve productivity and morale.

At the store level all over the US, Walmarts are full of surveillance cameras, monitoring not just the customers but also the stores' workers. Walmart security guards are stiffer than Army MPs. They are programmed to be the private police, keeping away peaceful demonstrators in so-called private shopping malls that were built on tax preferences and abatements.

If I had written our then-president on this issue in 2013, I would have put it this way:

Dear President Obama,

June 25 marks the seventy-fifth anniversary of the federal minimum wage law in the United States, known as the Fair Labor Standards Act. When President Franklin Delano Roosevelt signed this legislation, his vision was to ensure a "fair day's pay for a fair day's work," and to "end starvation wages."

More than seventy-five years later, there are 3.3 million Americans working for pay at or below the federal minimum wage. More extensively, *30 million low-wage workers are making less today, adjusted for inflation, than they did forty-five years ago in 1968.* They are working for a wage that does not even reach the federal poverty line for a family of three, and they cannot afford basic necessities like food, housing, transportation, and health care.

Each year that the federal minimum wage is not increased, you and Congress are effectively telling low-wage workers that they are not worth as much as they were the year before, and each dollar they earn gets stretched even further due to the effects of inflation.

Here's where you can make a moral executive decision. Under your watch, federally contracted low-wage workers walked off the job and participated in some of the largest strikes the nation's capital has seen in recent years. Despite the fact that they worked on company contracts for the federal government, they were still being paid poverty wages—some even explained that they were being paid *less than* the federal minimum wage, which invites your administration's immediate investigation! This is disgraceful; the federal government should be providing a shining example of fair and just treatment of their contracted workers for other employers to follow.

If you issued an executive order to get this done, you would move closer to FDR's vision of ending "starvation wages." Your decision would set a good example for the rest of the business community to follow and provide the type of determined and persistent leadership that our country's political class has lacked for decades. Especially if you also limit CEOs' and other top executives' pay on substantial federal contracts to an amount no greater than twenty-five times their entry-level wage. (Famed management guru Peter Drucker believed in this range as prudent corporate practice, and legendary investor Warren Buffett has been very critical of excessive executive compensation.)

According to a recently released report from Demos, a public policy organization, the federal government indirectly employs the largest number of low-wage workers in the country. More even than Walmart and McDonald's combined. The *Washington Post* reported in June 2013 that a study from the National Employment Law Project (NELP) surveyed a sample of 567 federally contracted jobs. Seventy-four percent of federal contract workers surveyed earned less than $10 per hour, 58 percent had no employment benefits, and 20 percent depended upon some form of public assistance.

In the absence of any serious movement in this disconnected Congress to increase the minimum wage, you have the potential to exert significant influence on the wages paid to millions of low-wage workers in this country. With a simple executive order, you can fix this shameful deprivation. I urge you to sign an executive order mandating that federal contract workers be paid no less than $10.70 per hour (the inflation-adjusted equivalent to 1968's minimum wage). Is this too much to ask of you?

This is, of course, no substitute for a lasting federal minimum wage increase. But an executive order provides you with an option to avoid the morass in Congress and effect real positive change in millions of low-wage workers' lives and to effect that change *now*. I hope that you will recognize and seize this opportunity.

This small but important example will make it easier for you to push Congress for a greater and bolder minimum wage increase than you did in your State of the Union address.

On the anniversary of the federal minimum wage, you should sign an executive order raising the minimum wage of those working for the federal government through corporate contractors. It is the federal government's—and your—responsibility to set the example for the rest of the country to follow.

When Franklin Delano Roosevelt signed the Fair Labor Standards Act into law, he showed courage in the face of the Great Depression as well as considerable opposition and criticism from businesses. Is it not time for you to leave your mark, to show Americans what type of president you want to be remembered as, and to be a leader on this issue? Millions of workers throughout the country deserve a minimum wage that, at least, catches up with that of 1968.

I'm sending a copy of this letter to Michelle Obama, who is said to have your ear.

Sincerely,

Ralph Nader

That letter might give you the erroneous impression that Obama was the only Democrat heel-dragging on this issue. Since Obama is out of office, let's turn to the highest Democrat in the House at this very moment, Rep. Nancy Pelosi (D-CA), the House Minority Leader.

Is her track record any better? I should say not. Glance over some of the innocuous mailings she sends to her constituents. Under the heading "Employment," there is *no mention* of boosting the minimum wage even to $10.10 per hour, though Rep. Pelosi ostensibly supports it. The closest option to check was "inadequate/or no salary increase."

This Pelosi mailing, uninspiring and defensive, is another product of the party's overpaid political consultants, who have failed them again and again in winnable House and Senate races against the worst Republican Party in history. These consultants, as former Clinton counselor Bill Curry notes, make more money from their corporate clients than from political retainers. Slick, arrogant, and ever reassuring, these firms are riddled with conflicts of interest and might just as well be Trojan horses.

The point here is more far-reaching than it may seem. Not only do the Democrats personally ignore the burning issue of the minimum wage today, but they have also set up an infrastructure that blocks their own access to vital information. By relying on consultants, they lock themselves into a corporate-dominated echo chamber where the cries of the people go unheard.

As you may know, Obama did eventually sign an executive order advancing the minimum wage to $10.10 an hour, *but this only applied to federal contract workers.* This was a step in the right direction and one place where he passed on a positive signal to the future—if not, going by Trump, the immediate future.

So, a livable minimum wage remains agenda item number one for a remade Democratic Party.

2.

When the People Were in the Streets, the Dems Were Behind Their Desks

A remarkable failure by Obama and the Democrats was their inability to take up the programs advocated by grassroots uprisings, such as those in Wisconsin or Occupy Wall Street's national actions in 2011, which signaled the younger public's disgust with the status quo and demand for progressive policies. Failing to join the Occupiers on the ramparts contributed further to the Democrats' loss of legitimacy. And, on the other side, the Occupiers' disinterest in politics, perhaps due to the lack of spirit shown by the Dems, proved fatal to advancing their agenda against inequality more concretely.

Imagine, if you will, in the following fictional narrative, how plutocrats—and perhaps the Democrats themselves—viewed the Occupy movement:

Stetson J. Bradford III met up with his fellow CEO, F. Reginald Lawless, for a brow-to-brow lunch at the Penthouse Reverie Room high above Wall and Broad Streets in New York. As charter members of the forty-year Corporate Supremes Club, they had serious business to discuss before Thanksgiving weekend in 2011.

Topic numero uno: Is the Occupy Wall Street movement and its sister occurrences all around the country the precursor to the giant peoples' upheaval that they and their brethren have feared ever since Wall Street collapsed the American economy in 2008 and sent the bill to the taxpayers?

Over their large whiskey sours, savored prior to consuming their lobster lunch, they shared their innermost thoughts in nearly whispered tones under grave visages:

Bradford: "I'm worried, Reg, that this could be the big one all of us have been dreading. It is always the ruffians and the demagogues who are the vanguard. Remember the sacking of the Bastille?"

Lawless: "I beg to differ, Stet. It is always the middle class that raises the banner of revolt, at least in the past couple of centuries. These people down at Zuccotti Park aren't relatable to the majority of people, what with their sanitation problems and the worsening influx of the homeless and vagrant crowd in their public spaces."

Bradford: "Maybe so, but look at the daily mass media coverage of these people calling themselves the ninety-nine percent. I've never seen anything like the TV and newspaper reports on these encampments everywhere. Also the polls show they have more support for their message against inequality than the Tea Partiers did for their push. Recall what Abraham Lincoln said about what can be done with the 'public sentiment.'"

Lawless: "Let me calm you, Stet. We know from our disheveled infiltrators what is going on in all these encampments, except maybe small ones like in little Niles, Michigan. It's our sort of jobs program. Barring some flashy provocation caught on video, like a sneering Wall

Street trader kicking a child beggar into the gutter, the Occupiers will soon be frozen out of the public consciousness by both the coming winter and a bored media."

Bradford: "Why do you say this? They must be very determined to stay and sleep in these uncomfortable parks night and day, setting up tables for first aid, legal aid, and even a library. You know, libraries with radical materials have historically been dangerous influences on the multitudes."

Lawless: "Time out, Stet. Let me show you why they are here today and why they will mostly be gone tomorrow. Do they have leaders? No, they proudly reject leaders and even the very trait of leadership. Show me a successful movement or business or union drive, and I'll show you leaders. It can't happen without leaders to give form and direction over time, no matter how unpleasant they may be."

Bradford: "You're right up to a point. But a mob doesn't have to have leaders. It just has to have emotion, motive, a target, and a sudden jolt or spark that can come from anywhere."

Lawless: "With modern, high-tech crowd controls, mobs can be spotted very early with corner surveillance cameras and dispersed in a hundred ways. Our good police—public and private—get tremendous adrenaline bursts in the face of advancing mobs.

"But, Stet, there is more. Occupy has no agenda or program that millions can relate to. Sure 'inequality, inequality, ninety-nine percent, ninety-nine percent' makes a good slogan because people believe it to be true. After all, don't we, really? But without either a religious fervor or some kind of ideological 'ism'—both out of tune with the times—all they're left with are actual reforms for which they have little interest or patience. This is where they're really missing the boat and the vehicle of change. Because they detest politics."

Bradford: "What do you mean?"

Lawless: "Stet, why do you think our higher class spends so much money and time and influence on Congress? Because that is where the desired action or inaction resides in our governmental system. Arouse Congress and we get tax breaks, subsidies, bailouts, contracts, giveaways, and little enforcement of the laws against us. Freeze Congress and the masses get nothing—worse, they get rollbacks of protections for their economic well-being, health, safety, children, and their shrinking pay, jobs, and pensions.

"So, by detesting politics, they avoid surrounding members of Congress at their offices back home or on Capitol Hill. They avoid the single victory that could be theirs in this election year. And that is raising the federal minimum wage to over ten dollars per hour to where it was, inflation adjusted, in 1968.

"And that doesn't count the doubled worker productivity since that time and the resultant wealth, which our class has regularly appropriated for our coffers. You know, Stet, over seventy percent of people polled support keeping the minimum wage raises current with inflation. Hundreds of groups of influence want it—at least they are on the record, like the AFL-CIO, the National Council of La Raza, the NAACP, social service and religious charity groups—just about everybody.

"But none are on the ramparts. Like a long train ready to go without the fuel. Guess who can supply the fiery energy? The Occupiers. And they can galvanize all these groups to pour it out on members of Congress. Imagine the gratitude of thirty million workers who are now making ten dollars or less per hour for their families. Imagine a victory in an ocean of gridlock to whet the appetite of tens of millions of Americans for more of what they call their 'fair share.' Once the masses really get moving, as you know, they're hard to stop."

Bradford: "Well, why don't they fight for all those tens of billions of dollars that can go into the pockets of these people now earning between $7.25 and $10.00 per hour? Seems obvious. And it's not going to affect our business. Our golfing buddies may be making several thousand dollars an hour, but none of our employees make less than $10.00, except maybe the janitors in our offices."

Lawless: "I'll tell you why, but pardon the repetition. The Occupy people are increasingly bickering among themselves in an imploding way while dispiriting themselves with the endless democratic assemblies where even majority rule is out. They do not want leaders, or a real-life agenda that needs the raising of funds. They are tussling with anarchists and hired provocateurs, and they disdain any discipline, much less paying full-time organizers. One might uncharitably say they are not serious about anything described as victory—even one right in their hands that would bring them great admiration."

Bradford: "You almost make me feel sorry for them. They could be our sons and daughters, Reg. They mean well."

Lawless: "Let them mean well. I'll give them that, any day, so long as they don't mean much more of anything else. How about another whiskey sour, Stet, before we get

to those credit default swaps in Greece."
Bradford: "Cheers, Reg. Cheers."

Those liberal Democrats who ignored Occupy had the excuses, which to them seemed like good ones, that Occupy's agenda was unclear or that it had no representatives to talk to; the occupiers had no reason not to listen hard to concerned citizens and activist groups that came forward with valuable proposals and fact-based discussions of pressing issues. Along with many others, I offered advice to these political leaders in letters.

This included many letters to Obama, none of which were answered. In fact, this gave me the idea, since I thought others might be interested in my thoughts even if he wasn't, of publishing these letters in book form. And, once they were published, I sent him a letter about it. Here are the contents:

LETTERS TO A PRESIDENT: RETURN TO SENDER

April 8, 2015

President Barack Obama
The White House
1600 Pennsylvania Avenue NW
Washington, DC 20500

Dear President Obama,
I am enclosing a copy of *Return to Sender: Unanswered Letters to the President, 2001–2015* (Seven Stories Press), which contains over one hundred letters that I sent to you and President George W. Bush (from 2001 to 2015). They were almost entirely unanswered and unacknowledged.
One of these letters asked you about the White House's policies regarding letters it receives. I raised this

issue early in your first term with the director of the Office of Presidential Correspondence, Mike Kelleher, who said there was no specific policy regarding responses, but that he would get back to me after the Office of Presidential Correspondence considered the matter. He did not.

Citizen correspondence is important both for you as president and for our nation's citizens. For the citizens, it is an opportunity to circumvent the barriers presented by the media and governmental institutions to directly access the White House. For presidents, letters help, as you have said, escape "the bubble" (e.g., the ten letters from the people you read each evening). Letters from citizens also convey ideas and observations that alert you to conditions, issues, and urgencies at hand and occasionally provide you with an opportunity to publicly discuss the points raised by an ordinary citizen who penned such a letter.

Just the other day, when you were visiting Ohio, a chance question to you from a person in the audience elicited your view that such mandatory voting as exists in a number of other democracies, such as Australia, would "be transformative." Those few words alone will stimulate a public discussion in an era of low voter turnout, which might include weighing the pros and cons of having a binding "None of the Above" (NOTA) option for voters.

Letters can be very valuable in asking questions that offer you an opportunity to respond on matters or issues not ordinarily addressed by the press corps or officials or members of Congress. (Incidentally, the first annual review of the White House press corps and its interaction with you appears in the March/April 2015 issue of the *Columbia Journalism Review*, funded by the Helen Thomas Fund. She would like that!)

There are many other potential benefits of sending letters to presidents. For example, during Secretary of Energy Steven Chu's entire four-year term, many of the major antinuclear power groups could not obtain a meeting with him. Although he had met numerous times with representatives from the nuclear industry, he would not respond to our letters and calls so that he could listen and respond to the empirical positions and recommendations of experienced groups whose overall views he did not share. I wrote asking if you could intervene and urge him to meet with us. Also, you needed to know about this rejection by your secretary of energy. There was no response.

I understand that you and your staff send courtesy responses to event invitations around the country and you respond to letters about highly visible issues, such as the auto industry bailout, with form letters. Of course, you also respond to political allies and affluent supporters in some fashion. But that still leaves out many letters reflecting the knowledge and position of many engaged Americans who should neither be stonewalled nor overlooked.

Here is what I recommend:

1. Issue a policy on responding to letters with whatever classification you choose to make, so that people can know what to expect.

2. At the very least, these active citizens should receive an acknowledgment of receipt of their letters and emails. This is what the prime minister of Canada does, regardless of whether the letters are supportive or critical. Additionally, the prime minister refers letters to the appropriate ministry for further review. Without even an acknowledgment, citizens might become cynical and/or stop writing.

3. Have your staff select the letters with ideas, proposals,

or suggestions that they think would contribute to a good annual public report to the American people. Include critical letters that point out shortcomings. This has a salutary effect on "the bubble," and goes beyond the few letters that all presidents use as political props.

I'll conclude with an invitation, which you may wish to consider (again), that appears in my previously mentioned book. On May 4, 2012, I sent a letter to you urging you to address a proposed gathering of a thousand leaders from the nonprofit civic community at a hotel ballroom near the White House, at your scheduled convenience. These leaders head diverse groups supporting justice for consumers, workers, small taxpayers, the poor, and other environmental, health, housing, transportation, and energy causes. These organizations represent many millions of Americans across the country who support them with donations and volunteer time. There was no reply. Then I sent the letter to first lady Michelle Obama's East Wing. Her staff at least responded, writing that you had no time. Well, what about any time this year?

Jimmy Carter addressed just such a group of civic leaders after his election in 1976. The event was very successful and helped give greater visibility to this very important civic sector in our society. I found your White House's response to the invitation disingenuous, inasmuch as you have traveled across the country and the world directly promoting by name for-profit US companies and the jobs these companies create. (In India, it was for Boeing aircraft and Harley-Davidson motorcycles.) Well, the nonprofit sector employs millions of Americans, and its growth and services are good for society, are they not?

I hope you and the family will enjoy perusing this book and possibly gaining some insights and ideas that will enhance your service to our country, its people, and its interactions with the rest of the world. This volume could have been called a "bubble buster," except we could only wonder whether these letters were ever given access through that self-described encasement.

Sincerely yours,
Ralph Nader

In September 2016, the civic gathering to which I invited Obama did occur (as foreseen) and Obama ignored it (not as foreseen). I say "not as foreseen" in that I wrote him a polite and, I think, convincing letter urging him to drop by. Here it is:

Dear President Obama,
There is much commentary these days about your legacy and your continued strivings to further extend your administration's reach in the remaining months of your second term of office. Your recent expansion of public land reserves and the large expansion of our country's ocean sanctuaries in the regions surrounding Hawaii and Guam are described as part of your environmental legacy.

I write once again to invite you to meet with the Washington-based, full-time nonprofit civic action and service community. On several occasions during your presidency, I have recommended that you speak to a thousand or more leaders of the national civic community in a downtown DC hotel ballroom or an auditorium such as the historic Constitution Hall.

Nonprofit organizations have millions of dues-paying members throughout the country supporting the fundamental bulwarks and seed corns of our beleaguered democracy.

They cover the important advocacy areas of peace, civil liberties and civil rights, antipoverty and health, consumer protection, environment, labor safety, access to justice, worker rights, and many traditional secular and religious charities that minister to the needy.

Yet there has been no response to these invitations, except for a reply by the office of Michelle Obama on July 17, 2011, saying the president was too busy.

Of course, presidents are very busy, but you found time to attend nearly five hundred fund-raisers around the country and to visit numerous factories and other corporate destinations. Even during a visit to India, you found time to extol Boeing airplanes and Harley-Davidson motorcycles.

Late in your second term, you could come to serve several other purposes. First, you can give necessary visibility to those committed people whose groups are left in the shadows during presidential election years despite their ability to enrich the content of such electoral activities with their exceptional hands-on knowledge and experience.

Second, you can make recommendations regarding various facilities, checkoffs, and new directions that can enlarge nonprofit membership and programs.

Third, you can educate the public about the critical role this "voluntary sector" has played in American history.

Fourth, you can herald the significant number of nonprofit jobs and economic activities—millions of staff and tens of billions of dollars coursing through the economy— which can only expand with larger philanthropy by billionaires, mega-millionaires, and regular citizens whom you might inspire to contribute to nonprofit organizations. Your address can become a presidential marker for your successors and for future generations of Americans inspired by your words and proposals.

It is difficult to understand why you have not yet embraced this opportunity. Certainly you have mentioned civic duty, civic engagement, and civic visions for posterity on a number of occasions. Especially now, when all elections are behind you, isn't it time to highlight the civic values and the civic heroes who reflect them in ways both dutiful and dramatic?

Lastly, such a presentation will set a finer, higher standard for your successor to inherit.

What say you, President Obama?

Yours,

Ralph Nader

Obama didn't respond or attend, losing another chance to prove he and his party were not divorced from the people's civic engagement.

I've already mentioned two places where progressives got together to work on their ideas and share their dreams, namely Occupy and the annual gathering of civic organizations in Washington, DC.

Another way progressive citizens might band together and call our legislators to account, an idea I floated years ago, would be to use the legislative summer recess as a time to buttonhole our representatives in town halls. It was practiced by the conservative Tea Party and has now been taken up by the resistance to Trump. Still, my original idea did add a new wrinkle. Let me explain it here:

There are many issues affecting our communities that need to be addressed by members of Congress. Over the years, it has become increasingly difficult to reach the legislators in Washington, DC, whether in person, on the telephone, or by letter correspondence. When they return to their districts and states, they often only attend public events and ceremonies where they do little more than shake hands and smile.

The in-person town hall meetings by members of Congress are diminishing, and often stacked and controlled. The locations, attendees, and sometimes even prescreened questions fail to provide citizens with an opportunity to make their case to their legislators. Politicians crave predictability; they are control freaks.

Our 535 senators and representatives need to be reminded that they were sent to Washington, DC by voters back home who entrusted them with the well-being of their communities and country. Many of these lawmakers become indentured to corporate campaign cash that they must constantly beg for, often compromising what is in the best interest of their constituents. For all this corporate campaign cash, these corporations want something in return—government contracts, giveaways, tax loopholes, weak corporate law enforcement, and other privileges and immunities, especially for giant multinational corporations that have tightened their grip of crony capitalism on Washington.

So what happened to our votes and trust in our elected representatives? They were nullified and replaced with ungrateful politicians who have forgotten that the sovereign authority lies with the people.

It is time for "We the People" to shake up the Congress and shake up politics across the land. If anyone is skeptical of this possibility, they should recall August 2009, when the Tea Party noisily filled the seats of some town hall meetings called by senators and representatives in a Congress run by the Democrats. That is how the Tea Party movement came to public visibility, with the help of Fox News.

After that experience, many members of Congress were forced to reevaluate the power and influence of town hall meetings. The anti-Trump forces renewed the fight in town halls across the country when the Republicans put forward their dreadful health insurance bill.

Here's my new wrinkle. Progressive activists, along with invading town halls, why not present a *Citizens Summons* to show elected legislators who is truly in charge, as befits the Preamble to the Constitution—"We the People." I am including below a draft *Citizens Summons* to your senators or representatives. It covers the main derelictions of the Congress, under which you can add more examples of necessary reforms.

Activists, your task is to start collecting signatures of citizens, and members of citizen groups, labor unions, and any other associations that want a more deliberative democracy. The ultimate objective is to reduce inequalities of power.

Shifting power from the few to the many prevents the gross distortions of our Constitution and laws, our public budgets, and our commonwealth that currently favor the burgeoning corporate state.

Your lawmakers deserve to be shown the workings of what our founding fathers called "the sovereignty of the people."

The *Citizens Summons* to a Member of the Congress

Whereas, the Congress has tolerated the expansion of an electoral process, corrupted by money, that nullifies our votes and commercializes both congressional elections and subsequent legislation, creating a Congress that is chronically for sale;

Whereas, the Congress has repeatedly supported or opposed legislation and diverted the taxpayer dollars to favor the crassest of corporate interests to the serious detriment of the American people, their necessities, and their public facilities—such as their access to safer consumer products, health care, clean air and water, and other basic social safety services. It has opposed fair taxation and raising the inflation-ravaged minimum wage, allowed endemic waste, fraud, and abuse by contractors, and authorized massive corporate welfare subsidies and giveaways;

Whereas, Congress has unconstitutionally allowed presidents to engage in costly, bloody, lawless wars worsening global and national security;

Whereas, the Congress has narrowed or blocked access to justice by millions of Americans, leaving them unprotected and defenseless in many serious ways, while giving corporations preferential treatment and allowing them full access to influence the three branches of government;

Whereas, the Congress has imposed trade treaty despotism over our democratic institutions—the courts, legislatures, and executive departments and agencies— subordinating our government's abilities to preserve and enhance labor, consumer, and environmental standards to the domination of global commerce's "bottom line," and endorsing the usurpation of our judicial process by secret tribunals under the WTO, and other similar invasions of US sovereignty;

Whereas, the access to members of Congress has increased for corporate lobbyists and decreased for ordinary citizens,

Therefore, the citizens of the [INSERT state (for senators) or congressional district (for representatives)] hereby *Summon* you to a town hall meeting(s) during the August recess (ending September [INSERT date and year]) at a place of known public convenience. Your constituents will establish an agenda of how Congress should enact a long-overdue shift of power from the few to the many, both in substantive policy and through the strengthening of government and civic institutions;

We deem this *Summons* to be delivered with the utmost seriousness as we gain grassroots support throughout your congressional district [or state for senators]. We expect to hear from you expeditiously so that the necessary planning for our town hall meeting can take place. This Peoples' Town Hall Meeting reflects the Preamble to the Constitution and the supremacy of the sovereignty of the people over elected representatives and corporate entities;

Be advised that this *Summons* calls for your attendance at a Town Hall Meeting run by, of, and for the People. Please reserve a minimum of three hours for this serious exercise of deliberative democracy.

Sincerely yours,

[The names of citizens and citizen groups]

If the Democratic lawmakers stand by their principles, they should welcome such summons.

3.

Trump Not the Only One to Roll Back Regulations

People with short memories may have forgotten, but the Obama administration quietly continued many Bush practices of dangerous deregulation and nonenforcement—which Trump in turn has made his own and shifted into high gear.

The Republican Party has a sense of humor, however inadvertent. Its ardent conservative advocates, both when Obama was in power and even now, regularly accused his administration of heavy-handed regulation of business.

Tell that to the hundred federal poultry inspectors who picketed outside the Department of Agriculture in 2012 in opposition to a proposal that would allow those crammed, bacterial poultry slaughterhouses to do their own inspections. The picketers feared that, with this weakening of oversight, the poultry bosses would speed up the slaughter rate to 175 birds per minute, up from the present 70.

Tell that to the Securities Exchange Commission, which Obama allowed to return to its notorious boiler-room practices. With little regulation, "start-ups" with up to $1 billion in annual revenues can sell stock to investors, just like in the old Wild West.

Tell that to David Michaels, the superbly qualified head of the Occupational Safety and Health Administration under Obama, who couldn't get the White House to approve issuance of long-overdue, vital safeguards for worker health and safety. Nearly sixty thousand workers lose their lives due to workplace-related illnesses and injuries every year.

Tell that to a strapped Environmental Protection Agency that at long last was trying to reduce the toxic materials in your air and water. If you really look back in history, you will see that President Obama personally intervened to stop two of their regulations from taking effect.

Tell that to the Food and Drug Administration (FDA) that was the subject of a front-page *New York Times* article on April 3, 2012, titled "White House and the F.D.A. Often at Odds." It seems that President Obama's deputy chief of staff, Nancy-Ann DeParle, had been leaning on FDA commissioner Dr. Margaret A. Hamburg to drop proposed rules requiring labeling of calories for foods served on airplanes and in movie theaters, as well as regulation of sunscreen and asthma inhalers.

The ObamaBush White House objected to what the *Times* said was "the enforcement of an agency decision on a drug to prevent premature births."

The FDA believed that the Obama "Hope and Change" campaign in 2008 would start a new day after the years of George W. Bush, who believed, for example, that the agency should not issue rules preventing contamination of eggs and other produce. Alas, said a top FDA official to the *Times*, "Employees here waited eight long years for deliverance that didn't come." Safety regulation of drugs remained tepid.

Mr. Obama, as with his other choices of White House staff, set himself up by choosing the "regulation czar," Cass R. Sunstein, who could and did give a thumbs-down on agency safety proposals. Professor Sunstein has a philosophy known as "libertarian paternalism." (Google it if you wish to discover its meaning.)

FDA scientists sadly recall Mr. Obama's White House ceremony to sign a memorandum in 2009 pledging to replace Mr. Bush's politicization of science in government with scientific integrity, and to listen to scientists "even when it's inconvenient—especially when it is inconvenient." Once again, words, words, words succumbed to the real power of corporatism.

Obama's regulatory agency officials received constant pressure from congressional corporatists on their meager enforcement budgets. They were made to behave as if they should fear the criminals and defrauders they were supposed to be catching to protect the American people.

All of them were envious of the new Consumer Financial Protection Bureau (CFPB), which was created by Congress to shield consumers of credit, mortgages, payday loans, and other financial transactions from the Wall Street–driven crime wave. You see, the CFPB resides inside the Federal Reserve and receives its $500 million budget from the Fed, which gets its budget from bank fees and is free of the congressional hammers.

Still, the CFPB and its sterling staff (with few exceptions) took a long time under Obama's reign to start producing long-needed rules of decent business behavior.

I used the term *ObamaBush* to label some of these bad policies. The Democrats sometimes *talk* differently from the Republican but *do* similarly. Trump's shutdown is, of course, off the charts.

4.

Obama's Unconstitutional Handling of the "War on Terror"

Another place where Obama's policies echoed Bush's and foreshadowed Trump's was in the war against stateless terrorism. None of these gentlemen looked much beyond military solutions, ones that failed repeatedly, as ways to handle the rise of such terrorism. In fact, the highly publicized killing, instead of capture, of a nonresisting Osama bin Laden was, in retrospect, another indication of how bankrupt is the policy of using guns to solve issues rooted in basic social and geopolitical conditions. As we see now, the death of this purported mastermind has done nothing to slow the spread of terrorist organizations around the world.

Imagine, if you will, what the shade of Osama bin Laden would have told Obama about the results of the extinguishing of his earthly body:

> The Ghost of Osama bin Laden swirled into the Oval Office, where Barack Obama was spending the evening going over a pile of requested sign-offs for armed drone missions.
>
> Osama's Ghost: "Mind if we have a conversation one year after you dispatched my body to the ocean sharks?"

With curiosity reigning supreme, President Obama replied, "Okay, so long as you remain hovering and do not alight to defile this solemn room."

Osama's Ghost: "Thank you. After your SEALs bravely shot, rather than captured, me while I was defenseless in my bedroom, you told your nation that 'for the first time in two decades, Osama bin Laden is not a threat to this country.'"

"Correct, the form of your presence now attests to that fact," the president curtly declared.

Osama's Ghost: "You completely misunderstood. You see, my work was completed by the evening of September 11, 2001. After that, the terror that I wanted to implant in American hearts was continued and intensified by George W. Bush, Dick Cheney, and you far, far beyond what our little, exaggerated al-Qaeda could ever dream of doing."

"How so? Make it short!" Obama demanded.

Osama's Ghost: "Okay, you want it short? For over a decade you and your predecessors have starved your domestic needs in favor of huge military adventures in Asia and Africa, and taken away the freedoms of your people and replaced them with fear and anxiety over the wildly overblown but very profitable war on terror. You destroyed the esteem of the world's people by reacting to 9/11 with aggressive attacks, torture, indefinite imprisonment without charges, secret laws, secret evidence, secret prisons, and routine violations of national borders. You backed tyrants in these countries who slay and loot their own people with US weapons, predatory corporations, and international political cover. You spy everywhere on the American people and watch your own soldiers commit suicide in record numbers. Do you know why these American soldiers are killing themselves, Mr. President?"

"You tell me, Dr. Freud," said President Obama.

Osama's Ghost: "Because when you send them to Iraq and Afghanistan for wars not of defense but of aggression, and they end up killing so many innocent women, children, and men, their consciences are traumatized. Your generals like to say their brains are physically traumatized. By what? Your adversaries have no loud artillery, bombers, or missiles to provoke that trauma. It is the trauma of their conscience when they see the burned, broken, and dismembered bodies of little children and their mothers and fathers in their homes, mosques, or markets. People were blown up while just gathering together to collect wood or participate in wedding processions. In addition, your soldiers see the daily suffering of millions who are maimed and homeless."

"You should talk, after the massacre of my people on 9/11," exclaimed President Obama.

Osama's Ghost: "But at least the attackers went 'down with the ship,' as you Americans say, and this attack was designed to make you suffer like you have made us suffer a millionfold over the decades. As a scholar and a son of Africa, you should understand what life is like under American-supported tyrants. Imagine American military bases—even in our holy lands—and the brutal suppression of any resistance to overturn these puppet dictators and expel their infidel masters from the West. If you were not in our backyard, for instance during the Palestinian *nakba*, or catastrophe, which the US made happen, our martyrs would never have gone to New York and Washington on 9/11."

"Do not lump me in with Bush and Cheney," said an irritated Obama. "'They lied this great nation into the invasion of Iraq, and played right into your hands,' as Bush's own counterterrorism adviser Richard Clarke wrote. I opposed this war but vowed to clear al-Qaeda out of Afghanistan by shifting our soldiers from Iraq. You know what happened to you all after that, don't you, Ghost?"

Osama's Ghost: "Yes, Mr. President. Al-Qaeda is not much in Afghanistan, having largely decided to migrate its activities to Pakistan and encourage our brothers in Yemen, Somalia, and North Africa. They are moving into Syria from Iraq, where they first surfaced thanks to your invasion. The word used by the CIA is *blowback*. But no one is furthering our basic mission of weakening the US more than the rulers of your country themselves. Look at your rich-poor economy; Wall Street's destructive greed; crumbling schools, roads, transit, clinics, drinking water facilities; and starved public budgets for the basic necessities of your poor people—food for the hungry, healing for the sick, shelter for the homeless.

"Even your people overwhelmingly say that America is going in the wrong direction, and they want out of Afghanistan. What is a democracy for anyway, Mr. President? Again, you're doing al-Qaeda's job—weakening and bankrupting your country until it can no longer continue 'messing around and meddling in the affairs of other countries,' as the presidential candidate Ron Paul says daily. You see, at my compound in Abbottabad, reading occupied me. There was nothing left to do because you Americans cannot resist doing it to yourselves year after year. As you can tell from my lack of precautions, I didn't care if I was executed because my mission was fulfilled. Near the end, grieving over Muslims killing Muslims, I became a fatalistic mystic."

"Are you finished, Ghost? I have to decide on some high-value targets in three countries. The hunt will never cease," said President Obama.

Osama's Ghost: "But Mr. President, you had the highest-value target of all and you eliminated the chance to interrogate me. Think what I could have told you about the past thirty years for your intelligence services."

"Tell me what, in a phrase. Your time is up!" declared President Obama.

Osama's Ghost: "Well . . . thank you, thank you for all that you, Mr. Bush, and Mr. Cheney have done, Mr. President."

Whereupon the Ghost evaporated into the ether and the president started signing.

I ended that imaginative piece with Obama signing drone strike authorizations. Rereading news stories about that time showed me that Obama both followed in the footsteps of Bush and cut a path for Trump to follow in his own free and easy attitude toward the Constitution.

While the Democrats complain that under Trump the rule of law is rapidly breaking down, this is something massive that can also be laid at their own doorstep.

Take the administrations of George W. Bush and Barack Obama. The conservative American Bar Association sent three white papers in 2005 to President Bush describing his continual unconstitutional policies. Then and now civil liberties groups and a few law professors, such as the stalwart David Cole, then of Georgetown University, and Jonathan Turley of George Washington University, have distinguished themselves in calling out both presidents for such violations and urging them to enforce the rule of law.

Sadly, the bulk of our profession, as individuals and through their bar associations, has remained quietly on the sidelines. They have turned away from their role as "first responders" in protecting the Constitution from its official violators.

As a youngster in Hawaii, basketball player Barack Obama was nicknamed by his schoolboy chums "Barry O'Bomber," according to the *Washington Post*. On May 29, 2012, the *New York Times* published a massive front-page feature article by Jo Becker and Scott Shané that demonstrated just how inadvertently prescient was this moniker. This was not an adversarial, leaked newspaper scoop. The article had all the signs of cooperation by the three dozen interviewed current and former advisers to President Obama and his administration. The reporters wrote that every week in office the president personally selected and ordered a "kill list" of suspected terrorists or militants via drone strikes or other means. The reporters wrote that this personal role of Obama's is "without precedent in presidential history." Adversaries pulled him into more and more countries—Pakistan, Yemen, Somalia, and other territories.

The drones have killed civilians, families with small children, and even allied soldiers in this undeclared war based on secret "facts" and local grudges (getting even). These attacks were justified by secret legal memos claiming that the president, without any congressional authorization, could without any limitations, other than his say-so, target far and wide assassinations of any "suspected terrorist," including American citizens.

The bombings by Mr. Obama, as secret prosecutor, judge, jury, and executioner, trample proper constitutional authority, separation of powers, and checks and balances, and, indeed, constituted repeated impeachable offenses, as Obama ignored the Constitution's Article I, Section 8, on Congress's war-declaring powers.

As if lawyers needed any reminding, the Constitution is the

foundation of our legal system and is based on declared boundaries of permissible government actions. That is what a government of law, not of men, means. Further, our system is clearly demarked by independent review of executive branch decisions—by our courts and Congress.

What happens if Congress becomes, in constitutional lawyer Bruce Fein's words, "an ink blot," and the courts beg off with their wholesale dismissals of constitutional matters on the grounds that an issue involves a "political question" or that parties have "no standing to sue"? What happens is what is happening. The situation worsens every year, deepening dictatorial, secretive decisions by the White House, and not just regarding foreign and military policies.

The value of the *New York Times* article is that it added ascribed commentary on what was reported. Here is a sample:

- The US ambassador to Pakistan, Cameron P. Munter, was quoted by a colleague as complaining about the CIA's strikes driving American policy, commenting that he "didn't realize his main job was to kill people." Imagine what the sidelined, endangered Foreign Service is thinking about greater longer-range risks to our national security.

- Dennis Blair, former director of National Intelligence, called the strike campaign "dangerously seductive." He said that Obama's obsession with targeted killings is "the politically advantageous thing to do—low cost, no US casualties, gives the appearance of toughness. . . . It plays well domestically, and it is unpopular only in other countries. Any damage it does to the national interest only shows up over the long term." Blair, a retired admiral, has often noted that intense focus on strikes sidelines any long-term strategy against al-Qaeda, which spreads wider with each drone that vaporizes civilians.

- Former CIA director Michael Hayden decried the secrecy: "This program rests on the personal legitimacy of the president, and that's not sustainable," he told the *Times*. "Democracies do not make war on the basis of legal memos locked in a D.O.J. [Department of Justice] safe."

Consider this: a liberal former constitutional law lecturer—Barack Obama—is being cautioned about blowback, the erosion of democracy, and the national security by former heads of super-secret spy agencies!

Secrecy-driven violence in government breeds fear and the surrender of conscience. When Mr. Obama was campaigning for president in 2007, he was reviled by Hillary Clinton, Joseph Biden Jr., and Mitt Romney—then presidential candidates—for declaring that, even if Pakistan's leaders objected, he would go after terrorist bases in Pakistan. Romney said he had "become Dr. Strangelove," according to the *Times*. But since then, all three of candidate Obama's critics have decided to go along with egregious violations of our Constitution.

Based on deep reporting, Becker and Shane noted that "[b]oth Pakistan and Yemen are arguably less stable and more hostile to the United States than when Mr. Obama became president."

In a world of lawlessness, force will beget force, which is what the CIA means by "blowback." Our vulnerable country has the most to lose when we abandon the rule of law and embrace lawless violence. That is only a deadly recipe for future revenge throughout the world.

The people in the countries we target know what we must remember. We are their occupiers, their invaders, the powerful supporters for decades of their own brutal tyrants. We're in their backyard, which more than any other impetus spawned al-Qaeda in the first place.

At least Trump has this excuse for his continuance of the legacy of putting the president above the law, one not available to Obama: Trump is not a lawyer.

Looking back at this whole seamy engagement in drone warfare, it makes one question what Obama's historical legacy will really be. At the moment, he is acclaimed for at least making a stab at getting the US national health care. But I wonder if historians will also remember and highlight his unremarked, unethical, and unconstitutional opting for drone warfare.

Let's focus here on his major expansion of drone warfare in defiance of international law, statutory law, and the Constitution. Obama's drones roamed over multiple nations of Asia and Africa and targeted suspects, both known and unknown, whom the president, in his unbridled discretion, wanted to evaporate for the cause of national security.

By November 2012, more than 2,500 people had been killed by Obama's drones, many of them civilians and bystanders, including American citizens, irrespective of the absence of any "imminent threat" to the United States.

As Justin Elliott of ProPublica wrote, "Under Obama . . . only 13 percent" of those killed "could be considered 'militant leaders'— either of the Pakistani Taliban, the Afghan Taliban, or Al Qaeda." The remaining fatalities, apart from many innocent civilians, including children, were people oppressed by their own harsh regimes or dominated by US occupation of their country. Apart from its importance for human rights and the laws of war, this distinction between civilians and combatants matters because it shows that Obama's drones became what Micah Zenko of the Council on Foreign Relations called "a counterinsurgency air force" for our collaborative regimes.

The "kill lists" were the work of Obama and his advisers, led by John O. Brennan, and came straight from the White House, according to the *New York Times*. Apparently, the president spent a good deal of time being prosecutor, judge, jury, executioner, and concealer. But he did so quietly; this was no dramatic "thumbs-down" emperor.

Mr. Brennan spoke at Harvard Law School in 2011 and falsely told a remarkably blasé audience that what he and the president were doing was perfectly legal under the law of self-defense—"self-defense" as it is defined, of course, by the president.

It appears that President Obama did not share the certitude boldly displayed by Mr. Brennan. On October 18, 2012, Obama told Jon Stewart and his *Daily Show* audience that "one of the things we've got to do is put a legal architecture in place, and we need congressional help in order to do that, to make sure that not only am I reined in, but any president is reined in, in terms of some of the decisions that we're making."

So in the absence of "a legal architecture" of accountability, do presidents knock off whomever they want to target (along with bystanders or family members), whether or not the targeted person is actually plotting an attack against the United States? It seemed that way, in spite of what is already in place legally, called the Constitution, separation of powers, and due process of law. What more legal architecture did Mr. Obama need?

Obviously what he wanted was a self-contained, permanent "Office of Presidential Predator Drone Assassinations" in the White House, to use scholar Bruce Fein's nomenclature. According to the *New York Times*, at that time President Obama wanted "explicit rules for targeted killing . . . so that a new president would inherit clear standards and procedures." Mr. Fein noted that "clear standards and procedures without accountability to the judiciary, Congress, or the American people" undermine the rule of law and our democracy.

Indeed, the whole deliberation process inside the Obama

administration was secret, a continual process of morbid overclassi-
fication containing internal legal opinions on targeted killings that
even today remain secret. The government refused at that time to
even acknowledge that a drone air force operates over Pakistan—a
fact that everybody knew, not least of all the hundreds of injured
and displaced Pakistanis. This drone air force used what the *New
York Times* called "'signature strikes' against groups of visually suspected, but unknown militants." Totally arbitrary mayhem.

Predictably, these strikes constantly terrorized thousands
of families who lived in fear of a strike anytime, day or night,
which caused a blowback that expanded the number of al-Qaeda
sympathizers and affiliates from Pakistan to Yemen. "Signature
strikes," according to the *Times*, "have prompted the greatest conflict inside the Obama administration." The former CIA director
under George W. Bush, Michael Hayden, publicly questioned
whether the expansion in the use of drones is counterproductive and creating more enemies and the desire for more revenge
against the US.

Critics pointed out how many times in the past departments
and agencies put forth misleading or false intelligence, from the
Vietnam War to the arguments for invading Iraq, or missed what
they should have predicted, such as the fall of the Soviet Union.
This legacy of errors and duplicity should restrain presidents who
execute by ordering drone operators to push buttons at bases in
the US that target people thousands of miles away, based on secret
so-called intelligence.

Mr. Obama wants, in Mr. Fein's view, to have "his secret and
unaccountable predator drone assassinations become permanent
fixtures of the nation's national security complex."

At the time, Attorney General Eric Holder astonishingly
maintained that there is sufficient *due process* entirely inside the
executive branch and without congressional oversight or judicial

review. Were Obama's actions any less those of an out-of-control presidency than Trump's so far? In this one context, Obama opted for a secret, violent, imperial presidency that shredded the Constitution's separation of powers and disposed of its checks and balances.

Sometimes when you are looking through old press clippings you'll come upon strange juxtapositions. In April 2013, in close proximity, the papers reported two tragedies: the Newtown massacre, in which twenty children were shot by a deranged gunman, and a drone strike in Afghanistan that accidentally killed ten children. Think of the different way these events were treated by the president and his fellow Democrats. Think of a president who could cry out of one eye, as it were, while looking at a list of targets for civilian- and child-killing drone strikes with the other.

An Associated Press photograph showed the American people the horror of little children lying dead outside of their home. At least ten Afghan children and some of their mothers were struck down by an airstrike on their extended family household by order of President Barack Obama. He probably decided on the strike during what his aides described as the weekly "Terror Tuesday" at the White House. On that day, Mr. Obama typically received the advice about which alleged "militants" should live or die thousands of miles away via drones or aircraft. Even if households far from war zones were repeatedly destroyed in clear violation of the laws of war, the president was not deterred.

These Obama airstrikes were launched with the knowledge that very often there is "collateral damage"—that is, a form of "so-sorry terrorism." How could the president have explained the vaporization of nine preteen Afghan boys collecting firewood for their families on a hillside? The local spotter-informants must have been disoriented by all those hundred-dollar bills in rewards. Imagine a direct strike killing and injuring scores of people in a funeral procession following a previous fatal strike that was the occasion of this mourning. Or the December 2009 Obama strike on an alleged al-Qaeda training camp in Yemen, using tomahawk missiles and—get this—cluster bombs, that killed fourteen women and twenty-one children. Again and again "so-sorry terrorism" ravages family households far from the battlefields.

At the time of that strike and for several years before, some White House officials, including retired general James Jones, declared that there was no real operational al-Qaeda left in Afghanistan to harbor anyone. The Pakistani Taliban was in conflict with the Pakistani government. The Afghan Taliban was in brutal conflict with the Afghanistan government and wanted to expel US forces, whom their members viewed as occupying invaders, much like the Soviet invaders their predecessors expelled.

Even a loyalist such as William M. Daley, Mr. Obama's chief of staff in 2011, observed that the Obama kill list presented fewer and fewer significant pursuits. "One guy gets knocked off, and the guy's driver, who's No. 21, becomes 20?" Daley said, describing internal discussions among the president and his advisers. "At what point are you just filling the bucket with numbers?"

Yet this unlawful killing by a seemingly obsessed Obama continued, and the killings included anyone in the vicinity of a "suspect" (called "signature strikes"), and mistakes, like the aerial killings of numerous Pakistani soldiers and Afghan policemen—considered our allies. The drone kill list goes on and on—in April 2013 the official fatality count was over three thousand, not counting injuries, and still less than the figures human rights groups recorded.

A few weeks later, the *Nation* magazine issued a major report on US-caused civilian casualties in Afghanistan.

Now switch the scene. The president, filled with memories of what his secret drone directives as prosecutor, judge, jury, and executioner have done to so many children, in so many places, traveled to Newtown, Connecticut. He commiserated with the parents and relatives of the twenty children and six adults slain by a lone gunman. Here he became the compassionate president, with words and hugs.

What must have been going through his mind as he saw the photo of ten little Afghan children and their parents blown apart in that day's *New York Times*? How could the president justify this continued military occupation in what amounts to a civil war? No wonder a majority of the American people wanted out of Afghanistan, even without a close knowledge of the grisly and ugly things going on there in our name that were feeding the seething hatred of Obama's war.

Maybe in his forthcoming autobiographical recollections, there will be a few pages where he explains how he endured this double life of ordering so-called precision attacks that kill many innocent children and their mothers and fathers while properly mourning domestic mass killings in the US and advocating gun control.

If in his autobiography he entertains such thoughts, then his reflections will differ markedly from the self-serving reminiscences of George W. Bush on the wars in Afghanistan and Iraq—being president means never having to say you're sorry.

A few comments on Bush's book. When it appeared in 2013, George W. Bush was riding high. A mega-millionaire due to his investment in the taxpayer-subsidized Texas Rangers company, he was making around $150,000 per speech, received a large presidential pension and support facilities, and was about to dedicate the $500 million George W. Bush Presidential Library and Museum.

President Obama was at the dedication, continuing to legitimize Mr. Bush, a war criminal, as he did from the outset by announcing in 2009 that there would be no investigations or prosecutions of Bush officials for their crimes.

In an interview with the *New York Times* at the time of the book launch, Mr. Bush continued to say he has no regrets about his presidency. "I'm comfortable with what I did," he said. "I'm comfortable with who I am." He added, "Much of my presidency was defined by things that you didn't necessarily want to have happen."

But he and Dick Cheney made them happen, although Mr. Bush attributed some military events to providence. One of the "things" he is comfortable with is his criminal, unconstitutional invasion and occupation of Iraq, which took over one million Iraqi lives—children, women, and men—created five million refugees, and committed overall sociocide of that country, which posed no threat to the US. The carnage continues to this day.

Apparently, Mr. Bush is "comfortable" with the price paid by the US soldiers and their broken families—nearly five thousand fatalities, suicides, more than two hundred thousand injuries, illnesses, and traumatic syndromes—and by US taxpayers, who over time will pay an estimated $3 trillion, according to Nobel Laureate and economist Joseph Stiglitz.

Former representative Ron Paul (R-TX) has said repeatedly that Bush and Cheney "lied us into invading Iraq." Such an understatement. Bush and Cheney not only lied about Saddam's weapons of mass destruction, they also deceived, covered up, corrupted, or intimidated the mass media, bullied an abdicating Congress, and delivered a false address to the United Nations via the now-regretful secretary of state Colin Powell.

Two secretaries-general of the UN subsequently declared Bush's war of aggression against Iraq to be in violation of international law.

Bush suffers no qualms about the brutal realities of his war and his recidivist violations of our Constitution, federal statutes, and international treaties. "One of the real challenges of life is that when you complete a chapter, you don't atrophy, that you continue to find ways to contribute," said Bush in an interview with the

Dallas Morning News. Army veteran Tomas Young was atrophying from his massive wounds in Iraq. He summoned his moral energy to write Mr. Bush a poignant letter calling him to account for his war crimes, saying, "I hope that before your time on earth ends, as mine is now ending, you will find the strength of character to stand before the American public and the world, and in particular the Iraqi people, and beg for forgiveness." Bush, however, never responded. After all, he's "comfortable" and that bloody "chapter" is closed.

The American people, not to mention law schools and the legal profession, have yet to come to terms with the reality that presidents are actually above the law. Presidents can commit repeated crimes in an outlaw presidency so long as they can invoke, however falsely and vaguely, national security.

Were presidents to engage in personal crimes or obstruction of justice, like Nixon's burglary of the Democratic Party's Watergate offices, the law and Congress can hold them accountable. But Bush and Cheney had bigger fish to fry with their destruction of justice. As the ancient Roman historian Tacitus wrote, "The worst crimes were dared by a few, willed by more, and tolerated by all."

Fortunately for our fragile democracy, there were dissenters. After 9/11, leading civil liberty groups objected to numerous provisions in the Patriot Act. Those provisions allow the government to search your home and business without telling you for seventy-two hours; prevent librarians and custodians of your financial or medical records from even telling you that the feds retrieved them; and have led to warrantless snooping on tens of millions of Americans.

In the months leading up to the invasion of Iraq in March 2003, more than three hundred retired generals, admirals, high-ranking officers, national security officials, and diplomats spoke out against any invasion.

Retired general and former director of the National Security Agency Bill Odom called the invasion the "greatest strategic disaster in United States history." Bush's father was privately opposed to the invasion, urging his retired top advisers, James Baker and Brent Scowcroft, to speak and write against the pending invasion.

In 2005 the venerable, conservative American Bar Association released three white papers declaring Bush's domestic surveillance and treatment of enemy combatants unconstitutional. Bush never acknowledged these reports. Also, a bipartisan report by the Constitution Project concluded that Bush/Cheney approved torture practices at Guantánamo.

All of the above, plus mass antiwar rallies in Washington, DC, and elsewhere, did not slow the march to war. The protests were not strong enough to penetrate the political and electoral systems. Until that happens, criminal, unconstitutional actions regularly conducted at top levels of our government will not, as a practical matter, trigger either the application of the rule of law or the impeachment authority of the US Congress. To the contrary, each succeeding president feels free to push the illegal, unconstitutional envelope further, gaining even more power through intimidation.

So the lawless legacy of George W. Bush was to continue under Obama—*sometimes worse, sometimes not.* Indefinite detention, arbitrary use of military rather than civil tribunals, secret evidence and secret laws, war crimes, secret courts, immunity from judicial review, continual snooping on citizens, extraordinary renditions to foreign countries—and even, for the first time, as President Barack Obama claimed in his sole, secret judgment as prosecutor, judge, jury, and executioner, the unilateral right to assassinate an American citizen, far from the battlefield.

As I noted, just above, "So the lawless legacy of George W. Bush was to continue under Obama—sometimes worse, sometimes not." Now that Trump is in power, I use the same phrase to refer to him, so far.

Still, in terms of fighting terrorism, so far Trump has done little but buff up the Bush, then Obama, plan to fight terrorism by drone striking and bombing away. You might call it the "boots off the ground" strategy. But bombing and drone blasting is a highly indiscriminate way of fighting a foe, one guaranteed to bring the collateral deaths of civilians. Although some in the military admit that this cost must be paid, they ignore another collateral cost: the production of new stateless terrorists against state-sponsored terrorism.

Take the Boston Marathon bombing of 2013. It was a horrendous action, but wasn't it—or something like it—predictable, given the carnage our collateral damage–causing drone raids were causing?

The words of the Scottish poet Robert Burns in 1786 come to mind:

"O wad some Pow'r the giftie gie us / To see oursels as ithers see us!"

2018 English translation:

"Oh, would some Power the small gift give us / To see ourselves as others see us!"

At the time of the Boston Marathon bombing, I wondered what the "ithers" in the Middle East theater of the American Empire must think of a great city in total lockdown from an attack by primitive explosives when Iraqis, Afghans, Pakistanis, and Yemenis experience far greater casualties and terror attacks several times a week—including what they believe are terror attacks by

US drones, soldiers, aircraft, and missiles that have killed many thousands of innocent children, women, and men in their homes, during funeral processions and wedding parties, or while they're working in their fields.

Here's what they were thinking: that America is very vulnerable and ready to shake itself upside down to rid itself of and protect itself from any terror attacks. The Bush regime, after 9/11, sacrificed US soldiers and millions of innocents in the broader Middle East, drained our economy, ignoring the necessities of saving lives and health here at home, and metastasized al-Qaeda into numerous countries, spilling havoc into Iraq and now Syria. We have paid a tremendous price in blowback because of Mr. Bush's rush to war.

The attackers, be they suicide bombers over there or domestic bombers here, are motivated by their hatred of our invasions, our daily bombings, our occupations, and our immersion in tribal preferences leading to divide-and-rule sectarian wars. Studies, such as those by Robert Pape, a professor at the University of Chicago and a former adviser to Barack Obama and Ron Paul during the 2008 presidential campaign, conclude that entry into paradise is not the motivation for these suicide bombers. What drives them is their despair and their desire to expel the foreign invaders from their homeland.

Still "ithers"—admittedly a smaller number—viewing the reaction of Obama and the media to the Marathon bombing must see a giant country going berserk with speculation, rumors, accusations, and random mobilizations of military equipment. There are enough of these younger people wondering if it is worth giving up their lives to make a nation more fearful—particularly in light of the staggering overreactions of America's rulers.

Why give these contorted young minds, frustrated by what they perceive as US attacks on their religion or their ethnic group in their home countries, such incentives?

Huge overreactions by the mass media to this and similar terrorist attacks crowd out coverage of larger and more preventable losses of life and safety in our country. Every day in the US there are preventable tragedies—such as the five thousand fatalities a week that result from preventable hospital errors, according to a Johns Hopkins University School of Medicine report—that receive no media coverage because they aren't part of the "war on terror."

Individually, many Americans intuitively understand the consequences of neglecting problems in our own country to engage in lawless wars and military adventures abroad. Unfortunately, Americans also collectively sing the song "Que Sera, Sera" or "Whatever Will Be, Will Be" because the big boys in Washington and Wall Street will always make the decisions. Be assured that they will often be stupidly harmful over the long run to our country, and not just to the millions of defenseless people overseas who have become victims of the aggregate punishment or random ravages of our modern push-button-weapon systems. All empires devour themselves.

In an impressive collection of writings, speeches, comments, and cartoons titled *Against the Beast: A Documentary History of American Opposition to Empire,* edited by John Nichols, the eminent historian Chalmers Johnson had this to say:

> ...where US-supported repression has created hopeless conditions, [and where] US-supported economic policies... have led to unimaginable misery, blowback reintroduces us to a world of cause and effect.

In 2013, the first-ever Senate hearing on the use of armed drones away from battlefields was initiated by Senator Richard Durbin (D-IL) and arrogantly boycotted by the imperial Obama administration. Farea Al-Muslimi, a young Yemeni from Wessab, a village recently attacked by a US drone strike, gave witness.

Al-Muslimi said, "When [my fellow villagers] think of America, they think of the terror they feel from the drones that hover over their heads, ready to fire missiles at any time. What the violent militants had previously failed to achieve, one drone strike accomplished in an instant: there is now an intense anger against America in Wessab."

Still today, in country after country, the terrifying, 24/7 whine of hovering drones and the knowledge that special US killing teams can drop from the skies at any time create a state of terror.

Jeremy Scahill, author of *Dirty Wars: The World Is a Battlefield*, who has been in these countries and spoken with these villagers, says that our government has created unnecessary enemies and stirred up desire for revenge among these people over the past ten years. "This is going to boomerang back around to us," he fears, adding that we're creating "a whole new generation of enemies that have an actual grievance against us . . . have an actual score to settle." Killing innocent men, women, and children creates blowback that lasts for generations.

In these overseas regions, the message prior to the bombing at the Boston Marathon was that the high-tech buttons were only being pushed by the drone operators to attack them. But after Boston they can see that low-tech buttons can be pushed in the US at any time to attack defenseless, innocent people.

For our national security, the American people must recover control of our runaway, unilateral presidency—first Obama's, now Trump's—that has torn itself away from constitutional accountabilities. The office of the president continues to be hijacked by ideologues who ignore our founding fathers' wisdom regarding the separation of powers and the avoidance of foreign entanglements that become costly, deadly, and endless quagmires.

It's no secret that Trump is a warmonger, but as of the winter of 2018 he hasn't started a war or a new military involvement. Rather, he's simply continued with the ones Obama had going. And let us not allow the positive vibes Obama communicates to blind us to the fact that he initiated new fights in the Middle East, adding to the quagmires Bush had jumped into. Obama got our nation embroiled in Syria and Libya.

I need hardly remind readers that Trump, reneging on his promise to stop meddling in this war, bombed Syria because he saw pictures of gassed children he believed were poisoned by Assad's troops. Some condemned this intervention, rightly, as it did nothing to cool the conflict in Syria's civil war. It was a one-off, leading to no further action. Interestingly, short-memoried Americans forgot that some of the same complaints had been leveled against Obama.

If I could have gotten Obama's ear in 2013, when he was first committing to Syria, here's what I would have said:

> Before you decide to attack Syria, yet another Arab or Islamic country that does not threaten US security, there are certain constitutional "niceties" that you should observe. Chronically violating the Constitution overturns the rule of law and can produce costly blowbacks.
>
> On August 28, you stated that bombing Syria was not about war but about accountability, obviously referring to the brutal gassing of neighborhoods outside Damascus. What about your accountability to receive authorization from Congress, which, under Article I, Section 8, of the Constitution, has the sole and exclusive power to declare war? Spare Americans the casuistry of your lawyers who "legalized" your war on Libya, with no declaration, authorization, or appropriation of funds from Congress, and

pushed the envelope of the "unitary presidency" beyond the unlawful and brazen extremes advocated by George W. Bush and his lawyers.

Nearly two hundred members of both parties of Congress—now on its August recess—demanded there be no attack on Syria without congressional authorization. These signers have so far included seventy-two Democrats. Merely secretly consulting with some lawmakers on the intelligence committees does not substitute for formal congressional authorization. The framers of our Constitution were unanimous in writing Article I, Section 8, so that no president could go to war on his own. To do so, as you have already done in the past, would be a major impeachable offense.

The media have reported that your lawyers are searching for legal justification for firing Tomahawk missiles into Syria. They need look no more, because there is none. The Constitution clearly states that the power to engage in war rests with Congress and Congress only. You cannot start another war! You cannot continue to be the prosecutor, judge, jury, and executioner, anywhere, at any time.

You may think the Constitution a mere formality. But the framers granted the Congress with the sole power to declare war for reasons beyond just thwarting a latter-day King George III tyranny. They wanted a deliberative, open process to avoid reckless presidential decisions that could be bad for our country or that could entangle us with warring foreign nations. Remember George Washington's farewell address on this point—truer today than in his day.

Remember what the nearly two hundred members of Congress said to you: "Engaging our military in Syria when no direct threat to the United States exists and without prior congressional authorization would violate the separation of powers that is clearly delineated in the Constitution." Congressional deliberations would ask the following questions:

1. Assuming the veracity of the argument that the Assad regime is the cause of the chemical attacks outside Damascus, how could a US attack not make a horrible situation even more horrible, both inside Syria and in the surrounding volatile region?

2. Why are so many in the US military—though they defer to civilian authority—privately opposed to such an action? Could it be due to the lack of any strategic purpose behind entering the war, or the violent plethora of uncontrollable consequences? See the oppositional stands, reported in the August 30 *Washington Post*, "from more than a dozen military officers ranging from captains to a four-star general."

3. How are you going to avoid the kind of awful continual civilian casualties that were produced in the first Iraq War in 1990–1991? US bombings broke open stores of chemical weapons, likely leading to the long-term sickness (called the Gulf War syndrome) that afflicted tens of thousands of US soldiers—many continue to suffer to this day.

4. How are you going to deal with the overwhelming majority of American citizens, as well as Muslims here and in the Middle East, who are opposed to your bombing Syria? Do you think that lack of domestic public support and even deeper hatred abroad are inconsequential? Your empire mentality seems to say yes.

One would think that receiving a detailed letter of inquiry and caution, citing congressional authority, from House Speaker John

Boehner (R-OH), of all people, should give you pause. Increasingly, you are coming across, even to your hardcore political supporters, as *impulsively aggressive*, too quick to order killing operations and too slow to contemplate the waging of peace. (Don't those italicized words remind readers of Trump to come?)

The Syrian civil war—riven by fighting rebel factions, sectarian revenge cycles, outside arms suppliers and provocations, and a spreading al-Qaeda force fighting the dictatorial Assad regime—can only get worse following a violent attack by your administration.

Listen to Hans Blix, the head of the United Nations weapons inspection team in Iraq during 2002–2003. Mr. Blix, former Swedish minister for foreign affairs, urges all governments supporting the various sides in Syria's civil war to attend an international peace conference under the UN Security Council's auspices. Since all fighters in Syria are receiving their weapons from outside nations, these "supplier countries have leverage," Blix writes, to demand "that their clients accept a ceasefire—or risk losing further support."

Achieving this goal will require strong leadership. While it is difficult for you to move from waging war to waging peace, history documents that the latter brings better outcomes and forestalls the slaughter and other blowbacks that security experts fear could reach our country.

When your own military believes you are moving into dangerous terrain and possible points of no return, you'd better start to rethink. You'd better reread the warnings in the measured memoranda given to you by the secretary of defense, Chuck Hagel, and the chairman of the Joint Chiefs of Staff, General Martin Dempsey.

More publicly, retired lieutenant general Gregory S. Newbold, who directed operations for the Joint Chiefs during the run-up to the second Iraq War, told the *Washington Post*, "There's a broad naiveté in the political class about America's obligations in foreign policy issues, and scary simplicity about the effects that employing American military power can achieve." He said that many of his fellow officers share his views.

General Newbold's words seem like a rebuke not just to the Bush neocons (pro-Vietnam-War draft dodgers) who pushed for the Iraq invasion, but also to you and your immediate circle of hawkish civilian advisers.

All weapons of violence—chemical, biological, nuclear, drone, or conventional munitions—are used to destroy lives and habitats. That the use of certain types of weapons may not technically constitute an international war crime is hardly consolation for their victims.

Aggressive arms controls should be the priority of the leading superpower in the world. Why haven't you made US ratification of the treaties on small arms, landmines, and cluster munitions, adhered to by most nations, a priority?

Before you violently embroil our country in yet another Middle Eastern country's tragic turmoil, visit the government-supported United States Institute of Peace for intensive tutorials. Then reread Article I, Section 8, and its originating history, which says that going to war is not your decision but the *exclusive decision of the Congress*. That may help you accept the imperative of your moral and legal accountability.

Not many of the people who voted for you in 2008 would have imagined that your foreign policy would rely so much on brute military force at the expense of systemically waging peace. Certainly, voters who knew your background as a community organizer, a scholar of constitutional law, and a critic of the Bush/Cheney years, never would have expected you to favor the giant warfare state so pleasing to many in the military-industrial complex.

Now, as if having learned little from the devastating and costly aftermaths of the military invasions of Iraq, Afghanistan, and Libya, you're beating the combustible drums to attack Syria—a country that is no threat to the US and that is embroiled in a complex civil war under a brutal regime.

This time, however, you may have pushed for too many acts of war. Public opinion and many members of both parties in Congress are opposed. These lawmakers oppose bombing Syria in spite of your corralling the cowardly leaders of both parties in Congress.

Thus far, your chief achievement on the Syrian front has been garnering support for your position from al-Qaeda affiliates fighting in Syria, the pro-Israeli government lobby, AIPAC, your chief nemesis in Congress, House Speaker John Boehner, and Dick Cheney. This is quite a gathering and a telling commentary on your ecumenical talents. Assuming the veracity of your declarations regarding the Assad regime's resort to chemical warfare (a form of warfare, one might add, that Winston Churchill introduced to the Middle East in the 1920s, when he advocated for "using poisoned gas against uncivilized tribes"), your motley support group is oblivious to the uncontrollable consequences that might stem from bombing Syria.

You argue that shelling Syria and drawing that "red line" will maintain "international credibility," yet you seem unconcerned about how that credibility might be affected by the loss of innocent Syrian civilian life, causalities to our foreign service and armed forces in that wider region, and retaliation against the fearful Christian population in Syria (about 10 percent of Syrians are Christian). But the greatest harm to US credibility would come from the violation of our own Constitution, the neglected needs of the American people, and the flouted standards of international law and the UN Charter (which prohibit unilateral bombing in this situation).

There is another burgeoning cost—that of the militarization of the State Department, whose original charter invests it with the responsibility of diplomacy. Instead of following that charter, Mr. Obama, you have shaped the State Department into a belligerent source of "force projection," first under Generalissima Clinton and now under Generalissimo Kerry. The sidelined foreign service officers, who have knowledge and conflict-avoidance experience, are left with reinforced fortress-like embassies as befits our empire reputation abroad.

Secretary of State John Kerry descended to gibberish when, under questioning by a House committee member the first week of September 2013, he asserted that your proposed attack was "not war" because there would be "no boots on the ground." In Kerry's view, bombing a country with missiles is not an act of war.

It is instructive to note how government autocracy feeds on itself. Start with unjustified government secrecy garnished with the words "national security." That leads to secret laws, secret evidence, secret courts, secret prisons, secret prisoners, secret relationships with select members of Congress, denial of standing for any citizens attempting to file suit, secret drone strikes, and secret incursions into other nations—and all this directed by a president who alone decides when to be secret prosecutor, judge, jury, and executioner. What a republic, what a democracy, what a passive people we have become!

Voices of reason and experience have urged the proper path away from the metastasizing war that is plaguing Syria. As proposed by former president Jimmy Carter, UN Secretary-General Ban Ki-moon, and other seasoned diplomats and retired military officials, vigorous leadership by you is needed for an international peace conference that brings all parties to the table, including the countries supplying weapons to the various adversaries in Syria.

Crowding out attention to America's serious domestic problems with yet another Christian military adventure (as many Muslims see it) in another nonthreatening Muslim country is aggression camouflaging sheer madness.

Please, before you recklessly flout Congress, absorb the wisdom of the World Peace Foundation's Alex de Waal and Bridget Conley-Zilkic. Writing in the *New York Times*, they strongly condemn the use of nerve gas in Syria, brand the perpetrators as war criminals to be tried by an international war crimes tribunal, and then declare,

> But it is folly to think that airstrikes can be limited: they are ill-conceived as punishment, fail to protect civilians and, most important, hinder peacemaking.... Punishment, protection and peace must be joined.... An American assault on Syria would be an act of desperation with incalculable consequences. To borrow once more from Sir William [Harcourt, the British parliamentarian who argued against British intervention in the American Civil War]: "We are asked to go we know not whither, in order to do we know not what."

To repeat, history teaches that empires always devour themselves.

This devouring is based on a double effect. Men, women, and wealth are being poured into unwinnable conflicts *and* all those lives and monies are directed away from domestic needs. Just as in the 1960s and 1970s, when the war in Vietnam began to take up so much of the US's energy and wealth that proposed domestic programs had to be shelved, so further escalation of US involvement in the Middle East would prevent the government from working on important domestic issues. Let me expound that point more fully:

Short of an ongoing "hot" war, the imbroglio over the proposed bombing of Syria occupied the precious time of President Obama, and therefore the mass media, more than anything else on his plate. In addition, it absorbed still more of his time and political capital in the weeks that followed.

Our country's misguided foreign policy caused our president to devote enormous time and influence to enlisting allies and members of Congress, and figuring out the many risks of another protracted, unlawful war-quagmire in the Middle East. Imagine how much time our president could have spent on our country's many domestic problems, such as reforming the corporate tax escapes, universalizing health care, or attaining living wages or electoral reforms.

As our involvement in the Syrian conflict was just beginning, Mr. Obama was scheduled to fly to California to address the largest annual convention of the AFL-CIO and its member unions. Chief labor leader Richard Trumka—an Obama loyalist—was unveiling a bold new plan to expand labor's big tent to include groups such as Working America (representing non-union workers), the Sierra Club, the NAACP, La Raza, and student organizations. Keynoter Barack Obama had to cancel his appearance. Reason: absorption with Syria.

After waiting months for a meeting with their president, the Congressional Black Caucus finally got their White House invitation. Did their political hero engage them over the domestic issues Caucus members wanted to discuss?

As noted by a disappointed representative André Carson (D-IN), Black Caucus members wanted to focus on programs targeted at the African American community: "summer jobs," "helping to empower small businesses, women-owned businesses, and minority-owned businesses," helping to "improve the health of our public school systems," along with civil rights and voting issues. Sorry. Barack Obama spent his hour trying to persuade them to support bombing Syria!

If at the time one took Mr. Obama at his often-repeated word that "the safety of the American people" was his top priority, the trajectory of that commitment would have seemed strangely skewed. Drone attacks or other techniques of wiping out stateless terrorists, alleged suspects, and an occasional American citizen produce backlash, and in the long run force our country to spend more on "guns" than "butter."

But whether campaigning or presiding, candidate and president Barack Obama seemed to seriously undervalue policies that would prevent the loss of over three hundred thousand American lives each year and avoid many more injuries and illnesses.

If you were a relative or close friend of any one of the nearly sixty thousand American workers who die every year, according to OSHA, from "work-related illnesses and injuries," you might have wondered what our president was doing about occupational health and safety problems. Well, during the 2012 campaign he was preventing OSHA and its director, Dr. David Michaels, from issuing long-overdue life-saving regulations.

If you heard about the 250,000 Americans who never leave the hospital alive due to "medical errors," hospital-induced infections, or malpractice—that is, about 5,000 fatalities a week—you would have had no choice but to patiently wait for Mr. Obama to someday mention options for preventing this vast, avoidable death toll.

The Centers for Disease Control reports that more than 250 Americans die every day from health care–associated infections. These deaths are preventable, and some progress is being made to reduce the number of infections by simply encouraging medical personnel to wash their hands more frequently. Obama didn't talk about that but rather spoke about Bashar al-Assad and the civil war in Syria.

At the time, it made me feel like calling, *Come back home, Mr. President!* Go to work and use your muscle to protect the safety of Americans by reducing the loss of life and injuries and illnesses stemming from preventable causes. The mass media will follow your activities, your activist "bully pulpit."

A word to the wise to Democrats in office now under Trump: true leaders, ones who want to get voters behind them, should apply the many solutions already available to all the neglected problems and deprivations in our country. They should be addressing rising child poverty and restoring taxes on the rich and corporations rather than automatically funding self-defeating, metastasizing, and very costly military operations.

It seems incredible that so many peace advocates, many even at the top in the military, were shut out from the conversation on this run-up to war. That might have been expected if such a narrow mind as Trump were running things. But Obama kept saying he wanted to govern with the people's input.

As the Obama administration pushed forward with the Syria effort in fall 2014, all the good arguments *against military engagement*—that it was counterproductive, leading to more, not less, terrorism and chaos, and that it drained needed resources from the country—were ignored. In President Obama's words, the US had to "degrade and destroy" ISIS. The Republican Party, led by war-at-any-cost senators Lindsey Graham and John McCain, wanted a bigger military buildup, which could only mean putting US soldiers on the ground.

This was another result of Bush's war in Iraq. Washington had already expended thousands of American lives, hundreds of thousands of American injuries and illnesses, and over a million Iraqi lives. The achievement: the slaying or capture of al-Qaeda leaders—but with that came the spread of al-Qaeda into a dozen countries and the emergence of a new al-Qaeda on steroids, the

Islamic State of Iraq and Syria (ISIS), which gained control over an area in Syria and Iraq roughly equal to the size of Great Britain.

Still, no lessons were learned. Under Obama's watch, we continued to attack countries and side with one sectarian group against another, which only created chaos and set in motion the cycle of revenge, which in turn sparked new internal strife. So, Democrats: if slamming a hornet's nest propels more hornets to start new nests, isn't it time to rethink this nest-slamming policy? The militarization of US foreign policy only increases the violent chaos abroad and the risk of blowback at home. Suicide bombings and other "retribution" attacks in heavily populated spaces are very hard to stop, as we have seen thousands of times overseas in Iraq and Afghanistan.

According to Richard Clarke, former counterterrorism adviser to George W. Bush, Osama bin Laden wanted Bush to invade Iraq, so that more Muslims would take up arms against the US and more Muslims would hate our country for its destruction of their land and people. Similarly, ISIS would like nothing better than to embroil the US and our soldiers in a ground war, so that it can rally more people to expel the giant US invader.

Then there is the massive overreaction by our government and its ever-willing corporate contractors. Political turmoil ensues, and our democratic institutions, already weakened in their defense of liberty, due process, and the rule of law, are further overwhelmed by the policing dictates of a profitable national security state.

Randolph Bourne, a hundred years ago, wrote an essay with these words about war:

> It automatically sets in motion throughout society those irresistible forces for uniformity, for passionate cooperation with the Government in coercing into obedience the minority groups and individuals which lack the larger herd

sense . . . Other values such as artistic creation, knowledge, reason, beauty, the enhancement of life, are instantly and almost unanimously sacrificed . . .

Benjamin Franklin understood this collective panic when he said that people who prefer security to liberty deserve neither.

These words were as applicable now as they were a few years ago. More so, in that our current president seems all too willing to find more wars, beyond those we already participate in, in which to embroil us. And these questions are just as pertinent:

During war, can our civil society defend the institutions critical to maintaining democracy?

Will our courts fold the rule of law before the overreaching panic by the executive branch and its armed forces?

Will our Congress and state legislatures stand firm against sacrificing our liberty and the public budgets that serve our civil society's necessities (poverty, climate change, health and safety solutions) in the face of a police/military state's overreacting ultimatums?

Will our media resist hyper-focusing on the "war on terror" and give us other important news about ongoing American life?

Will our government pay more attention to preventing the yearly loss of hundreds of thousands of American lives from hospital infections, medical malpractice, defective products, air and water pollution, unsafe drugs, toxic workplaces and homes, and other domestic perils?

Let's hope recharged Democrats can answer these questions in the affirmative.

The 9/11 atrocities resulted in a brutal reaction. In devastating two countries and their civilians, the US lost far more Americans than on 9/11, not to mention the trillions of dollars that could have been spent to save many lives here.

Regrettably, our democratic institutions and civil resiliency are not presently prepared to hold fast with the forces of reason, prudence, and smart responses that forestall a national nervous breakdown—one which happens to be very profitable and power-concentrating for the few against the many.

Consider what our leaders did to our democracy during their "war on terrorism": secret laws, secret courts, secret evidence, secret dragnet snooping on everyone, unauditable, massive secret spending for military quagmires abroad, secret prisons, and even censored judicial decisions that were supposed to be fully disclosed! Government prosecutors have often made a shambles of their duty to show probable cause and respect habeas corpus and other constitutional rights. Thousands of innocent people were jailed without charges and detained without attorneys after 9/11.

Only the American people—who do not benefit from these wars—can exercise their constitutional sovereignty to shape responses that promote safety without damaging liberty. And only a party that stands behind them can get us out of this draining, destructive, and endless involvement in no-win wars.

I was thinking about Obama's last days in office after his second term. This is the time when presidents often make grand gestures to cement their legacy. Obama pardoned Chelsea Manning as one of his going-away presents—a good start, but why couldn't he have done something even more dramatic? Thinking back, I drafted this imaginary letter:

Dear President Obama,

On November 28, 2016, Jimmy Carter, the president who negotiated the peace agreement between Israel and Egypt in 1978, wrote an op-ed for the *New York Times* titled "America Must Recognize Palestine." His urgent plea was directed to you to take "the vital step . . . to grant

American diplomatic recognition to the state of Palestine, as 137 countries have already done, and help it achieve full United Nations membership," before you leave office on January 20, 2017.

Mr. Carter referenced your reaffirmation in 2009 of the Camp David agreement between Israel and Egypt and United Nations Security Council Resolution 242, when you called for "a complete freeze on the building of settlements, constructed illegally by Israel on Palestinian territory." He noted that in 2011 you made clear that, in your words, "the borders of Israel and Palestine should be based on the 1967 lines," and that "negotiations should result in two states, with permanent Palestinian borders with Israel, Jordan and Egypt, and permanent Israeli borders with Palestine."

Former president Carter sees that the "combined weight of United States recognition, United Nations membership [for Palestine] and a Security Council resolution solidly grounded in international law would lay the foundation for future diplomacy."

With Israeli lawmakers moving, in December 2016, to annex more Palestinian land—the 22 percent left of old Palestine (prompting a plea by outgoing UN secretary-general Ban Ki-moon for them to reconsider)—and the forthcoming carte blanche for Israeli repression of the Palestinians promised by the incoming Trump administration, Mr. Carter sees your recognition of international law and the United Nations resolution as "the best—now, perhaps, the only—means of countering the one-state reality that Israel is imposing on itself and the Palestinian people" and "that could destroy Israeli democracy."

He adds that "[r]ecognition of Palestine and a new

Security Council resolution are not radical new measures, but a natural outgrowth of America's support for a two-state solution."

In the remaining post-election weeks of your final term, you are freer than you've ever been to make these decisions for peace and justice in that troubled area—moves rooted in pronouncements you made early in your first term.

You have, as president, approved the greatest transfer in US history of military weapons, research, and intelligence to the Israeli government. Unlike any other president, you have agreed to an unprecedented ten-year deal for Israel's multibillion-dollar military assistance program. No other country outside of wartime has ever come close to receiving that kind of gift, paid for by the American taxpayers.

More than any other president, you have been forbearing to the extreme when the Israeli prime minister, in an impetuous move widely criticized in Israel, circumvented the White House in 2015 by addressing a joint session of Congress, undermining your delicate, multilateral negotiations with Iran.

In return for all this largesse and astonishing self-restraint, you have been the subject of nonstop revilement in Israel, with ugly racist epithets and absurd accusations of anti-Semitism. This campaign of calumny has brought down your approval rating in Israeli polls—often to single digits—and diminished the Israeli peace movement.

Is it not time for action on behalf of regional peace? You'll have the support of the active peacemakers from both the Left and the Right—including numerous former heads of the Israeli domestic and foreign intelligence agencies (see *The Gatekeepers* documentary and the S.

Daniel Abraham Center for Middle East Peace), former cabinet ministers, and mayors and public intellectuals, not to mention stalwart Israeli human rights organizations, such as B'Tselem.

As if any further proof is needed for the urgency to act, you must be appalled by the declarations of Donald Trump and his selection for the next ambassador to Israel: David Friedman, Trump's own bankruptcy lawyer, a man privy to the president-elect's innermost business dealings.

Friedman, who has accused you of "blatant anti-Semitism," is a hard-liner on Israeli colonial expansionism and annexations in the West Bank. His bigotry against Palestinian Arabs is deep and long-standing, making him an anti-Semite against these Arabs whose Semitic ancestors have lived there since time immemorial (See James J. Zogby's *The Other Anti-Semitism: The Arab as Scapegoat*). If Friedman reflects Mr. Trump's policies, the uncontrollable eruption of the long-simmering conflict between Israel and Palestine is seen as a near certainty by expanding Jewish American groups advocating for peace, such as J Street and Jewish Voice for Peace.

What more foreboding signs do you need?

Many commentators who know you have described your last year in office as rounding out your historical legacy as president.

Jimmy Carter is experienced, prescient, and correct—he's earned that encomium—in believing that joining the international community in recognizing Palestine, allowing the UN Security Council resolution to be passed, and supporting UN membership for Palestine could be your most consequential contribution to Middle East

security, and our domestic priorities, with other likely collateral benefits for world peace.

The American people, for the most part, including
Jewish and Arab Americans, judging by the polls over
time, would applaud such statesmanlike actions.

Sincerely yours,

Ralph Nader

Readers may be thinking, after seeing Trump's flattery and
near-subservience (at times) to Putin, that at least Obama paid
no fealty to that oligarchic leader. And that much is true. But
while Trump has seemed at times to almost excuse Russia's illegal
annexation of Crimea, Obama, who did protest this usurpation,
could hardly do so in very ringing tones, seeing as he himself, as
I've noted here, was hardly a very credible defender of international laws on warfare. In other words, both presidents faced Putin
from compromised positions.

This is another instance in which our president's playing fast
and loose with international law and our Constitution could have
had an unexpected blowback. I can imagine writing a reproving
letter to Obama at the time of the Russian invasion of Crimea,
using these words:

Dear President Obama:

As you ponder your potential moves regarding President Vladimir V. Putin's annexation of Crimea, where a
large majority of the population is ethnically Russian, it
is important to remember that whatever moral leverage
you may have had in the court of world opinion has been
sacrificed by the precedents set by you and by previous
American presidents who did not do what you say Mr.
Putin *should do*—obey international law.

The need to abide by international law is your recent refrain, often delivered in an accusatory tone when discussing Mr. Putin's military entry in Crimea and its subsequent annexation, following a referendum in which Crimean voters overwhelmingly endorsed rejoining Russia. True, most Ukrainians and ethnic Tatars boycotted the referendum, and there were obstacles to free speech. But even the fairest of referendums, under UN auspices, would have produced majority support for Russia's annexation of the region.

Every day, your presidential actions violate international law because they infringe upon national sovereignties with deadly drones, flyovers, and secret forays by soldiers—to name only the most obvious violations.

President Bush's criminal invasion and devastation of Iraq in 2003 violated international law and treaties initiated and signed by the United States (such as the Geneva Conventions and the UN Charter).

And President Obama, what about your executive branch's war on Libya—with its spreading, violent chaos—which was neither constitutionally declared nor authorized by congressional appropriations?

"Do as I say, not as I do" is always hard to sell, and the Russians can hardly be blamed for interpreting your words of protest as disingenuous. This is especially the case because Crimea, long under the rule of the Ottoman Empire, became part of Russia over two hundred years ago. In 1954, Soviet leader Nikita Khrushchev gave Crimea to Ukraine, which was then part of the Soviet Union, possibly out of sympathy for what Ukraine endured under the Nazi invasion and its atrocities. The transfer mattered little then because both "socialist republics," Ukraine and

Crimea, were part of the Soviet Union. However, it is not entirely clear whether Khrushchev fully complied with the Soviet Constitution when he transferred Crimea to Ukraine.

Compare, by the way, the United States' seizure of Guantánamo Bay from Cuba during the Spanish-American War. The United States had no qualms about retaining that land after Cuba became independent over a century ago.

The Russians have their own troubles, of course, but they do have a legitimate complaint and fear about the United States' actions following the collapse of the Soviet Union. Led by President William Jefferson Clinton, the United States pushed for the expansion of the military alliance NATO to include the newly independent Eastern European countries. This was partly a business deal to get these countries to buy United States fighter aircraft from Lockheed Martin, and partly a needless provocation of a transformed adversary trying to get back on its feet.

As a student of Russian history and language at Princeton, I learned about the deep sensitivity of the Russian people regarding the insecurity of their Western Front. Hitler's attack on the Soviet Union took many millions of Russian lives. The prolonged Nazi siege of the city of Leningrad alone is estimated to have cost over seven hundred thousand civilian lives, which is nearly twice the total number of United States soldiers killed in World War II.

The memories of that mass slaughter and destruction, and of other massacres and the valiant resistance against them, are etched deeply in Russian minds. The NATO provocation is only one example of the West's arrogant treatments of post-Soviet Russia, as pointed out in the writings of Russian specialist and NYU professor Stephen Cohen. That sense of the West's disrespect, coupled with the toppling of the elected pro-Russian president of Ukraine in February 2014 (which was not lawful despite his poor record) is why Mr. Putin's absorption of Crimea and his history-evoking speech before the Russian parliament were met with overwhelming support in Russia, even by many of those who had good reasons to dislike his authoritarian government.

Now, President Obama, you are facing the question of how far to go with sanctions against the Russian government, its economy, and its ruling class.

Welcome to globalization. Russia is tightly intertwined with the European Union, as a seller and buyer of goods, services, and assets, and to a lesser but significant degree with the United States' government and its giant corporations such as oil and technology companies. Sanctions can boomerang, which would be far worse than just being completely ineffective in reversing the Russian annexation of Crimea.

As for sanctions deterring Russia's unlikely westward expansion into Ukraine, consider the following role reversal: if Russia moved for sanctions against the United States before US attacks against Afghanistan, Iraq, Libya, and Yemen, would that have deterred either you or George W. Bush from taking such actions? Of course not. Such an outcome, politically and domestically, would not be possible.

If you want continued Russian cooperation, as you do, on the critical Iranian and Syrian negotiations, ignore the belligerent, baying pack of neocons who always want more US wars (which they and their families always avoid fighting themselves). Develop a coalition of economic support for Ukraine, with European nations, based on observable reforms for that troubled government. Sponsor a global conference on how to enforce international law as early as possible.

Drop the nonsense of evicting Russia from the G8—a get-together forum of leaders. Get on with having the United States comply with international law, and our Constitution, on the way to ending the American Empire's interventions worldwide, as has been recommended by both liberal and conservative/libertarian lawmakers, and in accordance with much public opinion.

Concentrate on America, President Obama, whose long-unmet needs cry out "from sea to shining sea."

Yours,

Ralph Nader

5.

An Interlude: Fund-raising

Let me lighten the tone for a minute here by shifting my focus to a less weighty issue. Going through my files for June 2012, I found a handful of fund-raising letters from the president. The salutation is often "Dear Ralph." One of them asks me for twenty-five dollars, adding, "Ralph, this is that moment. This is the time to be in with me." "I need your voice," he writes, noting that America needs the "dreams and the energy and the determination of people like you."

Mr. Obama acknowledged that "[w]e may have differences in policy, but we all believe in the rights enshrined in our Constitution." (I mentioned previously just how much the president honors the Constitution.) He concludes one letter by saying, "Ralph, I need you to be part of that movement. Now I need you to be in. . . . Your dreams, your determination will drive this campaign."

Wow!

Wait, it gets better. Another letter starts, "Dear Ralph, each night, I get the chance to read about 10 letters from people across the country. Some are inspiring. Some are heartbreaking. But each one compels me to keep moving forward on this journey we started together. . . . People like you have been giving it your all."

He even included a comment card for me to offer my suggestions, thoughts, and ideas. He wants this feedback, he writes, "from citizens in the District of Columbia and across the country" to help him "stay connected to [his] priorities."

This is exciting, I thought at the time. I get to tell the president directly what we can do together to abolish poverty (and establish full Medicare for All), apply law and order against the corporate crooks, dramatically shift from fossil and nuclear fuels to solar, wind, geothermal, and other renewable, efficient technologies to lower the risk of climate change, and keep more dollars in family pocketbooks. I can remind the president about his forgotten 2008 promise to raise the minimum wage to $9.50 by 2011.

Since he mentioned the District of Columbia, I can remind him, as many in DC already have, about another forgotten promise in 2008 to end the colonial status of the nation's capital and to fight for its disenfranchised people to have voting representation in Congress.

His expressed desire to repair America and help students and patients made me wonder why at the time he did not mention cutting the vastly bloated and wasteful military budget, ending the spreading Afghan quagmire, and putting all those saved dollars toward "hope and change" here in America. He had plenty of space left over in his four-page letters to discuss such things.

Oh well, I guess being president is more than any one person can really handle these days. Which is why I welcomed another of his letters, which opened: "Dear Ralph, when you sent me to the White House, I pledged that I would always keep the lines of communication open—and I meant it. . . . My ability to lead the country depends on listening to you." He then advised me to "stay engaged. Listen, learn and use your voice to speak out for the issues that matter most to you." He said America needs me.

It is touching to see his regular letters. Who would have thought, I said to myself at the time, after I had sent him many substantive letters since December 2008 and not received a single reply, not even an acknowledgment from one of his assistants in the vast executive branch, that he was interested in my suggestions?

Appealing once to Michelle, the nice organic gardener and fellow Princetonian, I tried to enlist her help in getting a reply from her husband about his meeting with a large gathering of national civic organizations in DC, which have millions of members nationwide. (President-elect Jimmy Carter held such a meeting in 1976.) That request went nowhere. I even asked her and the president simply to explain their nonresponse policy guidelines.

Again, no response.

Hark! There was still hope, I thought when I received a missive from President Obama with an enclosed postcard featuring his signed picture. The letter started with "Dear Ralph," and built to a crescendo with these boldly underlined words: "I'd like to hear from you."

Quickly, before he changes his mind, I thought, and rushed to my trusty Underwood typewriter, starting, hopefully, with "Dear Barack, I am so pleased that you'd like to hear from me...."

By the way, before I wrote this letter, I published *Return to Sender*, consisting of many of my unanswered letters to George W. Bush and Barack Obama. I thought they might prefer to read the letters in hardback book form, so I sent each of them a personalized copy, but there was no acknowledgment of receipt.

6.

The Democrats Will Be Repeatedly Corporatized Unless They Battle for a People's Agenda

Obama carried the water for a dispirited and corrupted Democratic Party. The Democrats, from 2010 on, were in retreat before the Republican onslaught. In my mind, this was simply because they were letting slip chance after chance to promote a people's agenda.

Today, we are in the same no-win situation for the Democrats. Forget the obsession with Trump bashing, attractive as it is. Let's get behind single-payer health care, more not less environmental, health, worker, and consumer protections, and other recurring items on the people's empowerment list.

This is hardly a new idea. When I glance over the headlines from the Obama Years, I see two things. One, during campaigns, when the Democrats should have been blasting the Republicans for their anti-populist policies and deceptions, they wimped out, maybe afraid to offend corporate donors. Two, when a politician, Democrat or Republican, raised the people's banner high in an election contest, that candidate most often found an enormous swelling of support.

I'll go back over a little of the history. Take the 2012 election, when Obama was running for a second term. Yes, he won, but not without him and his party squandering innumerable opportunities for an even bigger victory, especially in the Congress.

If the congressional Democrats were all drinking water from the same faucet, that might explain their chronic fear of the craven and cruel corporatist Republicans who dominate them.

Their fear, defeatism, and cowering behavior continued in the face of the GOP's outrageous actions as the November 2012 election approached. Let's ponder that.

The explanations go back some years. The Democrats long ago receded from the Truman days of "give 'em hell, Harry!" But their political castration occurred in the late 1970s, when the Democrats were persuaded by one of their own, Congressman Tony Coelho (D-CA), to start aggressively bidding for corporate campaign cash.

Victory in politics often goes to those who have the most energy and decisiveness, however wrongheaded. The Republicans have been winning these races for years. To paraphrase author and lapsed Republican Kevin Phillips, the Republicans go for the jugular, while the Democrats go for the capillaries.

One would think that politicians who side with big corporations, as the Republicans do, would be politically vulnerable for endangering both America and the American people. These corrupt politicians promote corporate tax loopholes and side with insurance and drug companies on costly health care proposals. They defend the corporate polluters' unsafe workplaces, dirty air and water, and contaminated food, they push for more deficit spending in the Iraq and Afghanistan wars, they neglect Main Street–based public works programs that would repair America and create good jobs, they support high-interest student loans, they cover for oil industry greed at the pump, and they are hellbent on taking the federal cops off the corporate crime beats, while stifling the voices of the people and blocking their access to justice.

In 2012 the Democrats should have been landsliding the worst Republican Party in history. Talk about extremists! There were virtually no moderate or liberal Republicans left in Congress after they were driven out by their own party's hard-liners. So this Republican Party, united in their extremism, should have been very easy to challenge.

It didn't happen. Though rolling in promotional cash and capability, the Democrats of the time never bothered to come up with a clear list of the hundreds of disastrous Republican schemes— whether passed in the House or only proposed. These wrongful Republican drives should have been boiled down to their vicious essence for public diffusion. Instead, the blue dog Democrats were constantly, and with impunity, giving Republicans cover, even to the point that seventeen Democrats supported a rash political move by Representatives Boehner, Cantor, and Issa in citing Attorney General Eric Holder for contempt of Congress.

The list of all the times the Democrats have experienced a failure to launch grows longer by the day.

In December 2010, with senators all but unanimously committed to passing auto safety legislation, the Democrats let one senator, Tom Coburn (R-OK), sink it by preventing the bill from being put to a vote. President Obama, ready to sign this life-saving bill, declined to use his powers of persuasion on Coburn, his avowed close friend in the Senate.

Politics is about credibly answering two questions: "Whose side are you on?" and "Whose side is your opponent on?" That means drawing a bright line between the two parties. Unfortunately, as you're seeing, on military and foreign policy there isn't much of a difference. So the bright line will have to be drawn on domestic issues.

But what happened during Obama's two terms, and what went on happening in the 2016 campaign when it was Hillary's turn at bat, is that the Democrats relied on the omnipresent political consulting firms looking for their lucrative 15 percent cut for insipid political television spots, and exclusively focused on raising ever more money in quid pro quo deals with avaricious donors. These combined to form a lethal mix of strategic stupor, stale messaging ("to restore the middle class"), and time-wasting paralysis.

As I mentioned, in 2012 Representative Jesse Jackson Jr. and two dozen progressive cosponsors stood proudly behind a bill that would have raised the federal minimum wage from $7.25 to $10.00 per hour. Neither the Democratic leadership nor President Obama came out in support of such popular legislation (nearly 70 percent in the polls) that historically has been identified with the Democratic Party since the first minimum wage law in 1938.

At that time there was evidently an every-Democrat-for-himself-or-herself policy. Most of the elected Democrats seemed more interested in their own careers and less so in their party's mission for America. Attendance at the regular meetings of the House Democratic Caucus was way down according to the Caucus's leader, Congressman John Larson. President Obama operated as if he cared only about numero uno, even though not regaining the House and keeping the Senate would freeze his second term in acrimony and inaction.

This was one of the significant factors helping Trump toward his White House win. Obama very often sat out important Democratic races when his involvement could have helped bolster the Democratic ranks.

One trend from that time is the most telling: President Obama's reticence in his nomination of federal judges. In meetings between outside support groups and Justice Department staff, the nominees hailing from the ranks of labor and public-interest lawyers, as well as law professors, were received coolly. The Obama staff wanted what they themselves called "stealth candidates"—that is, corporate lawyers with some enlightened pro bono tendencies. Why directly take on the Republicans for the future of the federal judiciary when you can settle for the corporate status quo?

Let me underline this: if Obama and the Democrats dredged the same corporate swamp for their court appointees as the Republicans, then what distinguished Democrats *in the voters' minds* from their rival party? And even where Democrats were completely distinct from the Republicans, *if they didn't trumpet that fact, most voters didn't notice it.*

7.

When Will Democrats Stand by Their Convictions?

Should the Democrats also emulate their rivals in supporting the dishonest waste of taxpayer money involved in party conventions? Let me sound off, since even today people don't grasp how mendacious and venal these presidential nominating to-dos really are. Take the one in 2012:

While the 2012 conventions were under way, the tough times in America continued. Tens of millions of Americans were feeling the squeeze and were suffering from diminished livelihoods. More than fifteen million children went to bed hungry at night. Unemployment and underemployment affected more than twenty million adults. Yet Republicans in Congress regularly called for cuts to the core programs for the needy, the vulnerable, and the disadvantaged, and the Democrats did little to stop them.

These calls most insistently came from Republicans like representatives John Boehner, Eric Cantor, and Paul Ryan, and Senator Mitch McConnell, who were demanding severe reductions in effective social programs and more tax cuts for the wealthy and large corporations, many of whom already paid very little or no federal income tax.

Meanwhile, as they demanded that the poor should get along

on less, the two parties each took $18.2 million in taxpayer money for their national political conventions in Tampa and Charlotte. The money comes from taxpayers via the Treasury Department's "$3 Tax Checkoff," found on tax return forms.

Taxpayers who check the box are told that the money generally goes to "the Presidential Election Campaign Fund." Taxpayers are not told that the funding also goes to the party nominating conventions, not the general election nominees or primary election candidates.

Taxpayers who opt for this partial public funding of elections may not like funding political extravaganzas for the two parties, flaunting banners, musical entertainment, food, drink, and other amenities. They might not want their tax dollars associated with nearby lavish corporate hospitality parties loaded with lobbyists lusting for access, subsidies, and other special privileges.

They might not want to have their tax dollars mixed with corporate contributions to the two conventions from the oil, drug, insurance, banking, nuclear, military weapons, and agribusiness/food-processing giant multinationals.

When your two parties in Congress established this slush fund for the conventions years ago, they lamely tried to justify it by declaring that televised conventions were educational presentations—live democracy in action! That didn't pass the laugh test then or now. In 2012, the nominations were all wrapped up by the conventions, making them de facto coronations of Barack Obama and Mitt Romney. The party platforms were also done deals.

Party rituals, the mutual admiration exchanges, and the scripted, precleared laudatory speeches by selected speakers are the highlights of these uncontested, predetermined, rigged shows of inaction.

I have said for years that even if the Republicans, past masters at living it up at the public's expense, keep putting on these conventions, the Democrats should not take this money, but pay for their conventions themselves. The two parties, embarrassed by some of their objecting members and an adverse public opinion, dropped the conventions' subsidy for their 2016 campaigns.

In the conventions, as with many aspects of foreign policy, the Democrats differed little from their Republican colleagues. Their failure to stand up for taxpayers gave the voters the loud and clear message that politicians care little about their non-wealthy constituents. Little of what was said at these conventions would dispel such beliefs.

In 2012, it was the usual parade of insincerity and insouciance. If you glance over the coverage from the time, you'll see that the Republicans reiterated four themes in just about every speech: Tell your personal story, recounting your humble beginnings and describing how you pulled yourself up by your own bootstraps. Show the people you're human or at least humanoid, not corporatist. Keep heralding small business so you don't have to talk about big business, which has bad vibrations these days around the country. Also, praise, praise, praise Mitt Romney and Paul Ryan as family men with family values. Imagine if Republicans told the press the truth, that their convention was meant to "humanize" Romney and give the voters a warm, fuzzy feeling about him so as to forget that in his campaign he acted as a clenched-teeth mouthpiece for big business.

The Democratic Convention evoked only pity. The Democrats had remarkably similar scripts at the podium—narrate your humble, hardworking family beginnings, talk incessantly about jobs so you won't have to talk about wages. Especially muzzled was the ever-willing Richard Trumka, head of the AFL-CIO, who, since 2009, had been given the back of Obama's hand when it came to legislation for "card check" organizing rights or an inflation-adjusted minimum wage. Obama's staged remarks even withheld any mention of a $10 minimum wage or the raiding of worker pensions by corporate raptors.

The repetitive, overwrought praise of "el Presidente" in every speech became mawkish, reminding one of the "politics of personalism," present in many countries with underdeveloped political institutions. Michelle Obama found no time to mention her mission of growing America's nutritious food sources to keep Americans fit and help them avoid the ravages of corporate junk food–induced obesity. She was too occupied gushing over her aggressive drone commander's touching nightly reading of letters from Americans about their problems.

The mass obeisance ended when the commander-in-chief himself sprang onto the stage to speak the language of hope, meanwhile dodging every opportunity to address the manifold undesirable conditions that actively needed his attention.

Conservative *New York Times* columnist David Brooks, trying to be sympathetic, was looking for some significant specificity:

> ... what I was mostly looking for were big proposals, big as health care was four years ago. I had spent the three previous days watching more than 80 convention speeches without hearing a single major policy proposal in any of them. I asked governors, mayors and legislators to name a significant law that they'd like to see President Obama pass in a second term. Not one could. At its base, this is a party with a protective agenda, not a change agenda ...

Fortifying Brooks's observation was Obama's recounting of the differences between the Democrats and Republicans. They were almost all defensive in nature: defend Social Security, Medicare, and abortion rights from the Republican offensive.

Yes, this is old news, but here is the takeaway point, as relevant now as it was at the time of the convention: the Democrats are *not on the offensive*—they aren't getting tough on corporate crime, consumer gouging, bank abuses, or corporate tax evasions. They are *not on the offensive* in the fight for worker safety and labor rights, minimum wage increases, public services, or helping the poor earn more and pay less.

Even when Obama mentioned climate change—a recent no-no in the Democrats' lexicon—his words were defensive: "climate change is not a hoax." He did not elaborate.

At that time, this *defensive* attitude against the cruelest, most ignorant, corporate-indentured, anti-worker, anti-consumer, warmongering Republican Party in history was also seen in the debates and programs of Democratic congressional and state candidates.

But this is where they need to be now: on the *offensive*. On the ramparts. It should be easy to go on the offensive with an agenda standing for and with the people who are being economically driven, along with their country, into the ground by unpatriotic global corporations and their war-making political minions.

8.

Romney Lost, Yes, but Obama Should Have Been Cleaning His Clock

If only the Democrats would take up the cudgels for the lower and middle economic classes, they would be landsliding the Republicans. But they don't do it. At every turn in 2012—which, as you'll recall, led to a win at the top (for Obama) and massive Democratic losses at the bottom (for Congress and state legislatures)—the party of FDR acted feebly and inefficiently, letting the Republicans get away with ugly and cruel agendas that only benefited the rich and powerful corporatists.

Let me note some of the low points for Democrats in that season: for starters, look at the way they let the Republican candidate Mitt Romney complain in the most uninformed way about the economy under Obama. He should have been repeatedly challenged in plain language.

Not a day went by without Romney blaming Obama for every slumping or stagnant economic indicator. Unemployment, increases in the number of food stamp recipients, government borrowing and spending, home foreclosures, economic uncertainty for businesses, trade deficits—you name it. Only for droughts and hurricanes did Romney let him off the hook.

Here's the rebuttal Obama should have made during the campaign. He should have taken on Romney, one on one, and told him something like this:

I won't go into detail about what was inherited from your party's years in office. Deregulation, nonenforcement, cover-ups by the collapsing, avaricious financial industry, and subsidies and bailouts were that period's hallmarks. For me to be held responsible for the state of the plundered American economy, there would have to be a "command and control" economy enforced by the White House. You know full well that is not the case, for several reasons:

First, our economy is dominated by corporations that make their own investment and hiring decisions. Two-thirds of the millions of minimum-wage workers are employed by large corporations with over one hundred employees, such as Walmart and McDonald's. Thirty million American workers are laboring between the federal minimum wage of $7.25 per hour and what the minimum wage, inflation adjusted, would be now. These large companies are successfully opposing moves in Congress to increase the minimum wage to catch up with 1968's!

Moreover, the largest US companies are sitting on more than two trillion dollars in inactive cash reserves. I have no power to get more of that capital invested, other than to appeal to their corporate patriotism. I could also use that patriotic appeal to urge them to increase their dividends to shareholders, which would pump tens of billions of dollars into our consumer economy and encourage much-needed spending. Some of these successful companies, like Google, eBay, Amazon, and others, offer no dividends at all to their owners.

Second, I am not the Federal Reserve. The Fed has kept interest rates very low, which has limited the return on savings. Tens of millions of middle- and lower-income people could spend those interest payments on the necessities of life. But the Fed is its own dictator, and its catering to the capital investment community doesn't seem to be boosting the economy.

"Third, there is oppositional unanimity by Republicans in Congress to block any economic, job-producing measures, as they're hoping a long-term recessionary economy will help you defeat me in November. I tried to promote a major public works construction and repair program in Congress. The Republicans in the House blocked it under the aegis of representatives John Boehner and Eric Cantor. This program would have produced well-paid jobs, with multiplier effects, that could not be exported to China. Our communities have trillions of dollars in deferred maintenance afflicting schools, clinics, public transit systems, highways, bridges, dams, and water and sewage systems. I cannot make this happen without the Republicans in Congress.

I can almost imagine him saying most of this. But he would never have said anything to overturn Romney's statement that "Washington has become an impediment to economic growth." I just think Obama was too close to the establishment to have said, for instance, "You want to improve Washington's relation to the economy, Mitt? So why don't you support an end to the vast array of corporate subsidies, handouts, bailouts, and inflated government contracts, especially from the defense industry? Imagine what your friends on Wall Street and in Houston would think of you after such a burst of candor."

Vote-getting words, for sure, but the Democrats have been too establishment entrenched to use them.

And there's more to say about Romney and his crew. Recent uproar about the hardheartedness of the Republican zealots who are bent on stripping health care from millions of Americans shows short historical memory. The Republicans' monetized minds and flinty hearts have been on display for years.

And they certainly were during the 2012 election. Why didn't the Democrats strike some sparks off them?

I mean, in 2012 it was hard to imagine a more crazed, cruel, anti-people, corporate-indentured, militaristic, and corporatized Republican Party. A party devoid of minimal compassion. Failure to distinguish themselves from that lot shows how limited were the Democrats' fortitude and imagination.

Here are some examples of the Republicans' malfeasance at that time, which Democrats should have roundly denounced:

The Republicans seemed to have it in for women. They weren't content to merely oppose health insurance companies covering reproductive health care, and to threaten the privacy of the medical records of victims of rape and incest. The Republicans voted *en masse* to block legislation that would prevent companies from paying lower wages on the basis of gender.

On consumer protections—forget it. The Republicans were indentured to the worst of their corporate paymasters. At the time, the Republicans either did nothing to help or actually pushed for rollbacks of regulations that defended consumers' health, safety, and pocketbooks.

In a frenzy, House Republicans voted to repeal all or parts of the "Affordable Care Act" more than fifty times. Be assured their hatred for Obamacare was not because they wanted full Medicare for All. It was because they wanted to voucherize Medicare and hand patients over to the grasping Aetnas and Pfizers of America, who would return the favor with campaign cash.

House Republicans raged against *any attempts to stop* the outsourcing of American jobs to communist and fascist regimes abroad that know how to keep their workers in powerless penury. Why? Because that is what the unpatriotic US-based global corporations want them to do. Anything Big Oil wants, it gets: big subsidies, tax breaks, weakened pollution restrictions, leases everywhere, and even relief when these oil companies damage the Gulf Coast.

What about Republicans' environmental actions? Republicans voted to weaken the Clean Air Act and drinking water safety standards. They cut funding for programs that prevent cancer and protect public health while pushing for more military weapons and bloated Pentagon budgets. The Republicans went so far as to vote for polluters over children, pregnant women, and people who live in nursing homes and assisted-living facilities. These Republicans voted to block the EPA mercury and air toxics standards, regulations the agency estimated would save eleven thousand lives every year and prevent more than one hundred thousand asthma attacks.

With unseemly fervor, House Republicans worked to weaken the National Labor Relations Board and labor laws. But when it came to protecting the lowest tax rates and loopholes for the very wealthy, they were Horatius at the Bridge. When corporations and their paid allies engaged in financial fraud (credit cards, mortgages and student loans, abuse of seniors) or urged privatizing Social Security, the Boehners and the Cantors block-tackled anyone in the House who wanted to push law and order for the rich and corporate or keep the "security" in Social Security.

For the poor, the Republican plan is "Let them eat less." Hunger in America is real. But not real enough for the Republicans to stop wanting to cut food programs. While Republicans campaigned against Obama for not doing anything to lower gasoline prices, they were voting against measures to regulate oil and gas speculators who drive up gas prices.

Yes, I'm not talking about the Trumpicans. This is what we saw as the heritage the Republicans were running on in 2012. Even then many wanted to summarily abolish agencies such as the EPA, OSHA, and the IRS. The meat-axe Republicans had trouble telling the public how the important *functions* performed by these agencies would be handled. The Republicans dismissed the work of climate change researchers and health and safety agencies as junk science. Fortunately, the Senate has blocked most of their madness.

I ask you to ponder the fate of our Republic. Ask why we have almost unconditionally given up our enormous sovereign power as "We the People" and delegated it to those out-of-control, raging members of Congress. One percent or less of our citizenry, active and organized back home, representing public opinion, could have turned that legislature around.

How could the Democrats have lost when running against such avaricious advocates of harmful policies?

In 2012, while the Democrats needed to up their game in terms of shifting their programs to more people-friendly ones, their president needed to jump into the election ring, tag-teaming on close races for progressive Democrats. His failure on this count was a key factor that *eventually* contributed to the Democrats' failure against the Trump steamroller. Lack of party building and failure to turn out the vote was decisive in the later defeat.

When the dust settled after the 2012 season, I think any progressive would have asked, "Why can't the Democrats landslide these Republicans as FDR, Harry Truman, John F. Kennedy, or Lyndon Baines Johnson would surely have done?" The same question could be asked in 2016.

Let me say a little more about this bitter victory in 2012.

The president ran a "lone ranger" campaign instead of campaigning with the congressional Democrats as a team. Notice how he kept saying, as he did during his nomination speech in Charlotte, North Carolina, "Vote for me." This separation from the rest of his party created more than a little resentment among Democrats on Capitol Hill. Compare Obama's aloofness with Bill Clinton's propensity while campaigning for president to act with his allies in Congress when he was in their districts. At the time, House Democrats were also upset at the White House's refusal to direct some of its immense campaign cash toward hard-pressed Democrats in close House races.

But did the Democrats in Congress feel free to go it alone at that time? Just the opposite. Earlier, they would have opened up new issues, new reforms, and new fronts. Now, they decided to capitulate and wait for Obama to take the first visible step. Yet Obama, ever cautious and conflict averse, did not make the first move.

Obama's consultants, advisers, and pollsters said that he had to appeal to the 5 or 10 percent of the right-of-center voters. He already had the liberals, progressives, unionists, and the minorities well in hand, because they had nowhere else to go.

Given this tactical approach determining Obama's daily orations and the political ads, including how he went after Romney/Ryan, he made no room for demanding an inflation-adjusted minimum wage of $10. There was no room for a tough law-and-order campaign cracking down on corporate crime, fraud, and Wall Street abuses daily afflicting tens of millions of Americans.

As returning legislator Alan Grayson showed, in his winning campaign against the Republicans and their super PACs in central Florida, these can be vote-getting issues. But as I was told by many politicians backing Obama at that time, that was neither his game plan nor that of his consultants! They simply did not think that they could get a higher net voter turnout from their large non-voting base of lower-income workers. Thirty million low-income workers making under $10.50 an hour apparently do not have as much voter turnout potential as right-of-center undecided voters. Of course, there are more elements involved. Back then, when I asked a top House Democrat what the real reason was for deep-sixing the minimum wage increase, he rubbed his thumb and two fingers together and said, "They feel they'd raise less money if they did that." In this bizarre equation, money, it seems, counts more than the votes of the people with whom the party should stand.

When at the time I spoke to other leading progressive Democrats, urging them to assert themselves, jurisdictional turf presented itself. No senior Democrat in the House would run first on any labor issues. They'd instead wait for moves by Rep. George Miller, from the San Francisco area, because they felt that was his issue. Nor would any senior Democrats run on any energy or environmental issues other than ranking committee member Ed Markey. Markey and his allies were privately wringing their hands over Obama's silence on climate change during the president's daily campaigns.

Obama didn't move. If you were a Democrat in Congress, you would not want to show up the president's inaction, would you?

It seemed that personal career complacency meant there was no drive to vigorously propel the party to win back the House, regardless of what Obama chose to propose.

After Election Day, it became clear that congressional Democrats had waited too long on Obama, and wasted their chance to win back the House and gain more seats in the Senate.

I've heard of resting on your laurels, but don't fall asleep on them.

Lamentable was the fact that Obama wasn't getting out and mixing it up to help Democrats in House races, as Rep. Maxine Waters (D-CA) remarked to me.

For all his hundreds of millions of campaign dollars, President

Obama repeatedly missed out on opportunities to emphasize the most obvious flaws of the Romney/Ryan campaign.

If in 2011 people with a casual interest in politics were told that Obama's opponent would be a man with secret bank accounts abroad and various incomes maneuvered over to tax escape islands, who ran businesses that destroyed or exported jobs, declares contempt for the 47 percent of Americans receiving public benefits, and adopts Paul Ryan's budget to shred America's public services, corporatize Medicare, bloat the military budget, and further entrench the domination of the 1 percent over American workers at a time of overall declining livelihoods and growing poverty, wouldn't they conclude that Obama was a shoo-in for reelection? I would have.

The Democrats failed to follow a cardinal rule of politics: never let the public forget your opponent's most serious liabilities. Sure, Obama's televised ads battered Romney during the summer. Sure, when Romney picked Paul Ryan as his running mate, the Democrats portrayed the Ryan budget as cruel, dishonest, and economically destructive. But in the final eight weeks of the campaign Obama should have been repeating Romney and Ryan's grim and dim positions over and over again.

The Democrats should have been hammering Romney over his offshore accounts. They should have been pointing to the grisly details of the unhinged Ryan budget, and explaining exactly how it would grind down people's economic well-being, sense of security, and health and safety. They should have, until the final hour, been repeatedly calling out Romney's worst failings before the undecided voters. That's the recipe for victory. It also could have changed some decided minds and induced some Romney-leaning voters to stay home. Better yet, it would have thrown the Republicans on the defensive all the way down to the local elections.

Instead, the big jobs were left undone, including a stunning inattention to the Republicans turning the 2010 elections into ger-rymandering heaven for the GOP. But then what can you expect from a visionless political party with more money than strategic brains? Obama's advisers told him to run by himself and not with his Democratic members of Congress, whom he needed to retake the House and keep the Senate in order to get anything done in his second term. Worse, as Matt Bai wrote in the *New York Times Magazine*, Obama had no narrative for America's future.

The Democratic National Committee decided to let their chief nemesis in Congress—Speaker John Boehner—run unopposed in 2014 by a Democratic candidate in his Ohio district. Unop-posed! A free ride! Newt Gingrich never did that when, as a junior congressman from Georgia, he led the movement to dump Dem-ocratic House Speaker Jim Wright and shortly thereafter helped defeat the sitting speaker, Tom Foley, in Foley's own Washington state congressional district.

Again, I'm not simply saying this was a sign of the times. It is a sign for right now about how the Democrats should be com-porting themselves.

It's not only that 2012 was a failure. It's the fact that Democrats didn't learn from it. Here were the Republicans, now that they had a majority in the House and were gunning for it in the Senate, brazenly talking up a government shutdown.

The polls showed convincingly in fall 2013 that people blamed the stubborn Republicans more than the Democrats for the adverse effects of the impasse on workers, public health, safety, consumer spending, recreational parks, and government corporate contracts.

To repeat, why weren't the Democrats slamming the Repub-licans more strongly on this obstructionism? And this brings us back to my earlier question, already partly answered: Why didn't the Democrats landslide the cruelest, most ignorant, big-business-indentured Republican Party in history during the 2010 and 2012 congressional elections?

First and most obvious is that the Democrats were dialing for the same commercial campaign dollars, which, beyond the baggage of *quid pro quo* money, detoured the party away from concentrating on their constituents' needs and crafting responsive policies as if they meant them to be enacted.

Democrats like Rep. Marcy Kaptur (D-OH) have told me that when the House Democrats get together in an election year, they go into the meetings talking about money and walk out talking about money, burdened with the monetary quotas assigned by their so-called leadership.

In 2012, House Minority Leader Nancy Pelosi (D-CA) was reported to have attended four hundred fund-raisers in DC and around the country for campaigning Democrats. Helping Democratic candidates with fund-raising is a major way she asserts her control over them. Over 90 percent of the Democrats in the House deferred to her and did not press her on such matters as upping the federal minimum wage, controlling corporate crime, reducing corporate welfare giveaways, asserting full Medicare for All, diminishing a militaristic foreign policy, or fighting for any other policies reputed to be favored by the party's Congressional Progressive Caucus, numbering more than seventy-five representatives. Instead, the Progressive Caucus remained moribund, declining to press their policy demands on leader Pelosi, as the hard-core, much more energetic Tea Partiers do with their leaders.

So when election time comes around, voters do not know what the Democrats stand for other than protecting Social Security and Medicare from the Republicans. Former senator and presidential candidate Gary Hart, now living in Denver, told me in 2012 that the local Democrats in Denver didn't know what the national Democrats stood for.

The 2010 election brought crucial wins for the Republicans in state government races, giving them the upper hand in redistricting decisions for a decade. That meant more gerrymandered, one-party-dominated districts. The Republicans won a majority of those gubernatorial and state legislative races and took over the US House of Representatives with Speaker John Boehner (R-OH) and his curled-lip majority leader, Eric Cantor (R-VA).

And there was also President Obama's political selfishness, a key point I've mentioned already. Obama knew that he could not govern with a reactionary and obstructionist Republican House of Representatives. Yet he did not provide serious campaign support and progressive policy leadership for Democratic candidates. Consequently he was overcome in 2011 by the Republican demands for sharp cuts in federal budgets serving the people, while corporate entitlements were exempted from similar cuts. And during the first term of his presidency he was constantly haunted by the specter of government shutdowns and Republicans in Congress refusing to raise the government's debt ceiling to pay current debts.

So you'd think that in 2012 President Obama would run arm-in-arm with congressional Democrats. No way. He not only signaled his "going it alone" approach by turning down the House Democrats' request for $30 million from his billion-dollar campaign hoard, but he also had little interest in campaigning with local congressional candidates as he traveled around the country. The House Democrats were dismayed, but kept quiet.

So he got the Boehner/Cantor duo for another two years after the 2012 election. That meant another shut-the-government-down, don't-lift-the-debt-ceiling imbroglio—a clash that crowded out all the necessities and the matters of justice that our government is supposed to champion.

By 2013, you'd think the Democrats would have gotten wise and started pushing a more populist agenda, but it turned out that

House Democrats believed that they could win back the House in 2014. Even given the fact that many House-passed Republican votes since 2011 sided with big business and against children, student borrowers, workers, women, consumers, and small taxpayers.

From the 1940s to the 1990s, the Republican Party did not behave as badly as today's snarling version of the GOP. Yet the Democrats beat Republicans in most congressional races. Imagine what presidents Franklin D. Roosevelt, Harry S. Truman, John F. Kennedy, and Lyndon Baines Johnson would have done with today's crop of Republican corporatists and rabid ideologues.

Today's Democrats, with very few exceptions, are dull, tired, and defeatist as they have been for years. They regularly judge themselves by how bad the Republican Party is, instead of by how affirmatively good they could be for our country and its politically alienated people.

Rhetoric notwithstanding, each Democratic failure against the corporate-friendly Republicans, and now against the corporate-friendly Trump, rhetoric notwithstanding, says that it's time for Democrats to get off the corporate-backers bandwagon, at least if they want to get the voters behind them and shut out the Republicans. More broadly, it's time to break up this two-party duopoly blockade of democracy.

Over and over again, the Democrats listened to their corporate-conflicted, highly paid consultants rather than the cries of the people, and lost elections. They suffered the same rout in 2014.

You might well ask, looking back at 2014: Did the Republicans win these midterm elections? Or did the Democrats lose? The results showed that in contested Senate races, where the Republicans picked up nine seats, voters did not support the Democrats who were the most wishy-washy.

In their campaigns, the soon-to-be-defeated Democratic senators ran away from President Obama and often bragged about opposing his policies. But where did these senators run to? Certainly not to popular policies that appeal to Americans where they live, work, and raise their children.

Getting Senator Mark Pryor to support a minimum wage increase took many months. By the time he saw the popularity of a statewide citizen-driven initiative on the ballot and switched, he appeared more like an opportunist than a leader. Shortly after, his Republican successor, Tom Cotton, switched as well. All four initiatives to raise the minimum wage in conservative "red states" won. Including in Arkansas.

Looking back, we see that defeated Democratic senators tried to win votes by dumping on Obama and the national Democratic Party. They avoided siding with the people's demands for strong law and order in cases of corporate crimes against consumers, patients, workers, and community and environmental health. They avoided talking about rethinking the failed war on drugs, including Big Pharma, and the failed war on terror, policies that have resulted in more harmful drugs in our country and more violent anti-American groups around the world.

The ever-perceptive Washington Post columnist Steven Pearlstein wrote just before the election that the "Democratic candidates find themselves caught in a vicious cycle in which their refusal to embrace and defend their party's brand is discouraging the faithful and turning away the undecided, threatening their election prospects still further."

To turn out young and minority voters, candidates must articulate progressive visions for America, similar to what Bernie Sanders has offered, that will provide opportunities for improving the livelihoods of millions of low-paid, underemployed, or unemployed laborers. Low turnouts of these eligible voters in 2016 ensured Democratic Party losses.

People have to believe that their vote means something. The

billions of dollars spent on repetitive, negative, insipid political television ads created by both parties' political/corporate consultants don't motivate voters to show up at the polls.

The Mark Pryor senatorial campaign in Arkansas provided a teaching moment regarding political cowardice. He had everything going for him—plenty of money and a father who was a popular former senator and was visible in his campaign. Bill Clinton even came back to his native Arkansas and traveled to many districts to lavish praise on Senator Pryor.

Yet on Election Day, Pryor lost big. Why? Because he did not speak truth to power; he couldn't stand on his record in the Senate *because he didn't have one*. As chairman of the Senate Consumer Protection, Product Safety, and Insurance Subcommittee for some time, he was asleep at the switch; he did not return calls from civic leaders and did not have high-profile public hearings on the myriad corporate abuses involving cheating, stealing, and injuring consumers.

As happened in previous contests, President Obama, by not barnstorming the country, reinforced the stereotype that he was a liability to his party. As I have often said, Mr. Obama could have united the nation on such issues as minimum wage hikes (a restoration of purchasing power for thirty million workers).

At the same time, President Obama should have traveled the country saying,

> Give me a Democratic Congress, and I'll sign legislation that will create millions of jobs repairing and upgrading the public works of our neglected land. There will be non-exportable, well-paid jobs restoring our water sewage systems, our highways and bridges, our public transit systems, and our crumbling schools, ports, and public buildings. We'll pay for these critical public investments by

shrinking crony capitalism (taxpayer subsidies, giveaways, and bailouts) and by making hugely profitable companies like General Electric, Verizon, and Apple pay their fair share of taxes rather than shifting the burden onto the backs of middle-class taxpayers. And we'll impose a tiny sales tax, far less than you pay on your basic necessities, on Wall Street stock transactions, to raise about $350 billion in a year.

Every American can benefit from these community and policy improvements, strictly monitored as they develop with audits for honesty and efficiency. Every local chamber of commerce, every union, every worker, supplier, and every civic organization will support our programs, which I am going to call "Come Home America."

Instead, how did President Obama spend his six weeks before November 6? He flew to the salons of very wealthy campaign donors or went to support specific candidates mostly in safe states for Democrats. His presidential presence did not resound with "hope and change."

This turning away from the public's and even the party's needs simply smoothed the path for Trumpism's empty promises and jeremiads. Meanwhile, most of the party politicians were equally devoted to cultivating fat cats to the neglect of their own constituents.

Looking again at Obama's State of the Union address in 2015—a time when the need for fighting the good fight against the Republicans should have seemed fairly evident—I wonder if Obama had learned any lessons at all. To some extent, yes, but not enough.

The president's State of the Union addresses are rarely focused. They are written by numerous speechwriters and go through many drafts, each reflecting the urgings of interested parties to have their particular issues mentioned. Often, this makes the speech sound like a grab bag of lists.

But once up on the teleprompter before a joint session of Congress and a thousand reporters and commentators, the speech becomes a signaling presentation based on what the president says, how the president says it, and what the president does not say.

The Democrats of 2015 didn't have a message. Coming away from Obama's speech, I saw that he (as the Dems' main representative) was unsteadily moving toward a kind of populism, but only halfway.

While trying to resist the temptation to project what my colleagues or I would have included, it is remarkable to note how contradictory or inconsistent a number of President Obama's points were.

For example, he touted the increased production of oil and gas (though he did note the fast rise of solar/wind energy), then alluded gravely to the perils of climate change. Taken together, those opposing energy sources do not mix well in forming a national energy conversion policy that hopes to slow climate change's planetary devastation.

Mr. Obama spoke of cherishing civil liberties. But he did not mention support of any amendments to the so-called Patriot Act, up for congressional renewal in June of that year, such as ones to delete its atrocious anti-civil-liberties provisions, from search and seizure notification delays to snooping into sensitive personal, medical, and financial information, or even secret demands of people's library usage. Nor did he declare, while saying he was increasing "open government" policies, that the Senate Select Committee on Intelligence's 6,700-page, already-redacted report on the CIA's use of torture should be publicly released from his administration's censorious grip.

When he said that "we still need laws that strengthen rather than weaken unions, and give American workers a voice," it would have been more persuasive had he told us that he meant revising the notoriously anti-union Taft-Hartley Act, including his long-promised "card check." Instead, he contradicted his stated concern for workers by urging passage of the job-exporting Trans-Pacific Partnership (TPP) trade agreement, and by not fulfilling his 2008 support for revising the North American Free Trade Agreement (NAFTA) and other free trade agreements that have resulted in the loss of large numbers of jobs along with impairing labor, consumer, and environmental rights.

Catching up with what Western Europe has been doing for nearly sixty years, President Obama strongly urged more afford-able childcare, paid sick leave, and paid maternity leave. He also demanded higher capital gains and dividend taxes on the super-rich. So far so good, but it was all talk, no action.

Every year, the Republicans hypocritically push for lower defi-cits while at the same time raising military spending and corporate welfare, as if somehow convinced that shackling the Treasury Department's tax collections does not increase deficits. But the president didn't stick up for the IRS, whose budget is being annu-ally slashed so that it cannot collect more of the estimated $450 billion in yearly evaded taxes! (Again, by the way, this set a clear precedent for departmental budget cutting that Trump would make one of his hallmarks.)

President Obama wanted to increase the repair and expansion of public works (called infrastructure), but he didn't connect this initiative to a crackdown on corporations defrauding defense con-tracts or overbilling programs like Medicare and Medicaid. These could be big money savings that could help pay for America's infrastructure needs. It could also become a "law and order" drive against corporate crime.

When he came to the section of his speech that argued for

raising the minimum wage, the President specifically taunted Republicans by finally saying, "If you truly believe you could work full-time and support a family on less than fifteen thousand dollars a year, try it. If not, vote to give millions of the hardest-working people in America a raise." His rhetoric would have been more effective if he had said specifically what minimum wage per hour he wanted, as he was winding down his presidency.

With Obama, as with Clinton, one *rarely* got the feeling that he really meant what he said when speaking for progressive programs, such as zero tuition for community college students and other measures. Follow-through, a laser focus, and the building of coalitions would have been required for these proposals if they were to be seen as believable priorities rather than merely feel-good rhetoric.

This wishy-washy attitude might also be attributed to Obama's desire not to upset fat-cat donors with proposals on, say, cracking down on corporate wrongdoing. We see this again and again among Democrats. Even the more progressive ones quickly shed their principles when donors come calling. But there must be other factors, such as an ingrained lack of passion and care.

I make this comment after looking over a 2014 clipping about the retirement of Congressman John Dingell (D-MI), the longest-serving member of Congress in history (fifty-nine years). He did much good and much bad. Reports of his retirement stressed his work in championing Medicare, civil rights legislation, and several environmental laws. Less noticed were his misguided investigations of federal departments and agencies that were destructive of people's health and safety and mistreated whistle-blowers.

But Dingell had another, darker side to his otherwise liberal image. He was totally and cruelly indentured to the auto industry, even though he was from an overwhelmingly safe Democratic district. More than any other lawmaker, Democratic or Republican, he fought to make sure that the auto Goliaths got their way in Congress and at the EPA and the Department of Transportation.

I observed his tenacity in delaying the issuance of the life-saving airbag standard, in opposing noxious emission controls on motor vehicles, and, most irrationally, in freezing fuel-efficiency rules for many years. He did this with sheer stubborn willpower and by forging a mutually destructive alliance between the Big Three auto companies—GM, Ford, and Chrysler—of course with the support of congressional Republicans and at times with the United Automobile Workers (UAW) union.

In the greatest irony of his lengthy career, he helped mightily in sheltering the technological stagnation of Detroit's auto barons from innovation-advancing regulation, a move that eventually cost them massive market share to more fuel-efficient and high-er-quality foreign imports from Germany and Japan. This also cost the UAW tens of thousands of jobs.

When, in recent years, the domestic auto industry's demise was finally clear to him, he began to relent on fuel efficiency, but it was too late to save the industry from its own mismanagement, illusions, and bankruptcies.

The resultant impact on the health and safety of the American people was his most lasting and devastating legacy. Year after year people breathed more vehicle emissions, and lost their lives or were injured in less safe vehicles, because of Mr. Dingell's huge presence on Capitol Hill. He upset the balance in his party and thereby made his Republican colleagues more powerful in their opposition to updating health and safety rules.

At his retirement announcement, Mr. Dingell described service in the House of Representatives these days as "obnoxious" because of "the acrimony and the bitterness" and the lack of pro-ductivity. After the great congressman John Moss (D-CA) retired and Dingell became chair of the powerful House Energy and

Commerce Committee in 1981, I and other consumer advocates experienced Dingell's "obnoxious" and exclusionary dictatorial regime, laced with exceedingly foul language directed at anyone from the civic community who dared criticize him.

Congressman Dingell knows politics, however. He kept his seat in the family. His wife, Deborah Dingell, replaced him as congressperson from his home district in 2015.

Asked on the verge of his 2014 retirement by the *Washington Post* whether the condition in Congress "is fixable," he replied, "There's only one person that can fix it, and there's only one group of people that can answer that question, and that's the voters. If they want it to change, it will change." He was right there.

Yes, Congressman Dingell, it will change, but only if we have a more competitive democracy, with more choices of candidates and more voices for the voters. Party and candidate dynasties are not compatible with democratic elections.

Indeed, to step back a little after talking about the anti-democratic and industry-subservient attitudes of many Democrats (which don't win them many active friends among lower- and middle-class voters), it's ironic that even a Republican, even a Tea Party Republican, could win *if* he or she adopted (even in part) the people's agenda.

All politicians, if they ever got back to first principles and empowered our citizens to have more of a say in our democracy, would be stronger for it.

While Obama and his fellow Democrats repeatedly fell down on or ignored first principles in 2014, there were some exceptional scenes during this period. If properly viewed, these incidents give cause for hope. There was, for instance, the unlikely victory in the *Republican* primary in Virginia of a professor over the House's sitting majority leader. I was especially gratified by this event, in that it substantiated my claim that party labels are often misleading.

While this was a Republican race, the winner won by endorsing some progressive positions, such as jailing lawbreaking Wall Street bigwigs and reining in the surveillance state, though he also had other reactionary views.

The stunning defeat of House Majority Leader Eric Cantor (R-VA) by Professor Dave Brat, an economist from Randolph-Macon College, in the 2014 Republican primary had several takeaways for progressives.

First, among all the reasons for Cantor's fall, there were the ones encapsulated in John Nichols' description of Brat in the *Nation* as an "anti-corporate conservative." Repeatedly, Brat said he was for "free enterprise" but against "crony capitalist programs that benefit the rich and powerful." Dave Brat pointed out that Cantor and the Republican establishment have "been paying way too much attention to Wall Street and not enough to Main Street."

Brat supported "the end of bulk phone and email data collection by the NSA" and other government agencies on constitutional grounds.

Professor Brat attacked the Wall Street investment bankers who nearly "broke the financial system," adding the applause line: "These guys should have gone to jail. Instead of going to jail, where did they go? They went to Eric Cantor's Rolodex."

An advocate of ethical capitalism with Christian overtones, Mr. Brat went after the dealmaking in Washington, including Cantor's close relationships with the US Chamber of Commerce and the Business Roundtable. He especially berated Cantor for weakening the STOCK Act's ban on insider trading among members of Congress by exempting their family members and spouses.

He chastised Cantor on immigration, taking advantage of the latter's wavering appeal to voters who believe that large corporations, represented by Cantor, want a never-ending supply of cheap foreign labor to hold wages down.

In addition, Dave Brat, described as a "commanding orator who mixes fiery rhetoric with academic references and self-deprecating humor," wants a balanced-budget amendment, a "fair or flat tax," and is opposed to federal educational programs such as "No Child Left Behind."

Brat is a mixed bag for progressives. But in that mix is a clear populist challenge by Main Street against Wall Street and by ordinary people against the government's corporate subsidies and bailouts (called "corporate welfare" by the Left and "crony capitalism" by the Right). Therein lies the potential for a winning majority alliance between Left and Right, as my book, *Unstoppable: The Emerging Left-Right Alliance to Dismantle the Corporate State*, relates in realistic detail.

Second, Professor Brat spent about $230,000 to Eric Cantor's $5.7 million. However, Brat more than made up for the money deficit with energy, focused barbs, and the shoe-leather of his committed followers. On election night, Brat made a point that progressives would do well to heed, as they obsess over big money in politics: "Dollars don't vote," he said, "you do." Interestingly, Tea Party forces and donors claim they thought Cantor was so unbeatable that they didn't even fund Brat, even though he had two right-wing national radio talk show hosts speaking well of him. Not surprisingly, Rep. Brat found himself voting sometimes for Wall Street and big business in contrast to candidate Brat's orations.

I ask now: Can't progressives find that kind of *energy* with their many broader issues and larger support base? Can't they find capable so-called nobodies with hidden talent to become publicly heralded champions? There are fresh voices everywhere who can take on those corporate Democrats like the Clintons who defer to Wall Streeters, espouse crony capitalism, and go with neocons to advance militarism abroad, along with supporting corporate-managed, job-destroying trade agreements and offshore tax havens. Unfortunately, the driving energy of progressives, even now, is not showing up in the electoral arena.

The third lesson from the decisive Cantor upset is not to embrace the political attitude that calls for settling, from the outset, for the least-of-the-worst choices. Many progressives have expressed and harbored strong criticisms of the Democratic Party establishment and their adoption of corporatist policies. But election cycle after election cycle, fearful of the Republican bad guys, they signal to the Democratic incumbents that the least-of-the-worst is acceptable. Like the dominant party liberals they often consort with, progressives do not ask, "Why not the best?" with the expectation that they will either win or at least pull their party away from the relentless 24/7 grip of big-time corporatism.

The final takeaway from this fascinating Virginian contest in the seventh congressional district was that Cantor's tactics backfired. The more money Cantor spent on TV, radio, billboard ads, and mailings, the more Dave Brat became known and the more people were reminded that Washington and Wall Street really do not care about people on Main Street.

That is truly the nub of a successful Left-Right alliance. In recent decades, pollsters would sometimes pose a variation of the question, "Do you believe that X candidate or Y party or Z in Washington cares about people like you?" A sizable majority of people, regardless of their ideological or political labels, said no.

With the interest of the public, the community, and the country in the forefront, those "nos" can become "yeses" for a long-overdue rejuvenated and just society driven by reality and edified by its ideals.

9.

Thoughts on the Inauguration

Obama won twice, of course, but winning isn't everything for a president. The candidate has to win with the party, not without it. He won, but his party didn't win. After 2010 the Republicans became dominant in Congress.

One of the ironies of history is that for all the Republicans' Obama bashing, many of Obama and the Democrats' policies of those years, such as bending the law to promote drone strikes, were exactly of a type dear to Republican hearts. These no-win policies have to be called out, even if the Democrats were better than the Republicans in other areas.

I reread Obama's presidential acceptance speech for his second term and added my thoughts to underline some of his shortsighted positions, ones that are still hampering the Democrats.

Here are Obama's words and my reactions:

> Obama: "They [the patriots of 1776] gave to us a republic, a government of, and by, and for the people . . ."
> Me: The flood of money-shaping elections and politics has given us a corporate government of the Exxons, by the General Motors, and for the DuPonts.

Obama: "Together, we resolved that a great nation must care for the vulnerable, and protect its people from life's worst hazards and misfortune."

Me: In his first term Obama was indifferent to the nearly three hundred thousand preventable fatalities a year in this country caused by hospital infections and malpractice, adverse drug effects, and occupational disease and trauma, and he failed to anticipate and prepare for impending perils of viral epidemics from abroad.

Obama: ". . . our country cannot succeed when a shrinking few do very well and a growing many barely make it."

Me: Obama reneged and kept silent on his repeated 2008 campaign promise to push for a $9.50 minimum wage by 2011 and for a card-check system to facilitate the growth of unions. In his first term he actively discouraged Democrats from championing these measures in Congress, even though thirty million workers are making wages less than workers made in 1968. He also opposed a Wall Street financial transaction tax and declined to reduce gigantic corporate welfare programs that beg for repeal.

Obama: "We will respond to the threat of climate change, knowing that the failure to do so would betray our children and future generations."

Me: Obama and the emissaries he sent to international climate change conferences brought up the rear among nations, infuriating our allies who looked to the USA for leadership. He never pressed for a carbon tax that even Exxon and leading conservatives, such as Gregory Mankiw, supported.

Obama: "... enduring security and lasting peace do not require perpetual war. ... We will defend our people and uphold our values through strength of arms and rule of law."

Me: Hello! This coming from the ex-constitutional-law teacher who turned his imperial presidency into an institutionalized violator of the Constitution, federal statutes, and international treaties. He personally ordered many unlawful military attacks and slayings in countries that are not at war with the US, against people who do not constitute "imminent threats." (See the documentary *Dirty Wars*.)

The very week of his inauguration, President Obama sent drones to destroy "suspects," nameless young men standing together talking by a roadside, and whoever may have been with or near them, including children, without any concern for the rule of law. The alleged "secret laws" Obama set out in Justice Department memos were designed to strip the Congress and the courts of their constitutional roles, as well as to keep the American people in the dark about the drone attack decisions he made on what his aides casually called "Terror Tuesdays."

Obama: "We will support democracy from Asia to Africa, from the Americas to the Middle East, because our interests and our conscience compel us to act on behalf of those who long for freedom."

Me: What about attending to the deteriorating democratic protections and civil liberties in our country? Washington, DC, is corporate-occupied territory for all three branches of government. Never in the past half-century have the people, and concern for their necessities, been more shut out of their own government. It continues to be "pay-to-play" time in the nation's capital.

Obama: "You and I, as citizens, have the obligation to shape the debates of our time . . ."
     Me: Well, then how about working to shift more power away from the few and toward the many? How about campaign finance reform and federal ballot access reform, so voters can have a competitive electoral democracy with more choices from third parties whose candidates propose different agendas?

Granted, inaugural addresses are meant to be general and inspirational, not programmatic and revelatory, yet they do reveal a president's general orientation.

Tom Sherwood, a local commentator watching the inaugural parade up Pennsylvania Avenue from the sixth-floor balcony of the Newseum, decried "the extraordinary expense—financial and psychological—of turning America's Main Street into an armed camp where democracy is suspended for several days. . . . Protest groups are 'assigned' demonstration areas, and required to pay fees and adhere to strict assembly instructions. . . . This being the week of the Martin Luther King Jr. holiday, it makes you wonder what success would have been achieved if civil rights workers had acceded to police demands not to march here or there, or to pay to get detailed permits first."

Sherwood added, "But why not a parade that showcases the social services, arts and industries, and sciences along with our military services?" Why not, indeed.

10.

Shutting Down Keystone XL: A Positive Step

Once Obama was safely ensconced in office, he could turn to important policy matters. One place in which he did listen to the protesting public was the Keystone XL pipeline, which industry promoted but a growing segment of the environmentally aware condemned. Eventually Obama attempted to nix this project (for which I laud him). In fact, looking back, I believe he eventually came around to opposing the pipeline due to the informed pressures that activists put on the White House to cancel this project.

One such activist was Bill McKibben, a prolific writer on global warming and climate change. In August 2011 McKibben organized unprecedented demonstrations in front of the White House urging President Obama to deny a permit for the Keystone XL pipeline that would haul very dirty tar sands oil from Alberta, Canada, down to Illinois and Texas refineries, largely for export. More than 1,200 people were arrested in August and September for protesting the construction of the pipeline. These were the largest mass arrests before the White House in decades.

Then on February 13, 2013, forty-eight people, including McKibben and Robert F. Kennedy Jr., were arrested for open, nonviolent civil disobedience, mostly for refusing police orders

to keep moving on the White House's sidewalk (with some protestors actually attaching themselves to the fence in front of the
White House).

At the end of that same week, McKibben was back at the
White House with more than forty thousand anti-Keystone-XL
protestors demanding that Obama act on broader climate issues.
Protestors included leaders of Native American tribes, some legislators, corporate executives, farmers, students, workers, and
other Americans who think saving the planet from oil spills and
dangerous levels of carbon dioxide and other greenhouse gases is
worth some of their direct effort.

At that point, President Obama had twice postponed his decision on the XL pipeline, to the relief of Hillary Clinton, whose
State Department would have been blamed for approving the
pipeline, much to the detriment of her future political aspirations.

The Keystone XL pipeline's owner is TransCanada, which
busily bought up rights of way through the western US and called
on states to use their eminent domain powers when ranchers and
farmers resisted. Giant pipes had already been shipped to various
locations along the way, and actual construction was under way in
Texas as McKibben led those protests. The governor of Nebraska,
Dave Heineman, dropped his objection once the pipeline's route
was altered to go around the state's environmentally vulnerable
Sand Hills region.

You might wonder, since fracking was spreading rapidly in many
states to increase US oil production and natural gas extraction, why
would President Obama want to approve Keystone XL? What
about his State of the Union warnings regarding global warming
and its terrible costs in lives, property, and money?

Notwithstanding the lack of need for oil from Canada and Mr.
Obama's stated concerns about global warming, TransCanada,
backed to the hilt by Canada's prime minister at the time, Ste-

phen Harper, was confident that it would receive a permit from Obama.

Here are some of the facts Obama eventually faced up to.

First, the pipeline was promoted as a significant job creator. In reality, building a pipeline in these days of automation requires mostly short-term workers, and, following the construction phase, the pipeline would employ fewer than one hundred people. The exporting refineries are even more automated.

Second, even without the pipeline, TransCanada could, and does, still ship tar sands oil to the US via rail, barge, truck, and other existing pipelines. The company, with Canadian government backing, could also decide to build a pipeline westward through British Columbia for shipment to oil-hungry China.

Third, the "sleeper" argument that was on Obama's desk was that TransCanada, having already invested big money in the US, could invoke Chapter 11 of the North American Free Trade Agreement and sue the US government for big damages if its permit was denied. Incredible as it may seem, the notorious Chapter 11 has been used by numerous companies to seek billions of dollars in damages from the Mexican and Canadian governments. Companies have succeeded in obtaining settlements totaling hundreds of millions of dollars. Paid for by the taxpayers, of course.

These were the pro-pipeline arguments touted by the industry. But it was the force of McKibben's army throwing its nonviolent troops against the Keystone XL pipeline and tar sands exploitation, and rallying against potential environmental devastation from Alberta all the way down to Texas, that eventually persuaded Obama to do the right thing. Not surprisingly, TransCanada then filed suit against the US government under the notorious Chapter 11 of NAFTA, only dropping its case when newly elected president Trump reversed Obama's decision and granted them their permit.

11.

What the Democrats Have to Get Right

Attempting to block the Keystone XL pipeline was one of the few progressive policies that Obama got right, but the missed opportunities far outweigh the successes.

The uses of the mighty presidency and its bully pulpit have rarely been much above amateurish when it comes to helping people empower themselves. This has been the case even when the same party controls the White House and both houses of Congress.

Consider the times Clinton and Obama were in that enviable position, in 1993–1994 and 2009–2010, respectively. Both Clinton and Obama fell short, unable even to get adequate public works agendas passed through Congress that would have produced good, non-exportable jobs in many communities.

Obama had lots of excuses as to why this and that could not be accomplished. Due to his and the congressional Democrats' ineptitude, they consistently lost their battles with the vicious and corporatist Republican Party, with their Senate filibusters and stubborn public posturing, Obama missed the chance to push significant projects, like a popularly supported minimum wage hike, whose popularity would have overwhelmed Republican opponents who have their fingers to the wind.

So let's lower the bar and ask why, when he had the chance in 2009–2010, Mr. Obama didn't just use his high visibility to strengthen our democracy in ways that didn't require legislation or tax revenues. Here are some of the ways he might have helped:

1. Obama could have announced his desire to speak to a convocation of leaders of civic groups that have millions of members around the country. He could have highlighted their good works via the mass media. He could have prompted more philanthropy, especially from the very rich, to these worthy organizations that work to help the poor, children, the environment, beleaguered communities, and others in need. An annual increase of only $10 billion in private donations could create about three hundred thousand jobs and provide serious help for millions of people.

2. He could have openly supported Public Interest Research Groups (PIRGs). After graduating from Columbia University, young Barack Obama worked for a few months at the New York Public Interest Research Group—a large, well-regarded, student-funded public interest organization I helped start that has been involved in numerous community improvements around the state, advocating justice, not charity.

   PIRGs operate in about thirty states. Though Obama addressed countless business summits, not once did he address the gatherings of PIRGs. He could have urged all colleges and universities to provide check-offs for PIRGs that would enable millions of students to develop critical civic skills and have life-changing experiences while improving their society.

   Engaging civil society would have helped balance Obama's exhortations to students to seek occupational training at institutions of higher education. The president declined to use his community organizing reputation in Chicago and New York to direct the public and the media toward such simple ways of strengthening our weakening democracy.

3. The warring president might have expended some of his fame to bring attention to those Americans who are waging peace through direct field involvement, advocacy, and peace studies. The corporate-criminal class got the president to attend their trade association meetings, but not once did he visit the American Friends Service Committee or Colman McCarthy's Center for Teaching Peace, unique organizations successfully working to expand peace studies curricula at scores of high schools and colleges.

4. Couldn't Obama have attended events defending unions under attack by right-wing governors and their corporatist allies, or encouraged workers in large companies to unionize?

   Remarkably, President Obama studiously avoided going to Madison, Wisconsin, in 2011 to support the mass rallying of workers against Governor Scott Walker's moves to strip-mine workers' rights. Vice President Joe Biden (a self-styled "union man"), on White House orders, also turned down an invitation from the Wisconsin Labor Federation to visit at that critical time.

   By contrast, Obama *walked* across Lafayette Park in February 2011 to pay homage to the chronically selfish and anti-labor US Chamber of Commerce. He could have gone around the corner to visit the AFL-CIO, representing nearly thirteen million American workers, but he did not.

5. What about championing, through check-off facilities, ways for people to voluntarily band together around specific endeavors? This would have been easy for the president. He could have started by establishing check-offs for taxpayer watchdog associations on the 1040 tax return and periodic postal notices to residential addresses, inviting participation in postal consumers' groups to bolster the US Postal Service.

All companies receiving corporate welfare from taxpayers should be required, as a condition of getting these subsidies, hand-outs, and bailouts, to include in their bills and communications with customers invitations for consumers to band together and support nonprofit organizations with full-time consumer champions fighting for their rights.

Just about every industry in the country—banking, utilities, insurance, fuel, health care, food—is on the dole, one way or the other. This simple reciprocity would facilitate the organization of tens of millions of Americans to defend and extend their livelihoods.

This same advice goes out to the current Democrats. It's one way to rally the troops, the dismayed Democratic voters and independents who haven't seen the party taking up the issues vital to them. The party has got to redirect its energies to subjects that are high-priority items for the general electorate, while empowering people at the same time.

There are three areas where the people need the views and vision of any progressive politician:

1. A progressive politician should give a major address on the resources and preconditions necessary for the government to wage peace as a continual policy of statecraft rather than depending on sporadic initiatives between wars and other violent conflicts. Consider the enormous disparity between the time, power, and money allocated to preparing for or waging military assaults and the meager resources devoted to conflict prevention and other fundamentals of securing the conditions for peace.

We have military academies but no peace academies. Vast sums of money are allocated for researching and teaching war and military tactics, but very little for peace studies at our schools and universities.

2. Any progressive politician worth her or his salt should make it a point to address a large gathering of leaders of nonprofit civic organizations. A speech to them would talk about the importance and means of advancing the quality and quantity of civic groups and their chapters, which, taken together, are major employers.

3. Another speech focus should be strengthening democratic processes and expanding democratic institutions and participation by the people, by making it easy for them to band together.

As even President Obama noted, democracy is not a spectator sport. It requires a motivated citizenry, along with rights, remedies, and legal mechanisms that facilitate people banding together as candidates, voters, workers, taxpayers, consumers, and communities. Concentration of power and wealth in the hands of the few who decide for the many is the great destroyer of any society's democratic functions. As Justice Louis Brandeis was reputed to have said, "We can have democracy in this country or we can have great wealth concentrated in the hands of a few, but we cannot have both." And as another well-regarded jurist, Judge Learned Hand, declared, "If we are to keep our democracy, there must be one commandment: Thou shalt not ration justice."

As *politics* is increasingly seen as a dirty word and as the people move from cynicism about political institutions to greater withdrawal from public meetings, primaries, elections, and referenda, they need politicians who address these disabling symptoms of a weakening democratic society from the local to the state to the national levels of our political economy.

Opinion polls in early 2015 showed voters were largely in favor of a number of progressive moves that Obama had often talked about but chronically failed to take forward.

Had I been granted a meeting with President Obama at that time, I would have stressed the following:

Mr. President,
Abraham Lincoln once said, "With public sentiment, nothing can fail; without it, nothing can succeed." Presumably, he meant that presidential action on popular issues can and should overcome influential interests.

At long last, the "public sentiment" seems to be aligning with some causes you have advanced.

First, support is increasing for raising the federal minimum wage at least to account for the inflation that, since 1968, has greatly diminished its purchasing power.

Restoring the purchasing power of the minimum wage has over 70 percent public support and would lift the wages of thirty million hard-pressed American workers.

Second, the vast majority of Americans want corporations to pay their fair share. US-chartered giant companies like Pfizer, Medtronic, and, perhaps most foolishly, Walgreens—given its eight thousand exposed protestable stores—are planning to move their headquarters to countries that lure them with lower tax rates, such as Ireland and Switzerland, to abandon their US "citizenship" and reincorporate in those jurisdictions. This is all to gain another tax escape to add to their existing ones, including the large tax credits for Pfizer's and Medtronic's research and development that corporatist lobbies have written into the US tax code. [Walgreens stepped back from its folly in 2014.]

"I don't care if it's legal, it's wrong," you have indignantly exclaimed in recent speeches. Most impressively, you are questioning the "economic patriotism" of many giant US corporations who have received support (financial and otherwise) from US workers, taxpayers, and public laws and have benefited from the infrastructure of our country. The mere implication that these companies are *unpatriotically* abandoning their native country has outraged the US Chamber of Commerce along with the predictable *Wall Street Journal*. Again, this call to penalize such erring companies is a position that has large backing from the general public, which wants action, not just words.

That highly vocal reaction means you touched on an issue that has been on the minds of tens of millions of Americans. May you continue to promote the importance of insisting on the *patriotic* duties of US corporations, particularly since the US Supreme Court (by a 5–4 decision) keeps telling us that corporations are people.

Third, there's one more area where the public sentiment awaits your leadership. Large majorities on both the Left and the Right favor breaking up the "too big to fail" New York City banks; support cracking down on corporate crime and fraud (see the Senate's proposed Hide No Harm Act); and, the more they know about its benefits and fairness, the more they support a Wall Street speculation tax, a sales tax that could bring in over $300 billion a year, fund repairs of our public infrastructure, and make up for some of the financial institutions' reckless gambling with other peoples' money, such as with pension and mutual funds.

The many rallies in New York City, in front of the White House, and around the country—some of which have been led by National Nurses United—are pressing Congress for such a transaction tax. Such activities have laid the groundwork for your exercise of the "bully pulpit."

Fourth, as I pointed out in my book *Unstoppable: The Emerging Left-Right Alliance to Dismantle the Corporate State*, as a senator you cosponsored legislation with Senator Tom Coburn (R-OK) in 2006 to require that the *full text* of all federal government contracts above a minimum dollar amount be available online.

As I've written previously, putting the full text of these contracts online will result in both taxpayer savings and higher scrutiny of public works; let the media focus more incisively on this vast area of government disbursements to inform the wider public; encourage constructive comments and alarms from the citizenry; and stimulate legal and economic research by scholars interested in structural topics related to government procurement, transfers, subsidies, and giveaways.

There is already support for this measure from members of both parties in Congress. Online disclosure would provide for greater scrutiny of over $400 billion in annual contracts and grants, which might be conducted by the media, taxpayer groups, competitors, and academic researchers.

Yes, indeed, Mr. President, wondrous and beneficial changes can come to our country when you and Congress heed the long-standing "public sentiment," which you recently called "the voices of the people," and translate that "public sentiment" into beneficial action by our government.

Yours sincerely,
Ralph Nader

In addition to that preliminary list of issues that called out for and still calls out for attention, there are a couple of other issues to which the Democrats, then and now, should be putting their muscle, even under a Republican regime. They need to become enlightened about what their real priorities should be —namely, sponsoring programs to help the American people.

One such program would deal with the runaway pathogens that are taking down so many people.

Deadly invisible pathogens are on the march. Ebola, Zika virus, the ongoing cholera epidemics, and the enormous regular casualties from tuberculosis, malaria, and varieties of avian influenza are expanding their territories. All of these should be waking us up to the global spread of disease and the public health challenges of dealing with mutational virulence. Millions die every year. But the leaders of nations don't seem to respect the warnings from our scientists. *Pandemic*, the important book by Sonia Shah, is an urgent jeremiad, and should spark policy makers' public concern.

There are US hospitals with larger annual budgets than the entire beleaguered World Health Organization, which is tasked, by nearly two hundred nations, with heading off epidemics and pandemics or trying to limit their spread.

Errant microbes are getting assistance from environmental upheavals, global travel, poor sanitation, and starved public health facilities, as well as political corruption and dense urbanization.

Yet the big money still goes into redundant armaments, where the profits multiply. Presidents make speeches about terrorism and national security. Congress holds constant hearings, rubber-stamping gargantuan military budgets. But have you heard these bacteria and viruses—those most certain terrorist perils—discussed in a nationally televised address by any president or brought up in any major congressional hearings? Of course you haven't. They've received very little attention.

Over the years I have tried to get this country's leadership to wake up to a looming century of pandemic perils. True, public money and grants by some foundations have gone into reducing malaria and some other infectious diseases. But it has been too little and, for many men, women, and children, too late.

Frustration often leads to satire. Let me share with you an unanswered letter I wrote to President Barack Obama on June 3, 2011. I was told that some scientists at the Centers for Disease Control and Prevention were pleased with the message.

> Dear President Obama:
>
> My name is E. coli $O104:H4$. I am being detained in a German laboratory in Bavaria, charged with being "a highly virulent strain of bacteria." The police have accused me and many others like me of causing about twenty deaths and nearly five hundred cases of kidney failure—so far. We've garnered massive publicity and panic all around.
>
> You can't see me, but your scientists can. They are examining me, and I know my days are numbered. I hear them calling me a "biological terrorist," an unusual combination of two different E. coli bacteria strains. One even referred to me as a "conspiracy of mutants."
>
> It is not my fault, I want you to know. I cannot help but harm innocent humans, and I am very sad about this. I want to redeem myself, so I am sending this life-saving message straight from my Petri dish to you.
>
> This outbreak in Germany has been traced to food— location unknown. What is known to you is that invisible terrorism from bacteria and viruses take a greater number of lives by far than the terrorism you're trying to stop in Iraq, Afghanistan, and Pakistan. While fighting that terrorism has involved spending hundreds of billions of dollars and deploying countless armaments, the terrorism

from me and my contagious colleagues has been practically unopposed.

Malaria, caused by infection with one of four species of Plasmodium, a parasite transmitted by Anopheles mosquitoes, destroys a million lives a year. Many of the victims are children and pregnant women. Mycobacterium tuberculosis takes over one million lives each year. The human immunodeficiency virus (HIV) causes over a million deaths each year as well. Many other microorganisms in the water, soil, air, and food are daily weapons of mass destruction. Very little in your defense budget goes for operational armed forces against this kind of violence. Your agencies, such as the Centers for Disease Control and Prevention, conduct some research, but it's nothing compared to the research for your missiles, drones, aircraft, and satellites.

Your associates are obsessed with the possibility of your human enemies waging bacteriological warfare. Yet you are hardly doing anything about the ongoing silent violence of my indiscriminate brethren.

You and your predecessor, George W. Bush, made many speeches about fighting terrorism by humans. Have you made a major speech about us?

You speak regularly about crushing the resistance of your enemies. But you splash around so many antibiotics (obviously I don't like this word and consider it genocidal) in cows, bulls, chickens, pigs, and fish that your species is creating massive antibiotic resistance, provoking our mutations, so that we can help them breed even stronger progeny. You are regarded as the smartest beings on Earth, yet you seem to have too many neurons backfiring.

In the past two days of detention, scientists have subjected me to "enhanced interrogation," as if I have any will to give up my secrets. It doesn't work. What they will find out will be from their insights about me under their microscopes. I am lethal, I guess, but I'm not very complicated.

The United States, together with other countries, needs more laboratories where scientists can detain samples of us and subject us to extraordinary rendition to infectious disease research centers. Many infectious disease scientists need to be trained, especially in the Southern Hemisphere, to staff these labs.

You are hung up on certain kinds of preventable violence without any risk-benefit analysis. This, you should agree, is utterly irrational. You should not care where the preventable violence comes from except to focus on its range of devastation and its susceptibility to prevention or cure!

Well, here they come to my Petri dish for some more waterboarding. One last item: You may wonder how tiny bacterial me, probably not even harboring a virus, can send you such a letter. My oozing sense is that I'm just a carrier, being used by oodles of scientists taking advantage of a high-profile infectious outbreak in Europe to catch your attention.

Whatever the *how*—does it really matter to the need to act *now*?

E-cologically yours,

E. coli O104:H4 (for the time being)

The danger of the natural health-damaging effects of germs leads to another danger undermining our health. That is, manmade contaminants. Here is another place where a Democrat could stand tall for the people, distinguishing himself from the deregulating, defunding, health-endangering policies openly trumpeted by the Republicans.

Obviously, we had a better chance of getting laws to combat this threat under a Democratic Party regime, but, hopes aside, nothing happened on this front under Obama. One of the terrible accidents involving hazardous substances occurred under his watch:

Dear President Obama,

As senators, you and Joe Biden were leaders in highlighting the threat of America's hazardous chemical plants—and in calling for solutions that included moving these facilities to adopt inherently safer technologies. In 2006, you bluntly stated that "these plants are stationary weapons of mass destruction spread all across the country."

Unfortunately, after the West, Texas, ammonium nitrate explosion, after you spoke at a memorial service for the fifteen deceased individuals, and after you issued an executive order demanding action, your EPA released a *proposed* rule that does too little to require a shift to safer technologies.

That is damaging, given the risk of more catastrophes by negligent accident, natural disaster, sabotage, or terrorism. Since the West, Texas, fire of 2013, which federal investigators determined was deliberately set, there have been more than 430 chemical incidents and 82 deaths. *The EPA has identified 471 US chemical facilities that each put 100,000 or more people at risk.*

In 2004, the Homeland Security Council estimated that a major attack on just one of these chemical facilities would kill 17,500 people and injure tens of thousands more. Many of the first victims would be plant workers and people in the low-income communities that often are located near these dangerous facilities.

Numerous experts have been urging the EPA to issue a rule that focuses on safer technologies, often called "materials substitution." They include your former EPA head Lisa Jackson; President Bush's EPA head, former governor Christine Todd Whitman; retired generals like Russel Honoré and Randy Manner; the US Chemical Safety Board; and a broad coalition of environmental, community, and labor groups.

You know who the opposition is: avaricious corporate interests like the Koch brothers. They don't want to pay to shift to safer materials and technologies, even though other companies like Clorox, which eliminated the use of chlorine gas in favor of a safer process for making bleach, have already made the switch and are thriving.

How would our country view a weak EPA rule if one day there was a chemical catastrophe that killed thousands of Americans? More than twenty thousand people died and hundreds of thousands more were injured as a result of the 1984 gas leak at a plant in Bhopal, India. A US company, Union Carbide, owned the plant.

If the plant were in the United States, and twenty thousand Americans died, would not our country already have responded to this problem? We can't wait for such a tragedy to explode before we take action.

Communities where the most dangerous plants are located—from Newark to Detroit, Mississippi to California—cannot wait any longer. For the facilities that have converted, the result is reliable protection for employees and communities against catastrophic disasters, and at low cost. Wherever this can be done, it should be a requirement.

The *proposed* EPA rule does offer an important first step by mandating that certain high-risk chemical plants conduct a safer technology and alternatives analysis (STAA) and feasibility assessment on the use of inherently safer technologies. Perhaps that is one reason why Republican congressman Mike Pompeo of Kansas [appointed secretary of state in 2018 by President Trump], in whose district Koch Industries is located and who has taken extensive campaign contributions from company officials, is pushing legislation to prohibit the EPA from issuing any rule at all.

But the current administration should not simply resist this industry-backed amendment; it should dramatically improve the EPA's proposed rule by:

1. Requiring all so-called Risk Management Plan facilities—those that use extremely hazardous substances and thus are required to develop a Risk Management Plan (RMP)—to assess safer alternatives to existing chemical processes. The inadequate proposed EPA rule exempts 87 percent of the approximately 12,500 Risk Management Plan chemical facilities from requirements to conduct a safer technology and alternatives analysis. The exempted facilities include, for example, water treatment plants, some of which put major cities at risk of a catastrophic release of chlorine gas.

2. Requiring all these especially hazardous RMP facilities to send their safer technology and alternatives analyses (STAA) to the EPA and readily share the information with nearby communities and other interested parties, such as emergency responders, vendors of safer technologies, facility employees and contractors, and safety researchers.

3. Establishing a publicly accessible clearinghouse of safer available alternatives that could encourage and support the adoption of safer substitutes by more facilities as soon as practicable.

4. Requiring chemical facilities—starting with those that pose the highest risk—to actually substitute safer alternatives to their industrial processes, wherever feasible, that will eliminate or significantly reduce the consequences of a catastrophic release. The coalition of community, worker, and environmental groups that has engaged the EPA on these issues has recommended that the EPA at the very least begin a pilot program to require inherently safer technologies to be implemented in a subset of RMP facility categories, such as waste water and drinking water treatment plants, bleach plants and refineries that use hydrogen fluoride, and the two thousand highest-risk facilities cited in the EPA's National Enforcement Initiative proposal.

The people demand that your EPA issue a stronger rule that moves industry to proven safer technologies and protects the public in every endangered community.

Sincerely yours,

Ralph Nader

While ignoring public and expert sentiment on issues such as the danger of infectious agents and hazardous materials, Obama and his fellow Democrats were quick to listen to the advice of the corporate powers on critical financial issues.

12.

Obama's and Democrats' Weak Appointments and Policies Pander to Wall Street

An area where Obama and the Democrats could have, but didn't, empower citizens was in appointing a conscientious chairman of the Federal Reserve and by "socking it to" financial firms that were caught with dirty hands.

In August 2013, Obama was on the verge of appointing Lawrence Summers as head of the Fed. Things didn't go well at the Summers hearings and he withdrew his name. Even so, the fact that such a corporate-friendly scam artist was pushed forward says a lot about the corporate orientation of Obama and his advisers.

When Obama was placing Summers's name in the ring, a widening circle applauded the mega-millionaire of Harvard University, Washington, DC, and Wall Street, agreeing on one word to describe this colossal failure: *brilliant!* That circle included Barack Obama, who appointed Summers as his chief economic adviser in 2009, Bill Clinton, who made him secretary of the Treasury in 1999, and the Harvard Board of Overseers, who named him president of Harvard University in 2001.

With his promoter, Robert Rubin, who preceded him at the Treasury post before making over $100 million at Citigroup, Summers *brilliantly* deregulated Wall Street in 1999 and 2000, thus setting up one of corporate capitalism's most disastrous speculative binges and collapses.

With Bill Clinton's approval, these men pushed for the repeal of the successful Glass-Steagall Act of 1933, which separated investment banking from commercial banking. They also blocked necessary regulation of the mounting speculation in complex, risky derivatives that led to the tanking of Wall Street in 2008. The collapse, caused by the plutocrats, cost eight million jobs, drained away trillions of dollars in pension and mutual fund assets, received a huge taxpayer bailout, and plunged the country into a "Great Recession."

At Harvard, Summers remained *brilliant* in placing much of the university's huge endowment into risky investments that lost billions of dollars. His *brilliance* also led him to say that women just weren't cut out for heavy-duty scientific work.

Wall Street likes people labeled *brilliant*. It hides their greed. So firms like Goldman Sachs, JPMorgan Chase, and Citigroup shelled out over $100,000 per visit to hear Summers speak his *brilliance*. While heading for bankruptcy and taxpayer bailouts (decided in one secret weekend in 2008 by Robert Rubin, Federal Reserve Chairman Ben Bernanke, and Treasury Secretary Henry Paulson, fresh from the lucrative chairmanship of Goldman Sachs), Citigroup was receiving, in its own words, *brilliant* "insight on a broad range of topics including the global and domestic economy." Soon thereafter, this shaky bank went belly-up into the lap of the American taxpayer.

Clearly, Summers's *brilliance* did *not* light a path toward banking prudence and productivity for the economy. But it sure did help Summers's bank accounts. He reaped huge salaries from the hedge fund D. E. Shaw and from Silicon Valley startups, including the Lending Club, a company that charges its debtors interest rates reaching as high as 29 percent.

Summers has cultivated *brilliance*. He speaks fast and can be bombastic as he exhales his experience with international crises, government, Wall Street, and academic life. He is quick with statistics and has a way of making vulnerable, smart persons around him feel inferior. That intimidating style did not work with former Federal Reserve chairman Paul Volcker, who came to the Obama administration at the same time as Summers, but as a lesser-titled economic adviser. So Summers worked the White House to marginalize Volcker, who soon left. Later, when Volcker's proposal to develop criteria to slow banking speculation with other people's money started moving through Congress, Summers went ballistic. But his *brilliance* could not stop it from becoming law.

This was the person Obama put forward for the chair of the powerful Federal Reserve.

Noam Scheiber, author of *The Escape Artists: How Obama's Team Fumbled the Recovery*, who is often admiring of Summers, writes, "My own view is that Summers is too fond of big shots— he's always wanted to be part of the most exclusive club that will have him. . . . In my book, I describe the pleasure he took from attending dinners with top Wall Street executives as a Treasury official in the 1990s."

Such awe of Wall Street—that has and will butter his bread— means that he would be more "credible" in the financial markets, though his *brilliance* may get under the skin of the Federal Reserve governors who set interest-rate or monetary policy.

Obama backed Summers for the chairmanship of the Federal Reserve only to see Summers withdraw from the nomination, brought down by complaints by fellow Democrats that Summers was too closely associated with the policies that eventually led to the great recession.

But the Obama regime still caved to the forces of the financial community left and right. For example, Attorney General Eric

Holder's sweetheart settlement with Switzerland's second largest bank, corporate criminal Credit Suisse, sent the wrong message to other corporate barons. Senators John McCain (R-AZ) and Carl Levin (D-MI) put it well at the time: "[T]his agreement provides no direct accountability for those taxes owed. Nor does the plea deal hold any officers, directors or key executives individually accountable for wrongdoing, raising the question of whether it will sufficiently deter similar misconduct in the future."

Mr. Holder, of course, touted the deal as tough. Credit Suisse was fined a nondeductible $2.6 billion for their long, elaborate plan to provide tax evasion services for many thousands of wealthy Americans. The bank agreed to plead guilty to criminal wrongdoing—a rare demand on the usually coddled large financial institutions. In addition, Credit Suisse acceded, in Mr. Holder's words, that it failed "to retain key documents, allowed evidence to be lost or destroyed, and conducted a shamefully inadequate internal inquiry" through a "conspiracy" that "spanned decades."

The bank also agreed to a "statement of facts" that detailed the nature of this conspiracy, which is worthy of an international crime thriller and involved hundreds of Credit Suisse employees, "secret offshore accounts," and "sham entities and foundations." In short, this was a coordinated, sizable, ongoing, premeditated financial criminal enterprise.

Credit Suisse agreed to submit to an outside, independent monitor for two years.

In return, here is what the corporate lawyers King & Spalding, on behalf of Credit Suisse, extracted from the Justice Department:

1. The bank retained its permits and licenses to remain fully operational in the United States.
2. Top management and directors emerged unscathed and were allowed to keep their lucrative positions.

3. State and federal regulators, including the SEC and the Federal Reserve, agreed to issue only slap-on-the-wrist penalties in related actions against the bank.

4. Credit Suisse did not have to give the Justice Department and the IRS the names of some twenty-two thousand US customers who engaged in their schemes, citing prohibitive Swiss laws which tough US officials could have challenged with a waiver demand.

These remarkable concessions mystified both Senator McCain and Senator Carl Levin, the latter having conducted an early inquiry into these banking crimes.

Credit Suisse's American CEO, Brady Dougan, immediately issued a statement regretting "the past misconduct," and the bank's British CFO, David Mathers, then said that the deal would assuredly produce no "material impact" on "our operational or business capabilities."

For the sake of comparison, let's imagine that such crimes were committed by a community bank or a credit union. The government would have shut them down and their executives would have been prosecuted, convicted, and sent to jail, as hundreds of officials were during the savings and loan scandals in the eighties and nineties.

In short, Credit Suisse is not only too big to fail, but the schemers at the top rungs of the company are apparently *too big to jail*. Eight lower-level supervisors were indicted. Six of them remained in hiding, allegedly in Switzerland, to avoid being extradited.

There is another problem that needs attention, as James Henry, former chief economist at McKinsey & Co., described on *Democracy Now!*:

Eric Holder used to be an attorney at Covington & Burling, after he left the Clinton administration. He was handling UBS [Switzerland's largest bank] as a client. The chief IRS legal counsel, Mr. Wilkins, used to be a registered representative for the Swiss Bank[ers] Association in Washington, when he was a partner at WilmerHale. You have the US treasury secretary, [who] was in charge of Citibank's global private banking department when he was at Citibank in 2006. . . . [And] one of the key golfing partners of the president of the United States, Robert Wolf, used to run UBS America. He was a big fundraiser for Obama in 2008. So this administration is permeated with people who are basically very sympathetic to Wall Street and to Swiss interests, as well.

These previous relationships paint a troubling picture. Would these government officials be willing to state publicly that they'd never go back through the revolving door to these same law firms or large businesses? It is unlikely that they would ever deny themselves such a routine return to lucrative positions, using the experience they built up, at taxpayers' expense, to represent future corporate clients in deep trouble with law enforcement.

Shuttling between governments and law firms has always been a tradition, most prominently exhibited by the powerful Lloyd Cutler in the seventies and eighties. A recent issue of the *Corporate Crime Reporter* published the names of the thirty top corporate criminal defense law firms responsible for arranging 60 percent of corporate deferred- and non-prosecution agreements. It helps mightily for lawyers to bring their government regulatory experience to these giant power brokers.

Bad as the Credit Suisse slap-on-the-wrist deal was, this lenient treatment of big company transgressions was common practice under Holder and the Democrats. They were generating the climate for tax escapes and deliberate tax evasion that would characterize Trump's path to the White House.

What Credit Suisse did, according to a Department of Justice news release, was to "aid and assist" in tax evasion by "assisting clients in using sham entities to hide undeclared accounts"; "soliciting IRS forms that falsely stated, under penalties of perjury, that the sham entities were the beneficial owners of the assets in the accounts"; "failing to maintain in the United States records related to the accounts"; "destroying account records sent to the United States for client review"; "using Credit Suisse managers and employees as unregistered investment advisors on undeclared accounts"; "facilitating withdrawals of funds from the undeclared accounts by either providing hand-delivered cash in the United States or using Credit Suisse's correspondent bank accounts in the United States"; "structuring transfers of funds to evade currency transaction reporting requirements"; and "providing offshore credit and debit cards to repatriate funds in the undeclared accounts."

These elaborate illegal acts show a deliberate willingness by Credit Suisse AG officials to knowingly engage in profitable activities that defrauded the United States Treasury and burdened honest taxpayers. Credit Suisse paid a $2.6 billion fine—small compared to the size of its crimes and the company's large revenues. More broadly, these crimes were yet another sordid chapter in the ever-burgeoning tax-evading business catering to wealthy Americans and massive corporate entities. But the Credit Suisse story does not end there.

The Employee Retirement Income Security Act of 1974 (ERISA) was enacted to protect the pensions of retirement plan participants. The law, in theory, automatically disqualifies institutions like Credit Suisse AG that have committed serious crimes or pled guilty to serious crimes from serving as a "qualified professional asset manager" (QPAM) of ERISA assets or pension plans.

Unfortunately, the Department of Labor has not adequately enforced this law or its regulations in this area. Between 1997 and 2015, twenty-three firms were granted exemptions from this disqualification rule and were allowed to continue their business of advising pension and other investment funds. In 2016 alone, five of these waivers were granted to companies that, like Credit Suisse AG, violated serious laws either in the United States or abroad. Remarkably, in this century only one waiver request has been rejected, for Royal Bank of Scotland in 2016, following its banking affiliate's criminal conviction for currency and price fixing.

In 2014 the DOL granted Credit Suisse a temporary waiver to continue conducting their pension management business. On January 15, 2015, the DOL held a public hearing—where I testified—to discuss whether Credit Suisse and its affiliates should be allowed to continue this troubling trend of avoiding the consequences of their actions indefinitely. Credit Suisse AG is hoping to completely sidestep the mechanisms of justice for their serious crimes and carry on business as usual—a result that in itself is, unfortunately, business as usual. Is it not astounding to think that a company that knowingly engaged in such illegal activities would not be deterred from engaging in activities that could be harmful to retirees as well?

Public Citizen's Bartlett Naylor wrote in a public comment to the Department of Labor:

> Firms that engage in criminal activity should face real consequences. Where those consequences are excused, the firm is invited to become a repeat offender; and the deterrence effect for other firms is nullified. Pension fund beneficiaries are especially vulnerable to Wall Street abuse

because their savings may be managed by firms they do not even choose, let alone control. As overseer of the nation's ERISA-governed funds, the Department of Labor bears the heavy responsibility of policing the integrity of the pension fund management industry. The DOL must apply all its tools to achieve this lofty goal. They should be used, not routinely discarded.

This routine ability to evade proper punishment is at the root of so much corporate and Wall Street crime—a slap on the wrist leads to a perpetual cycle of wrongdoing with no end in sight. Their corporate lawyers turn laws into "no-law" laws. Corporate crime pays.

James Henry, former chief economist at McKinsey & Co. and current chair of the Global Alliance for Tax Justice, estimates that the United States loses between $170 billion and $200 billion a year in tax revenues through offshore tax havens and corporate tax loopholes. He told the *Corporate Crime Reporter* in 2013:

> The idea that you would actually permit big ticket tax dodgers to walk off of the stage with a slap on the wrist— like the proposed [Credit Suisse] settlement—or that you would let companies like Apple and Microsoft, General Electric and Google . . . shift their most valuable corporate assets to places where they have almost no activity and evade corporate income taxes at a time when we are slashing aid to kids in schools, money for seniors—this is outrageous.

13.

Obama's Bad Ideas on Free Trade

The Obama administration's gratuitous espousal of the oligarchic Trans-Pacific Partnership (TPP)—a trade and foreign investment treaty between twelve nations (Australia, Brunei, Canada, Chile, Japan, Malaysia, Mexico, New Zealand, Peru, Singapore, the United States, and Vietnam)—would have lost us jobs while helping multinationals concentrate power against US laws. The partnership would have lowered standards for workers, raised prices for consumers (especially drug prices), and harmed the environment—and any attempts even to fight such results could have been considered violations of the TPP's "non-tariff trade barriers."

Trump spoke out against the TPP in an attempt to please his hard-core followers, perhaps not even knowing that he was doing something many progressives also saw as being of long-term benefit to US citizens. Here Trump inadvertently made a change that was better for the general populace.

However Democrats and progressives must recognize how bad such agreements are for the general public, despite Obama's championing of the TPP. Obama and his corporate allies campaigned to manipulate and pressure Congress to ram through the "pull-down-on-America" TPP—meaning pull down our regulatory standards to allegedly "meet the global competition."

The first skirmish was a fast-track bill to have Congress formally strip itself of its constitutional authority to regulate trade and surrender this historic responsibility to the White House and its corporate lobbies. While Congress balked at the bill, a revised version of the fast-track legislation was later signed into law.

If you think the TPP was too commercially complex to bother about, think again. This mega-treaty was the latest corporate coup d'état undermining American consumer, labor, and environmental standards by bypassing the sovereignty of our three branches of government in favor of secret tribunals biased toward corporate commerce decisions.

Trade treaties like NAFTA or the General Agreement on Tariffs and Trade (GATT), the precursor to the establishment of the World Trade Organization, already have proven records of harming our country through major job-exporting trade deficits, unemployment, the freezing or jeopardizing of our consumer and environmental rules, deregulation of giant banks, and the weakening of US labor protections.

How does the corporate state, with its "free traitors," construct a transnational form of autocratic governance that bypasses the powers of our branches of government and accepts the decisions of secret tribunals run by corporate lawyers-turned-judges? Well, first they establish autocratic congressional procedures, such as fast-track legislation, that facilitate the creation of an absentee transnational autocratic government. These procedures betray the American people by going far beyond reducing tariffs and quotas to erode our domestic health, safety, and economic safeguards.

That's how the TPP proceeded toward multinational signatures. The TPP treaty was cynically classified by the White House as an "agreement" requiring a simple majority vote, not a treaty requiring two-thirds of the Congress for passage. Fast-track legislation then limited debate on the TPP to a total of twenty hours in each chamber. Then, Congress let the White House tie Congress's hands by agreeing to prohibit any amendments and limiting their participation to just an up or down vote.

Meanwhile, the campaign cash flowed into the abdicating lawmakers' coffers from the likes of Boeing, General Electric, Pfizer, Citigroup, ExxonMobil, and other US multinational corporations that show a lack of loyalty to the United States (no corporate patriotism), doing business with communist and fascist regimes that allow them to get away with horrible environmental abuses and labor repression in the name of greater profits.

Many of the Pacific Rim countries included in the TPP, for example, have bad labor laws and practices, few if any consumer or environmental protections that can be enforced in courts of law, and precious little freedom of speech.

A 2007 treaty with South Korea was pushed through Congress on false predictions of jobs and win-win solutions. In fact, the agreement resulted in a ballooning of the trade deficit that the US has with South Korea, costing an estimated sixty thousand American jobs.

The majority of these corporate-managed trade agreements come from the demands of global corporations. They exploit developing countries that have cheap labor and lax laws, unlike more developed countries, such as the US, that have greater protections for consumers, workers and the environment, including in courts of law. Under NAFTA and the WTO multinational trade agreements, countries that seek better protections for their workers and consumers can be sued by corporations and other nations. Remarkably, better protections, such as safer motor vehicle standards, can be ruled as obstructive trade barriers against inferior imports.

As just one example among many, under the WTO, the US cannot keep out products made by brutal child labor abroad, even though US law prohibits child labor in this country. This is how our sovereignty is shredded.

Under the WTO, in the secret tribunals in Geneva, Switzerland, the US has lost most of the cases brought against its public interest laws, including consumer and environmental protections. If the TPP had passed, it would have produced similar autocratic outcomes for the Pacific Rim countries, enforceable by major fines and other sanctions.

At the time Obama was pushing the fast-track bill, Congressman Lloyd Doggett (D-TX), a former Texas Supreme Court justice, told *Politico*, "I do not believe that Congress should relinquish its trade oversight authority. This really is a fast track—seeking to railroad the Trans-Pacific Partnership through while USTR [the United States Trade Representative] hides from Congress the most important details."

This is why Senator Elizabeth Warren opposed the TPP. She wrote in the *Washington Post* that the TPP "would allow foreign companies to challenge US laws—and potentially to pick up huge payouts from taxpayers—without ever stepping foot in a US court."

Under the TPP, if a company doesn't like our regulatory controls over cancer-causing chemicals, it could skip the US courts and sue the US before a secret tribunal that hands down decisions that can't be challenged in US courts. If a company won before this secret kangaroo court, it could be given millions or even hundreds of millions of dollars in damages, charged to you, the taxpayer. Again, the big-business "free traitors" are shredding our sovereignty under the Constitution on the grounds that the US has agreed to these terms.

Scores of such cases have already been brought before the WTO. Senator Warren explained that "recent cases include a French company that sued Egypt because Egypt raised its minimum wage, a

Swedish company that sued Germany because Germany decided to phase out nuclear power after Japan's Fukushima disaster, and a Dutch company that sued the Czech Republic because the Czechs didn't bail out a bank that the company partially owned. . . . Philip Morris is trying to use ISDS [Investor-State Dispute Settlement] to stop Uruguay from implementing new tobacco regulations intended to cut smoking rates."

Senator Warren upset President Obama, who, talking on a business panel (he wouldn't talk TPP before a labor or consumer gathering), called Warren "wrong on this." Really? Well, why didn't he debate her then, as Al Gore debated Ross Perot on NAFTA? She read the fine print; I doubt whether he read more than the corporate power tea leaves. He seemed to have forgotten his severe criticism of NAFTA from when he ran for president in 2008.

In the lead-up to the vote on the fast-track bill, the Democrats should have done things to show that they were a party of healthy debate, not a party of obedience and subordination to a single leader who clearly hadn't taken the time to read the text of the WTO agreement, and didn't see the need for adequate open debate on it on Capitol Hill.

A debate clarifying the issues before a skeptical public and others who are downright confused would have sent a signal of internal party democracy that would have been laudatory.

This would have been the time to engage the American people by putting on a debate. They would be the ones paying the price in many dire ways if the mega-corporate promoters of TPP turned out to be as wrong as they were with prior trade deals, like 2007's disastrous US-Korea Free Trade Agreement.

Consider also these salient points:

1. President Obama and Senator Warren have both been teachers of the law. A debate between them would have been delibera-

tive and, assuming both had read the thirty chapters of the TPP, revelatory, far beyond the narrow prisms reflected in the mass media.

2. Like NAFTA and the World Trade Organization, the TPP would have established a transnational system of autocratic governance that subordinates and bypasses our own judiciary in favor of secret tribunals whose procedures contravene our country's system of due process, openness, and independent appeal. Such trade agreements, as Obama knew at the time, have enforceable provisions for the privileges of corporations. Obama's rhetorical assurances for labor, environment, and consumer rights had no such enforcement mechanisms.

3. Notwithstanding all the "win-win" claims of promoters of past trade agreements, our country's trade deficit has grown over the past forty years to well beyond half a trillion dollars each year. Enormous trade deficits mean job exports. Given this evidence, the public would have been interested to hear Obama's explanation of this adverse effect on US workers and our economy.

4. Obama believed Elizabeth Warren was wrong on the facts relating to the "investor-state dispute settlement" provision of the TPP. She claimed the provision would have allowed foreign companies to challenge our health, safety, and other regulations, not in our courts but before an international panel of arbitrators. Obama claimed, without citing any evidence or precedents from previous transnational trade agreements, that it allowed nothing of the sort. A perfect point/counterpoint for a debate process, no?

5. Over the years, it has become abundantly clear that very few lawmakers or presidents actually read the text of these trade agreements involving excessive surrender of local, state, and federal sovereignties. They generally rely on memoranda prepared by the US Trade Representative (USTR) and corporate

lobbies. Given the mass of fine print with portentous consequences for every American, a worthy debate topic would have
been whether to delay the vote on the TPP until copies could be
made available to the American people to discuss and consider
it. Instead, Obama urged Congress to pass the TPP with very
limited debate and without any amendments being permitted.
Why such a rush before the ink was even dry on the page?

Some may wonder why Obama didn't call the TPP agreement a
"treaty," as other countries typically refer to similar deals. Could it
have been that an "agreement" only requires 51 percent approval in
Congress, rather than a two-thirds vote in the Senate, for a treaty
ratification? Of course.

Obama was quoted in the *Washington Post* in the lead-up to the
vote on the TPP, decrying "misinformation" that was circulating
on the TPP and pledging that he was "going to be pushing back
very hard if I keep on hearing that." Fine. In a letter I wrote to him,
I told him that if he really stood behind this cruel agreement, he
would stand before tens of millions of people with Senator Elizabeth Warren as his debating counterpart and allow the democratic
process to take its course. "If you agree," I wrote to the president,
"be sure that interested Americans have a copy of the proposed
TPP deal first, so that they can be an informed audience."

Instead of debating her, Obama, of course, went in the opposite
direction—to say, in effect, "Trust me."

The reason I would refer to President Obama as "King Obama"
in this case is that he, with his royal court of massive corporate
lobbies, sought to circumvent the historic checks and balances
system of our founding fathers that is the very bedrock of our
government. They sought to severely weaken the independence
of the primary branch of our government—the Congress—and
fought off any court challenges with medieval defenses—claiming,

for instance, that no American citizen has any standing to sue for harm done by such a treaty, or that transnational trade is a political, not judicial, matter.

President Obama weakened two branches of our government in favor of the third, his executive branch, to allow secret negotiations with eleven other nations, some of which are brutal regimes.

In the mid-nineties, I opposed the creation of NAFTA and the World Trade Organization. President Obama and some members of Congress said that the TPP would be different from NAFTA and the WTO, but I doubt that they read the entire draft of the TPP. They again relied on summary memos by the US Trade Representative and corporate lawyers, for example, from drug companies that sugarcoated the TPP's complex monopolistic extension of pharmaceutical patents, conveniently failing to mention that it would have resulted in higher prices for your medicines.

Hundreds of pages of cross-references and repeals of conflicting existing laws could not hide the TPP's primary purpose: *the subordination of our protective laws for labor, consumers, and the environment—impersonally called "non-tariff trader barriers"—to the supremacy of global commercial traffic.* (See Public Citizen's Global Trade Watch for detailed analyses of the effects the TPP would have had on US regulations).

One example—by no means the worst possible—of global trade trumping US law occurred in May 2015. After Congress passed a popular "country-of-origin" labeling requirement on meat packages sold in supermarkets, Canada and Mexico, both exporters of meat to the US, challenged this law before a secret (yes, literally secret in all respects) WTO tribunal in Geneva and won.

"Many Americans will be shocked that the WTO can order our government to deny US consumers the basic information about where their food comes from and that if the information policy is not gutted, we could face millions in sanctions every year," said Lori

Wallach, director of Public Citizen's Global Trade Watch, at that time. "Today's ruling spotlights how these so-called 'trade' deals are packed with non-trade provisions that threaten our most basic rights, such as even knowing the source and safety of what's on our dinner plate." A May 2013 survey by the Consumer Federation of America found that 90 percent of American adults favored this "country-of-origin" requirement, which meant an overwhelming convergence of liberal and conservative Americans.

Still, fearing billions of dollars in penalties under the WTO, the US Congress raced to repeal its own law. That is how the straightjacket works: foreign countries trying to pull down our higher regulatory standards can take conflicts to secret tribunals with three trade judges, who also have corporate clients and can say to the US, "Get rid of your protections or pay billions of dollars in tribute." Outrageous, no? Fortunately in 2017 President Trump pulled the US out of the TPP negotiations—at least for the time being.

PART II

THE PRESIDENTIAL
PRIMARIES

The Democrats, by not championing a people's agenda, left the field open for a contrived ersatz-populist like Trump to gain the presidency, albeit due to the Electoral College rather than the popular vote. Of course Trump had no intention of delivering on his promises to the little guy, but he left specious room for them to hope. Hillary Clinton, deemed almost as "untrustworthy" as Trump in national polls, didn't even do that, nor did she consistently attack the Republicans where it hurts, targeting their selfish, pro-business, anti-consumer, and anti-worker policies. Had the Democrats set out to win, strategic attacks on Republican corporatism would have been essential coming out of the primaries. Many higher-ups in the Democratic Party knew this, but they also knew that tactic would have alienated most of their big donors. Since Trump didn't have to rely on special interests and corporate campaign donors, he had the autonomy to run his mouth and attack the rich, even while furtively assembling a deeply corporatist cabinet, ready to betray all but the wealthiest of Trump's voters.

14.

Hillary on Her Record

Let's go back to the Hillary Clinton for President 2016 campaign, a bandwagon that started very early and purposefully. The idea was to get large numbers of endorsers, so that no Democratic competitors would dare make a move in the primaries. Clinton's earliest supporters included Senator Chuck Schumer (D-NY), financier George Soros, and Ready for Hillary, a super PAC that mobilized with great specificity (in Iowa, for instance, as early as 2014).

Given this early bird launch, one might have wished to ask at the time a rather pressing question: Would the future of our country benefit from Hillary, another Clinton, another politician whose policies are almost indistinguishable from Barack Obama's militaristic corporatism, another candidate whose war chest is garnished by big money donors from Wall Street and other plutocratic canyons?

There is no doubt the Clintons are syrupy political charmers, beguiling many naïve Democrats who have long been vulnerable to a practiced set of comforting words and phrases camouflaging contrary deeds.

Everybody knew that Hillary was for women, children, and education. She said so every day. But during Clinton's time in the Senate, Democrats and other family advocacy groups could not get her to support raising the federal minimum wage to $10.10, which would have raised the wages of thirty million workers. It just so happens that almost two-thirds of these Americans are women, many of them single moms struggling to support their impoverished children. And nearly a million of these workers labor for Walmart, where Hillary Clinton once sat on the board of directors. Words hide her deeds and inactions.

As a senator on the Senate Armed Services Committee, Hillary had to prove that women can be just as belligerent as the macho men. Never did she see a weapons system that she opposed. Never did she demonstrate any real interest in de-bloating the massive, wasteful, duplicative military budget so as to free up big monies for domestic public works programs or other social welfare necessities.

As a senator she also admitted that she didn't have time to read a critical National Intelligence Estimate report, whose caveats might have dissuaded her from voting in October 2002 to support war criminal President George W. Bush's invasion of Iraq. War-mongering and imperialism never bothered her, then or now. She was photographed giving the recidivist war criminal and Republican Henry Kissinger a big, smiling hug at a public event. It was all part of the bipartisan image she cultivated under the opportunistic banner of "cooperation."

As secretary of state, Hillary Clinton accelerated the department's militarization, belting out far more war-threatening assertions toward governments of developing countries than the secretaries of defense. She loved to give speeches on "force projection"—the latest synonym for "imperialism"—and "the pivot" toward East Asia, against the asserted looming threat of China. Taking due note, the Chinese generals demanded larger budgets. She didn't mind provoking another costly, risky arms race.

The secretary of state's highest duty is diplomacy. Not so for Hillary. Despite her heavy traveling, she made little or no effort to get the government to sign on to the numerous international treaties that already had over a hundred nations as signatories. These included stronger climate change agreements and, as Human Rights Watch reported, unratified treaties "relating to children, women, persons with disabilities, torture, enforced disappearance, and the use of anti-personnel landmines and cluster munitions." Such tasks bored her.

Much more exciting was military action. Against the expressed wishes of Secretary of Defense Robert Gates, she pulled Barack Obama into the Libyan war. There were consequences. Libya is now in violent chaos, with its extremist militias smuggling munitions into Mali and other neighboring countries. Hillary did not think of the consequences of overthrowing Gaddafi, the dictator who had recently disarmed from weapons of mass destruction and was making peace with Western nations and deals with oil companies.

A Yale Law School graduate, Hillary was not in the least bothered that the attack on Libya occurred without any congressional declaration, nor authorization, nor appropriation of funds—the classic Madisonian definition of impeachable "high crimes and misdemeanors."

Like her husband, Hillary was an unabashed cheerleader for corporate globalization under NAFTA, the World Trade Organization, and the proposed sovereignty-stripping, anti-worker Trans-Pacific Partnership. Secretary of State Clinton, in the words of trade expert Jamie Love, "put the hammer to India when the government took steps to grant compulsory licenses on cancer drug patents," urging them not to issue life-saving compulsory licenses of expensive drugs that would allow low-income people and their children to have access to more affordable medication.

Hillary Clinton also, while serving as secretary of state, fired whistleblower Peter Van Buren, a twenty-four-year foreign service officer, who exposed waste and mismanagement by corporate contractors in Iraq.

Worse yet, Secretary of State Clinton ordered US spying on top UN officials, including secretary-general of the UN Ban Ki-moon and diplomats from the United Kingdom. She ordered her embassies around the world to obtain DNA data, iris scans, and fingerprints along with credit card and frequent flier numbers. Not only was this a clear violation of the 1946 UN convention, but after admitting what happened she didn't even make a public apology to the affected parties. Hillary does not apologize. She does not apologize even for her disastrous Iraq invasion vote. Very infrequently she'll use her preferred word for it, a "mistake."

Under her watch, the advice and status of the State Department's foreign service officers and aid workers were marginalized in favor of the militarists—and not only in Iraq.

Many Wall Streeters do like Hillary Clinton. Expecting their ample contributions, and socializing with their business barons, Hillary Clinton unsurprisingly avoided going after the crooked casino capitalism that collapsed the economy, drained investments, pensions, and jobs, and took huge taxpayer bailouts. Hillary Clinton is a far cry from the stalwart senator Elizabeth Warren in combating this pattern of unaccountable corporate abuse.

The surreal world of Hillary Clinton includes charging $200,000 for speeches, collecting prestigious awards she does not deserve—including one from the American Bar Association, no less—and basking in the glory of her admirers while appropriately blasting the Republicans for their "War on Women"—the safe refrain of her 2016 campaign.

It is true that the cruel, rabid, ravaging Republican madheads make it easy for any Democratic candidate to appear comparatively wonderful. But is that the kind of choice our country deserves? That Clinton was essentially crowned the Democratic nominee nearly two years before the 2016 elections stifled any broader choice of competitive primary candidates, and, more importantly, it precluded a more progressive agenda that would have been supported by a majority of the American people. But then, out of the blue, came Senator Bernie Sanders.

As you can see, Clinton resembled Obama in her tendency to embrace military solutions and in her obeisance to the dictates of Wall Street. These were not just individual failings, but the failings of the Democratic Party.

A June 2014 *New York Times* interview was very revealing about Hillary in terms of her desire to (verbally) try to please everyone and, at the same time, test her audience's credulity. In the interview, Mrs. Clinton was asked about her current reading list and she offered a transparently manufactured response that reflected the fundamental inauthenticity that would characterize and later doom her campaign.

My first reaction to looking at her list was "Can anybody believe this? How can such a super-busy person have the time to absorb such a staggering load of diverse books?"

The *Times* sends questions in advance to the person they are going to interview each week. This gives the person being interviewed enough time to think about their favorite books and be precise about titles. The titles Hillary said she was reading could have been poll-tested for the 2016 presidential race.

First, Hillary declared that she was reading three books at one time, which she explained were among the "pile of books stacked on my night stand that I'm reading." They included *Mom & Me & Mom* by the late Maya Angelou.

To the question "What was the last truly great book you read?" she listed not one but four of them: *The Hare with Amber Eyes* by Edmund de Waal, *The Signature of All Things* by Elizabeth Gilbert, *Citizens of London* by Lynne Olson, and *A Suitable Boy* by Vikram Seth.

Revving up, she took on with gusto the question "Who are your favorite contemporary writers," including "any writers whose books you automatically read when they come out?" She replied that she reads "anything by Laura Hillenbrand, Walter Isaacson, Barbara Kingsolver, John le Carré, John Grisham, Hilary Mantel, Toni Morrison, Anna Quindlen and Alice Walker," plus she "automatically" reads "the latest installments from Alex Berenson, Linda Fairstein, Sue Grafton, Donna Leon, Katherine Hall Page, Louise Penny, Daniel Silva, Alexander McCall Smith, Charles Todd and Jacqueline Winspear."

Whew! That's not all of her responses. I have read some of this popular *New York Times* column's interviews over the years, many with professional authors of fiction and nonfiction, and not one replied with such an oceanic immersion, even though many of these authors regularly read many books for their craft.

The former first lady explained that she finds time to indulge in "guilty pleasures and useful time fillers" that include "[c]ooking, decorating, diet/self-help and gardening books." Time fillers? For one of the busiest people on earth? Has Hillary discovered the seventy-two-hour day?

It gets better. When asked her opinion on the best books about Washington, DC, she chose *Our Divided Political Heart* by E. J. Dionne Jr., as it "shows how most everybody has some conservative and liberal impulses, but just as individuals have to reconcile them within ourselves, so does our political system if we expect to function productively."

To the question "Is there one book you wish all students would read?," Hillary could not hold back from providing three: *Pride and Prejudice* by Jane Austen, *Out of Africa* by Isak Dinesen, and *Schindler's List* by Thomas Keneally.

As for the "one book that made you who you are today," Hillary replied, as she does often, that it was the Bible, which, she elaborated, "was and remains the biggest influence on my thinking." It isn't clear which parts of the Bible she's influenced by, but presumably she has read the ones about "an eye for an eye," "turning the other cheek," and "the golden rule."

More insights into her eclectic interests came from her response to the question "Which books might we be surprised to find on your shelves?" "You might be surprised," she admitted, "to see memoirs by Republicans such as *Decision Points*, by President George W. Bush"—whose criminal Iraq War she voted for—"and *Faith of My Fathers*, by Senator John McCain"— chief saber rattler in the Senate.

Perfecto! With this interview Hillary used her literary interests to pander to homemakers, ethnic groups, poets, lovers of fiction, adversaries, hard-line Republican leaders in Congress, religious groups, and the swooning credulous.

Why was Hillary Clinton unable to resist straining our credulity?

Prior to the publication of her prodigious exploits in the literary world, Hillary told Diane Sawyer of ABC News that she and Bill left the White House "dead broke." This comment prompted the press to report on their combined $23 million book contracts, Bill's ample presidential pension, their $200,000 speeches, and other rewards and perks provided to them by wealthy friends.

Sure, politicians are calculating, even cunning. Those are their occupational traits. Maybe Hillary thought she could push the envelope into prevarication and distortion with impunity. After all, as a Wall Street corporatist and a warmongering militarist, she had gotten away with much worse.

Rocky Anderson, the former two-term Democratic mayor of Salt Lake City, addressed Clinton's "recognized reputation for lying, distorting, and evading," citing polls and previous examples, and suggested important questions for the media to ask Hillary on her North American book tour.

One questionable episode involved her trip to Bosnia as first lady in 1996. By her account she and her daughter, Chelsea, landed under sniper fire and had to run "with our heads down to get into the vehicles." This narrative was contradicted by the videos and the report from the CBS reporter who accompanied them, *Sharyl Attkisson*. The video shows Clinton and daughter Chelsea, in *Attkisson's* words, at "a greeting ceremony when the plane landed.... There was no sniper fire."

The *New York Times* noted that on June 10, 2014, the lines of people seeking autographed copies of Hillary's book *Hard Choices* started lining up before 3 a.m. in front of the Barnes & Noble bookstore at Union Square in New York City, where she was launching her book tour. The *New York Times* reported that "dozens of Secret Service agents" were establishing orderly processions and examining the gear of "hundreds of journalists, cameramen and photographers." Retired presidents and their families are given a small permanent Secret Service detail. A private citizen doesn't have "dozens of Secret Service agents" to help sell her books. The reporters didn't push this subject. It is a small wonder that Hillary's seeming march to the White House was being described by commentators as "a coronation."

With so many people curtseying instead of inquiring, how could her path be anything but queenly?

I remember talking to someone about Hillary Clinton in August 2014. "Hillary works for Goldman Sachs and likes war. Otherwise, I like Hillary," he said sardonically. The man was Bill Curry, the former counselor to President Bill Clinton. First, he was referring to her cushy relationships with top Wall Street barons and her $200,000 speeches to the criminal enterprise known as Goldman Sachs, a major player in the US economy's crash in 2008 that burdened taxpayers with vast, costly bailouts. Second, Curry was calling attention to her hawkish foreign policy.

At that time, Clinton commented in an interview with the *Atlantic* that Obama's response to the Syrian civil war wasn't forceful enough, and that he did not have an organized foreign policy. She was calling Obama weak despite his heavy hand in droning, bombing, and intervening during his presidency. While Obama was often wrong, he was hardly a pacifist commander. It's a small wonder that, since 2008, Hillary the Hawk was generally described as, in the words of the *New York Times* journalist Mark Landler, "more hawkish than Mr. Obama."

In the *Atlantic* interview, she chided Obama for not involving the US more deeply with the rebels in Syria, who themselves are riven into factions and deprived of strong leaders and, with few exceptions, trained fighters. As Mrs. Clinton well knew, from her time as secretary of state, the White House was being cautious because of growing congressional opposition to intervention in Syria, as Congress sought to determine the best rebel groups to arm and how to prevent US weaponry from falling into the hands of enemy insurgents.

She grandly told her interviewer, "Great nations need organizing principles, and 'Don't do stupid stuff' is not an organizing principle." Nonsense. Not plunging into unconstitutional wars could have been a fine "organizing principle." Instead, she voted for the criminal, unconstitutional invasion of Iraq, which boomeranged back, resulting in costly chaos and tragedy for the Iraqi people, American soldiers, and the American taxpayers.

Moreover, Hillary ended her undistinguished tenure as secretary of state in 2013 with an unremitting record of militarizing a department that was originally chartered over two hundred years ago to be the expression of American diplomacy. As secretary of state, Hillary Clinton made far more bellicose statements than Secretary of Defense Robert Gates. Some career foreign service officers found her aggressive language unhelpful, if not downright hazardous to their diplomatic missions.

Mrs. Clinton had no "organizing principle" for the deadly aftermath of Gaddafi's assassination, with warring militias carving up Libya and smuggling arms and mayhem into Mali and the resultant violent disruption in Central Africa. The Libyan assault was Hillary Clinton's undeclared war—a continuing disaster that shows her touted foreign policy experience involved just doing more "stupid stuff." She displayed dangerous ignorance about the quicksand perils for the United States of post-dictatorial vacuums in traditional, tribal, sectarian societies.

After criticizing Obama, Mrs. Clinton then issued a statement saying she had called the president to say that she did not intend to attack him and anticipated "hugging it out" with him at a Martha's Vineyard party. Embracing opportunistically after attacking is less than admirable.

Considering Hillary Clinton's origins as an anti-Vietnam-War youth, how did she end up such a war hawk? Perhaps it was a result of her overweening political ambition and her determination to prevent accusations of being soft on militarism and its empire because she is a woman.

After her celebrity election as New York's senator in 2000, she was given a requested seat on the Senate Armed Services Committee. There, unlike her hawkish friend, Republican senator John McCain, she rarely challenged a boondoggle Pentagon contract; never took on the defense industry's waste, fraud, and abuse; and, as noted, never saw a redundant or unneeded weapons system (often criticized by retired generals and admirals) that she did not like.

President Eisenhower's prescient warning about the vaunted military-industrial complex apparently did not get through to Hillary Clinton.

Energetically waging peace was not on Secretary of State Clinton's agenda. She preferred to talk about military might and deployment in one geographic area after another. At the US Naval Academy in 2012, Clinton gave a speech about pivoting to East Asia with "force posture," otherwise known as "force projection" (one of her favorite phrases), of US naval ships, planes, and positioned troops in countries neighboring China. She was chief diplomat of the secretary of state, not the secretary of defense.

Of course, China's response was to increase its military budget and project its own military might. The world's largest superpower should not be addicted to continuous provocations that could produce deadly unintended consequences.

As she went around the country with an expanded, publicly funded Secret Service corps to promote the sales of her book, *Hard Choices*, Clinton should have pondered what, if anything, she as a presidential candidate had to offer the war-weary, corporate-dominated American people.

After all, Hillary Clinton was insulated—spending her time with the splendors of the wealthy classes and the culpable Wall Street crowd, when she wasn't pulling down huge speech fees for pandering to closed-door giant trade association conventions around the country. This created distance between her "high-society" life and the hard-pressed experiences of the masses.

15.

The Attempt to Sideline Sanders

While plans for Hillary's preemptive coronation as the Democratic Party presidential candidate were under way, Sanders threw his hat into the ring, making a formal announcement for the presidency before five thousand cheering supporters in Burlington, Vermont, in May 2015. He was starting from the region that launched the American Revolution, and he promised to "begin a political revolution to transform our country economically, politically, socially and environmentally," with "the support of millions of people throughout this country."

He would be taking on the corporate plutocracy and its servile political oligarchy with numerous assets. In his long, scandal-free elective career, from mayor of Burlington to member of the House of Representatives to US senator, Sanders could woo voters with progressive rhetoric backed by a consistent voting record.

At that point, he had a large number of progressive supporters who were not "Ready for Hillary" because of her corporatism and militarism. This assured his ability to raise $73 million, mostly in small donations, by the end of 2015. This level of contributions could fund a competitive grassroots campaign drive, especially since he was running as a Democrat—to get into the party's primary debates—and didn't have to expend money and time getting on each state's ballot.

Moreover, if you read the positions he took—summarized in his Burlington campaign speech—you could conclude that they already had majoritarian support in this country. Sanders's "Agenda for America" was an outline of some key issues our country faces, complete with concrete facts to back up his stances. The other candidates preferred to campaign on abstractions and to avoid articulating detailed solutions to our country's problems.

Sanders stood for a national program to repair and renovate America's public facilities, which would create thirteen million well-paid jobs that could not be exported to China. He opposed the corporate-managed trade's corrosive supremacy over domestic protections of workers, consumers, and the environment, and pledged to end America's participation in transnational trade deals that circumvent our open court and regulatory system with literally secret tribunals. He has been a longtime challenger of the price-gouging, taxpayer-subsidized pharmaceutical industry. He advocated raising the minimum wage to "$15 an hour over the next few years." He wanted tuition-free college education, full Medicare for All with free choice of doctor and hospital, and "paid sick leave and guaranteed vacation time for all"—much of which Western Europe has had for decades!

He was pressing for the breakup of the too-big-to-fail banks, calling them, as did conservative columnist George Will, "too big to exist." He was also pushing for an end to "huge tax breaks while children in this country go hungry" and while this "billionaire class" continues "sending our jobs to China while millions are looking for work."

When Sanders began his campaign I foresaw that he was not without his vulnerabilities. He would be dismissed by the corporate mass media as a gadfly going nowhere, as was another recent good Democratic presidential candidate, former congressman Dennis Kucinich. Sanders had to ensure that his speeches stayed fresh and current, while touching on regional issues that vary, depending on where he was speaking, to avoid being tedious to the dittohead press that doesn't apply the same standards to the repetitive tedium of the mainstream front-runners.

His case was based not just on current public needs but on the long-term needs of the American people, as workers and taxpayers. For many, material income, adjusted for inflation, stalled in the early 1970s, and the vast gains from growth and productivity since then have gone to the wealthiest 5 percent, and especially to the wealthiest 1 percent.

Furthermore, Sanders needed to give visibility to the massive, preventable, silent violence afflicting innocent, undefended Americans. This includes occupational trauma and disease, hospital-induced infections and medical malpractice, deadly side effects of overused or dangerous medicines, toxic, cancer-producing pollution, and product defects. He needed to show that he was ready to tackle the cycle of poverty, where the poor pay more and die earlier.

Sanders was going to have a number of people and organizations bidding for his time to give him their opinions on any number of matters. At the time I would have said that to win, he should welcome advice with an open mind. Many of his political supporters have stuck with him for decades; it would have been highly beneficial for him to listen to them. But according to eyewitness accounts, he is *not* a good listener. The late senator Paul Wellstone provided a fine example of how to network with citizen groups for the common good. I wrote at the time that, as a presidential candidate, Sanders should follow the example of Wellstone.

The nagging problem facing the Vermont senator right from the start was how to compete with and challenge Hillary Clinton. In 2015, he said that he had "never run a negative political ad," and that he respected his former senatorial colleague. And yet, while progressives may not like negative ads, they do want a candidate who clearly articulates his or her differences from other candidates in direct ways that draw voters away from those competitors. Assuming, of course, that the candidate is *really* running to win.

Sanders had to take on Hillary Clinton and the other candidates with the issues that matter—the ones that truly show the difference between their voting records and their rhetoric. Sanders's task was to hold Clinton accountable for her illegal, disastrous, brute force foreign policy. He needed to point out her record of favoring Wall Street and the military-industrial complex. He also had to, in his way, convince Democratic and independent voters not only that he would be good for America but that he would support many issues that Hillary did not, such as shifting power and control of wealth, income, and our commonwealth from the plutocratic few to the many.

The rise of Sanders, not strictly speaking a Democrat till he ran in the primary, illustrated the salience of the idea that a candidate can truly run for the people, and broke down the long-held assumption that political campaigns must necessarily be beholden to wealthy special interest groups. Here was a senator who had consistently won with a pro-people, anti-corporate message and practice. Which is not to say he never showed any weaknesses. In August 2015, as Sanders's campaign was just ramping up, I wrote him the following letter:

> Dear Senator Sanders,
>
> You've come a long way without my advice, but now that you are running for president, you may be interested in these suggestions:
>
> 1. You've taken progressive positions on "decent-paying job" programs, such as investing in repairing our country's

public works, raising the minimum wage, strengthening labor laws, opposing the good-job-exporting, corporate-managed trade treaties like NAFTA and the WTO, and creating a Youth Job Corps. Now you need to make major addresses in greater detail on each topic before large audiences. The media coverage of these events will be very helpful during primary season.

2. You need to identify with local and regional issues as you travel around the country and appear with the citizen or labor groups championing these pathways to justice. Just about all major presidential candidates assiduously avoid such identification with citizen groups, for fear of some taint or gaffe when dealing with less common topics. You shouldn't have this worry.

3. As your popularity rises in the polls and your audiences get larger, your opponents will challenge you for being a self-identified "socialist." It is best to preempt them. Your socialist beliefs seem in line with those of social democratic parties in Western European nations. So, while there is wide bipartisan support for certain socialist institutions— for instance, municipally or regionally owned utilities, or federally owned utilities like the giant Tennessee Valley Authority—you are not interested in nationalizing industry and the banks. You are interested in breaking up giant "too big to fail" banks and reforming the governance of giant multinationals. The vast majority of the American people favor the breakup of large banks; want the Wall Street crooks prosecuted, convicted, and jailed; and oppose bailing out powerful big businesses. This is a Left-Right convergence issue—of Main Street against Wall Street.

4. You need to expand your efforts to reach out to racial and ethnic minorities. Campaign in the low-income neigh-

borhoods. Get to know the dynamic community groups and listen to the issues that they have been struggling with for decades. Your support of credit unions and well-equipped schools, call to curb harmful junk foods, focus on community policing, emphasis on tenant rights and building code enforcement, and concentration on good day care and accessible community health clinics through full Medicare for All will resonate with their community interests.

5. Emphasizing that you are campaigning *with* the people, not on stage *before* the people, is what helps build a movement that will continue after the election—win or lose.

6. In addition to your smaller-denomination *fundraisers*, why not have *time-raisers*—people pledging to support your campaign with hours of volunteer time? This creates opportunities for wider voter involvement.

7. Since you are a US senator, why not develop a unified contract for America? Look how far Newt Gingrich got in 1994 with a contract that was *against* America—he deceptively packaged a list of anti-people, pro–big business proposals and empty rhetoric as the focal point of the election, and, with little opposition from listless Democrats, engineered a landslide Republican takeover of the House of Representatives.

8. Look for advice and return more calls from your imaginative supporters. Being a lone ranger worked in Vermont, but campaigning across fifty states—and you *must* be the only presidential candidate to go to *every* state—requires more congeniality and openness to the problems of many different constituencies.

Sincerely,
Ralph Nader

Subsequent disclosures revealed obstruction of Senator Sanders primary campaigns by the National Democratic Party apparatus, loaded with pro–Hillary Clinton operatives. This sabotage might well have tilted this close contest in Hillary's favor.

16.

The Trump Rampage

When Trump first entered the race in June 2015, his brash, boorish, outsized personality had never been tested in politics, and few accurately predicted how far he would go in upending the Republican primaries.

Many of us thought at the time that if he were to survive the first three months of the mass media drubbing him and his notorious affliction of "leaving no impulsive opinion behind," he would be big trouble for the other fifteen or so Republican presidential candidates.

Already at the start of his campaign the commentators were deriding his massive egotitis—he said "I" 195 times in his announcement speech, not counting the 28 times he said "my" or "mine" or the 22 mentions of "me." But Trump reveled in self-promotion, and, as one commentator wrote, he "plays the media like a harp."

Back then, I predicted that he would be a big nightmare for Republican contenders—from Jeb Bush to Ted Cruz, from John Kasich to Scott Walker—for the following reasons:

1. Many American voters love to vote for very rich candidates, whether they are Republicans or Democrats. They believe they

can't be bought. They love business success stories. And the media and polls keep the very rich candidates in the limelight.
2. Trump was able to pay for his own media. Remember billionaire Ross Perot and his purchase of national television airtime to show his charts on deficits? People laughed. But Mr. Perot got more than nineteen million votes in 1992, even after dropping out of the campaign in the summer and being labeled a conspiracy theorist before again becoming a candidate in the fall!
3. Trump regularly and personally attacked the other candidates, which made for consistent news. The other candidates did not at first like to engage in personal attacks, though many of them sank to his level briefly and too late when they felt cornered.
4. Trump turns liabilities into assets. For instance, he changed the lack of disclosure of his tax returns into a running promise that he would disclose the information eventually. While Jeb Bush and Mitt Romney before him tried to play down their wealth, Trump absurdly insisted he's worth over ten billion dollars. He even ridiculed Jeb Bush for announcing his run for president without wearing a jacket and tie. To the many accusations that he has taken public subsidies and eminent domain protections for his giant projects, Trump replied that his projects create jobs, more businesses, and "beautification."
5. Trump crowded out other candidates from valuable TV, radio (Rush Limbaugh thinks highly of him), and print space. To adjust, the other candidates had to become more flamboyant, further expanding the circus-like atmosphere of the Republican primaries, while the Democratic Party leaders chortled.
6. Some of Trump's positions have sizable support among Republican voters. He believes in public works programs on a big scale. He talks jobs, jobs, jobs, and said on the campaign trail that he was the only one among the candidates who has created many

jobs. He objects strongly to transnational trade agreements, including the Trans-Pacific deal that was a hot topic during the campaigns, on the grounds that other countries, such as Japan and China, are superior negotiators and are taking us to the cleaners. He wants to build a tall wall on the Mexican border. He is against Common Core and federalizing education. He said he warned against invading Iraq in some detail, predicting it would expand Iran's influence (though, in fact, he originally publicly supported the invasion of Iraq). He is for a strong military and talks about the mistreatment of veterans. He exudes self-confidence and attaches it to American national interests.

7. Having survived tough, acidic New York journalism for years, his public persona is relatively unscathed by derailing scandal despite many (underreported) unsavory dealings. Attacks from his business and political enemies have helped to immunize the big-time scrapper from serious reporting. He feeds off public cynicism about politics.

8. If the Republican bigwigs had attempted to exclude or humiliate him, Trump had the means to run as an independent candidate for president—as Mr. Perot essentially did under the banner of his Reform Party. Just the prospect of that raised nightmare-induced caution at the top levels of the GOP.

9. He is not going to run out of money and, unlike his competitors, he didn't have to spend any precious campaign time dialing for dollars or making campaign promises to big-money donors and PACs.

As Trump proved his mettle on the campaign trail with enormous, free mass-media publicity, Sanders was increasingly gaining positive attention, making it clear not only that this was a campaign season like no other in recent memory but that populist agendas were back on the table.

17.

Trump and Sanders

It is not often that Democratic and Republican insurgent candidates for president achieve such prominence and maintain such staying power against the establishment "pols" of the party duopoly that manages elections for the campaign-financing plutocracy. By December 2015, the media was taking the insurgents seriously, which meant that the polls were being done regularly on these candidates' positions alongside matchups with other primary candidates.

Both Bernie Sanders and Donald Trump started out with the first signal of viability the mass media demands—money to spend on campaigning. Sanders surprised the pundits with his ability to attract an immense number of small contributions, which put him on the road to raising a remarkable $73 million in 2015 alone. He was not dependent on the fancy fat-cat fund-raisers that cater exclusively to the very wealthy in New York City, Los Angeles, and other watering holes for rich partisans.

Billionaire Trump, on the other hand, actually exaggerated his wealth as a campaign tactic, bragging that he could finance his entire presidential run if necessary. His "nobody owns me" image resonated with more than a few voters, who may not have realized that "The Donald" is a card-carrying member of the New York plutocracy.

The loud and raging Trump campaign showed us what can happen when voters follow their impulses without doing their homework. The burst of headline-grabbing, braggadocious phrases from Mr. Trump left his dubious business dealings, mistreatment of workers and consumers, acceptance of corporate welfare, and various tax escapes in the shadows. Words trumped his deeds.

As the campaign progressed, Trump held or raised his poll numbers with each outrageous remark that appealed to the hardcore Right—not all of them voters, by the way—who loved his bashing of minorities, his sexism, and his personal ripping into other candidates.

The Republican establishment—the ones who went for the Bushes, Mitt Romney, Ronald Reagan, and Richard Nixon—feared the continued success of Trump's provocations.

Karl Rove, the arch-strategist for George W. Bush, wrote a column in December 2015 for the *Wall Street Journal* titled "Trump is the Democrats' Dream Nominee." Rove cited poll after poll to support his thesis—Trump had low overall favorability ratings, low trustworthiness rankings. Rove said that Hillary Clinton trumped Trump on "three important characteristics," according to the Quinnipiac survey. She had sizable leads on such questions as which candidate has "the right kind of experience to be president" (never mind what kind of judgment), which candidate "cares about the needs and problems of people like you," and which candidate "shares your values."

Rove went on to imagine the kinds of television ads the Democrats would release should Trump get the Republican nomination. During the Cleveland debate, Trump asserted that he took his companies to bankruptcy four times, having, he brazenly asserted, "taken advantage of the laws of this country." Rove writes that the "footage might be followed by compelling testimony from contractors, small-business people and bondholders whom he stiffed."

Other Republican strategists worried that, should he head the ticket, Trump could bring down candidates from Congress and state legislatures, and even governors and mayors.

At the time, people wondered when the establishment Republicans were going to make their move. The plethora of well-funded primary candidates was complicating any quest to back a single challenger. But simply publicizing Trump's business record and hoping and waiting for Trump to increase the self-destructive severity of his outrageous statements was all Republicans seemed able to do.

Bernie Sanders offered a different kind of challenge. Polling a solid second to Hillary Clinton nationwide and running very close in Iowa and Nevada, he had to constantly freshen and broaden his message. Over a six-month period, he demonstrated, with a tiny campaign staff and a swelling campaign treasury, that he could attract larger audiences than Hillary.

Back at the beginning of 2016 Bernie had to increase the number of full-time people on the ground to organize and get out the vote to win Iowa and New Hampshire before Hillary's advantage in the southern state primaries registered on March 1, 2016 (the date that eleven states and American Samoa cast their votes in the primaries, known as "Super Tuesday"). More pressingly, Sanders had to educate the public about the vast differences between his voting/policy record and Clinton's when she was a senator and secretary of state. Some of his supporters believed he had not been doing this strenuously or sharply enough.

Finally, Senator Sanders needed to start diversifying his strategy by becoming more receptive to the opinions of those outside of his team. His campaign got repetitive and unimaginative, depending heavily on cyclical and often abstract talking points. Needless to say, he had enormous material to work into his daily stump speeches and special subject addresses. Sanders also had to make more news, especially because anti-Sanders Democratic Party operatives were not allowing more than six debates, thereby limiting the occasions in which he could be contrasted against Hillary Clinton before very large television-viewing audiences. Senator Sanders needed more prominence if he really wanted to overtake Clinton. His followers felt that Sanders's promise to endorse the eventual Democratic nominee could create a ripe opportunity to get the winner of the Democratic primary to specifically endorse much of the Sanders agenda beforehand.

18.

The Media Was Letting Us Down in Covering the Election and the Debates

The public's view of the candidates during the primaries was not helped by a media that was obsessed with unveiling the latest scandal or outrage. In this environment, Trump had somewhat of an edge, given his tendency to say or do outrageous things multiple times a day.

The mass media, with the usual exceptions, allowed itself to be pulled down to the level of the political circus and, in doing so, gave Trump a daily platform. It was hard for the Republican presidential candidates to resist the temptation to hype an entertainment circus led by the chief circus barker—Donald Trump. If the Republican Party's early primary campaigns for the presidential nomination had featured an elephant and a clown car, Ringling Bros. would have been in trouble. There were seventeen Republican candidates in total—after the inexplicable exclusion of Mark Everson, the former IRS commissioner under George W. Bush and one of the first to announce—all of them hurling hyperbolic epithets, warmongering bravados, and assorted boasts against one another. After their so-called debates, the media emphasized the insults of Trump and others against each other. Reading the coverage and watching the TV clips, one came away with the impression that snarls, quips, ripostes, and gaffes now passed for news.

How rancid! How demeaning to our country and its people! It was bad enough that voters were reduced to spectators watching a reality show where the reactionary candidates bid to become the most powerful person on earth. It was bad enough that the ever-hovering super PACs and their indentured candidates, save Rand Paul and John Kasich, didn't seem to want to be serious, knowledgeable, or at all compassionate toward the powerless and deprived.

This potpourri of poseurs made it possible for Carly Fiorina to rise briefly to the "top tier" of Republican nominees on the basis of a few statements that exude the feigned confidence of the failed corporate CEO she once was. The "roman candle" moment that had the political pundits calling her the debate winner after one free-for-all was her response to Donald Trump's brutish questioning whether anyone would vote for "that face." She calmly responded: "I think women all over this country heard very clearly what Mr. Trump said," just before Trump exercised his usual recovery ploy and exclaimed, "I think she's got a beautiful face. I think she's a beautiful woman." Will Rogers or Jon Stewart would have had a field day with that exchange.

Culpable as these candidates were, to varying degrees, of debasing the most fundamental electoral expressions of the people—that is, the delegation of their sovereignty and power to elected representatives—the media accentuated the dismal trivia with questions that matched the vacuity of the format.

The only business explicitly protected from government by our Constitution is the media—their right of free speech is based in the First Amendment. But just look how the media handled this public trust! As Jamie Larson, a reporter for the website Rural Intelligence, said on viewing the Republican debates, "The media ask questions about what candidates are saying but are not asking the questions they independently should be asking."

I would have suggested such questions as, "What is your record and specific position(s) on corporate crime enforcement, and what would you specifically change so as to punish and prevent corporate criminality?" Or, "People everywhere feel powerless toward government and business; half do not even vote. How would you specifically shift power from the few to the many so that the citizens can have more real choices of candidates and can better control the abuses of electoral politics, government, and big business?" And, "Have you ever supported specific empowerment strategies for the people?" And, "How would you increase voter turnout—say, by having a voting holiday, more days for absentee voting, enacting a binding none-of-the-above option for voters, or reducing or eliminating burdensome and meaningless voter registration rules?"

When voters decide they will no longer be mistreated and begin to summon candidates to their own scheduled citizen-powered debates, the dynamics behind the campaigns will shift toward the citizenry. There are about two hundred million *registered* voters in America; it would not take more than five hundred thousand people seriously connecting with each other in all congressional districts to enact real change. The media can indirectly create the climate for this civic engagement and can help shape a presidential campaign befitting a deliberative, democratic society serious about its future and its children.

First, however, the press, TV, and radio have to reduce their endless appetite for focusing on political gossip, tactics, and who has raised more money.

And the media ought to have a higher estimation of their own significance. What say you, publishers, editors, and reporters? It's your country, too!

The Republicans' ludicrously posturing, nearly substanceless debates served as a prime illustration of how the mass media is doing little to elevate the quality of the discussions in these contests. Consider this question: Who thought up giving private corporations (CNN and Facebook) control of a presidential debate? In one Democratic presidential debate, for example, CNN and Facebook controlled which candidates were invited, who asked what questions, and the location, Las Vegas—the glittering, gambling temple of America's love affair with consumption. This is a mirror image of the control Fox News, also teamed up with Facebook, exercised during the Republican candidates' circus.

Corporatism aside, the debate with Bernie Sanders, Hillary Clinton, Martin O'Malley, Jim Webb, and Lincoln Chafee was not a debate. With few exceptions—most notably Hillary Clinton going after Bernie Sanders on gun control, an issue on which she is reborn—the stage was the setting for a series of interview questions to each candidate by Anderson Cooper and his colleagues.

Granted, the quality of the questions was higher than has been the case with other debate spectacles in recent years. Yet CNN's self-censorship—in part reflected in the content of the questions and the favored positioning given to Hillary Clinton over Bernie Sanders—was not obscured.

For example, our country has been plagued by a corporate crime wave from Wall Street to Houston. These crimes are regular occurrences, often with recidivist corporations such as giant oil, drug, insurance, auto, banking, munitions, and mining companies corrupting our politics. Such chronic violations are reported far more often than they are properly prosecuted.

Corporate crimes affect American workers, consumers, children, taxpayers, and community residents. Unfortunately, corporate criminal law is woefully weak, prosecutions are minor, and enforcement budgets are scandalously tiny. Moreover, corporate lobbyists ensure that corporate privileges and immunities are preserved and expanded in corporate-occupied Washington, DC.

Somehow, in presidential debate after presidential debate, "corporate crime and punishment" and "law and order for corporations" almost never get mentioned either by questioners or candidates. Wonder why?

Another perennial omission in the debates is the question of how the candidates plan to give more power to the people, since all of them are saying that Washington isn't working. I have always thought that this is the crucial question voters should ask every candidate running for public office. Imagine asking a candidate: "How are you specifically going to make 'We the People' a political reality, and how are you going to give more institutional voice and power to people like me over elected representatives like you?" Watch politicians squirm over this basic inquiry.

The most remarkable part of the Democrats' "debate" was how Hillary Clinton got away with her assertions and then got rewarded—not necessarily in the subsequent polls, but by the pundits and malleable critics, like the *Washington Post*'s usually cynical Dana Milbank, who fell very hard for the Clintonian blarney.

Well-prepared and battle-tested in many superficial political debates, Hillary knows how to impress conventional political reporters while limiting their follow-up questions. She started with her latest political transformation early on: "I don't take a backseat to anyone when it comes to progressive experience and progressive commitment. . . . I'm a progressive."

And the moon is made of blue cheese. Arch-militarist Hillary Clinton, a progressive? She is the steady Wall Street corporatist, who hobnobs with criminal firms like Goldman Sachs for $200,000 a speech, and goes around the country telling closed-door business conventions what they want to hear for nearly $5,000 a minute!

As a senator, she did not challenge the large banks and insurance companies whose avarice, willful deceptions, and thefts set the stage for the economy's collapse in 2008–2009. In fact, she supported Bill Clinton's deregulation of Wall Street with its painful consequences for single mothers and children who suffered the most from the deep recession.

A progressive would not have waited year after year, while receiving the entreaties of women's and children's assistance groups and her own Democratic Party in Congress, to endorse a modest minimum wage increase to $10.10 per hour. She finally took the plunge and endorsed this minimum wage in April 2014, during a speech to the Simmons Leadership Conference in Boston. If CNN's Democratic lovefest in Las Vegas had been a real debate, Bernie Sanders, who voiced domestic progressive positions all evening long, would have intervened and sent her packing. What everlasting hubris the Clintons exude!

An embedded militarist during her tenure as senator and secretary of state, Hillary Clinton never saw a boondoggle, obsolete weapons system or boomeranging war she didn't like. She delivered belligerent speeches against China, and overruled, through her White House contacts, the opposition of Secretary of Defense Robert Gates to overthrow the Libyan dictator. This illegal war opened up the savage chaos, bloodshed, and havoc in Libya that continue to spread into huge areas of central Africa. She has never subsequently expressed any regrets or changes of mind for these continuing war crimes in Iraq and Libya, other than to cavalierly call the slaughter in Iraq a "mistake."

Hillary's war didn't seem to interest anyone on stage except former senator and governor Lincoln Chafee (D-RI)—an antiwar stalwart—who was promptly marginalized despite making much sense in his brief declarations.

Senator Bernie Sanders missed opportunities to highlight

Hillary Clinton's true corporatist and militarist identity. Most unfortunately, she placed him on the defensive by questioning his self-declared socialism. Next time, Bernie Sanders should tell the millions of voters watching the "debates" that local socialism is as American as apple pie, going back to the eighteenth century, by mentioning as examples post offices, public highways, public drinking water systems, public libraries, public schools, public universities, and public electric companies.

He then could add that global corporations are destroying competitive capitalism with their various bailouts and corporate-state crony capitalism, despised by both conservatives and progressives.

There was one question—"Which enemy are you most proud of?"—that Hillary Clinton did not anticipate and had about a minute to ponder. Her answer: "Well, in addition to the NRA, the health insurance companies, the drug companies, the Iranians." The Iranians? An entire people, her enemy? Is this what her self-touted foreign affairs experience has taught her?

Astonishingly, and this bears repeating until heard, candidates for public office, especially at the state and national levels, are never asked this central question of politics: "Since the people are sovereign under our Constitution, how do you specifically propose to restore power to the people in their various roles as *voters*, *taxpayers*, *workers*, and *consumers*?" Politics, after all, is about power—who has it and who doesn't have it.

Imagine that inquiry starting the so-called debates of both the Republican and Democratic presidential candidates. I'm not sure any of the candidates—so used to saying "I will do this" and "I propose that"—would even know how to respond. Regardless of their affiliation with either of the two dominant parties, politicians are so used to people being spectators rather than participants in the run-up to Election Day that they have not thought much about participatory or initiatory democracy. Too many candidates and elected officials, backed by the concentrated wealth of plutocrats, have perfected the silver-tongued skills of flattery, obfuscation, distraction, and deception. Many voters oblige candidates by not doing their homework on the candidates, their voting records, and their opinions on issues the voters want addressed. Such passivity lowers expectations of what voters should demand from the elected officials who, after all, are supposed to hold the people's delegated power in trust and not sell it to big-money donors.

Let's begin with *voters*. How could elected officials systematically empower the people they represent?

Restoring power to the voters would mean eliminating the private money that currently finances public elections. Big commercial interests nullify votes, and turn most elections into low-grade ditto days of tedious repetition. Well-promoted voluntary checkoffs, for example, on the 1040 tax return, up to, say, three hundred dollars, can make public financing of elections into a more politically acceptable reform. Plus a certain amount of free time on radio and TV stations as a condition of their licenses on our public airwaves and cable networks. But to strengthen the power of voters there must also be more voices and choices on the ballot lines, the Electoral College should be abolished, and state legislators must stop gerrymandering districts that ensure seriatim one-party domination. Same-day voter registration and a binding none-of-the-above choice can give voters more significant leverage as well. Voters themselves must demand that their representatives' legislative votes be immediately posted and justified on their public website. Universal voting as a civic duty (as in Australia) should be deliberated in campaigns.

Taxpayers lack the tools and resources to challenge the many hundreds of billions of federal tax dollars being used illegally, corruptly, or shockingly wastefully each year. Taxpayers have no standing, under our federal laws, to sue to stop such abuses. They are rendered weak and meek by this exclusion. When will voters hear a candidate pledge to give them their day in court? One way to increase taxpayer power is to provide for a voluntary checkoff on the 1040 tax return that makes it easy for taxpayers to voluntarily contribute funds and band together with a full-time staff of watchdogs focused on curbing the government's waste, fraud, and abuse. Big-time leverage is likely with this persistent taxpayer searchlight.

Workers are empowered when they demand that candidates stand for the repeal of the notorious Taft-Hartley Act of 1947—the most handcuffing, obstructionist law against union organizing and union rights in the Western world. Enforcing fairer labor standards that are already on the books, protecting pensions from looting by corporate management, establishing full, improved Medicare for All, and lifting the minimum wage—all of these initiatives increase the power of workers.

Finally, how can it be that the "customer is always right" when the *consumer* has no might? Consumers are becoming serfs in many ways—penalized at will, deceived and tied up by fine-print contracts that exclude them from the courts by forcing them into biased, compulsory arbitration, even if they are wrongfully injured. There are even loopholes that allow vendors, using the same fine print, to unilaterally change contract terms whenever they want to end any contract and replace it with dictates. Recently, in 2017, a hack of the consumer credit reporting agency Equifax exposed 143 million American consumers' personal information, all due to Equifax's complacency about securing the data. Nearly half of all American adults were left vulnerable to identity theft or fraud due to Equifax's incompetence, and yet, because of their boilerplate contracts, those consumers have no agency with which to easily band together and collectively restore the exercise of trial by jury.

Corporate power, led by the cruel US Chamber of Commerce in Washington, DC, is stripping consumers of class action remedies, imposing severe penalties and fines in the marketplace, and intimidating consumers into quiet acquiescence through threats against their credit ratings and credit scores. Add to this the price-gouging of drugs and health care, medical malpractice, near-zero interest rates on consumer savings, high rates on credit cards, and unregulated foreign imports of hazardous food, medicines, and other products, and you have a compelling case for a power shift from vendors back to consumers.

Consumers are backed into a corner, but there are methods of recourse. For example, to repeat, requiring vendors—such as banks, insurance companies, and electric, gas, and water utilities—to provide inserts in billing envelopes or online, inviting consumers to band together in nonprofit advocacy organizations with full-time champions, can be a great step forward in getting consumers seats at the tables of power.

Consider how much of your money and assets the government spends to enrich business organizations—with subsidies, handouts, bailouts, and giveaways, with tax credits and deductions, and with privileged bankruptcy laws to give mismanaged or reckless companies second and third chances. Consumers and taxpayers pay for all these goodies. *Where is the reciprocity*, where is *the modest payback for all these exactions*? At the very least let consumers have easy ways to organize, with full-time advocates, as bank customers, insurance policyholders, car owners, energy and credit users, and those simply wanting food that is safe to eat. When enough consumers organize, through easy checkoffs, they can defend themselves and make for an efficient and equitable economy.

The appeal of these power shifts is that they come at little or no cost to citizens. These resets for a functioning democratic society would cost far less than the equivalent of one week of the Pentagon's budget. By their own accomplishments, they would save consumers, workers, taxpayers, and voters more than is spent on the entire Pentagon budget. Not to mention the improvements in quality of life, peace of mind, and life-saving justice that cannot be measured just in dollars.

The flip side of the disenfranchisement of the average voter is the disproportionate power allotted to the wealthiest people in America. The massive flow of donors' money into the coffers of politicians, who need these sums to buy ads and for other expenses, has warped our democracy and tragically disempowered the unmoneyed populace.

Both parties spend much time "dialing for dollars" from wealthy donors, but at the same time the media and the debate process are beholden to and taken over by similarly insidious interests.

Presidential debates, for example, are controlled by the Commission on Presidential Debates (CPD)—a private corporation—created by the Republican and Democratic parties and funded by beer, auto, telephone, and other corporations whose patronage includes lavish hospitality suites. Thus, through the cover of the CPD, the two big parties, and vicariously, large corporations, control the number of debates, who is invited to participate, and which reporters ask the questions before an approved audience.

In 2015, the monetized minds went further. Now commercial cable or network television companies decide the formats and who is in tier one, tier two, or not included at all. The Big Media sponsors (Fox, CNN, NBC, and others) decided that Mark Everson, who was the first presidential primary candidate to go to all of Iowa's ninety-nine counties, should be excluded from the competition, evidently because he did not have a rich PAC sponsor and hadn't raised enough money. Yet he was one of the only Republican presidential candidate with executive branch experience.

Under George W. Bush he was head of the IRS, and prior to that he was deputy commissioner of the Immigration and Naturalization Service. Monetizing elections has predictable consequences. The dittohead reporters, obsessed with tactics and gaffes, never ask about corporate crime, corporate welfare, the American empire's un-auditable Defense Department, the over $300 billion a year in computerized billing fraud in the health care industry, or why corporations are allowed to freely exploit our public property—such as gold and silver mines on public land, the public airwaves, or the trillions of dollars of federal research given away free to the drug, aerospace, computer, biotech, and information technology industries. Therefore, the candidates get away with totally ignoring these huge, abhorrent abuses.

Commercializing elections leads to an astonishing similarity among reporters traveling with candidates and among those asking questions during the so-called debates.

For example, Donald Trump always brags about his business prowess as an asset in realizing his campaign promise to "make America great again," but, with few exceptions, he was not pressed by reporters and editors to voluntarily release his thousands of pages of annual tax returns or the sordid details of his companies' bankruptcies to prove whether his boasts were justified.

The pretentious Marco Rubio, fresh from the Florida legislature and a few years in the US Senate, repeatedly flaunted his difficult previous experience with student loans and living paycheck to paycheck. No reporter asked why, then, was he opposed to raising the inflation-gutted minimum wage, and why did he have no practical proposal to deal with the massive yoke of $1.3 trillion in student loans with very high interest rates?

The brazen PAC-created Senator Ted Cruz told his audiences that the time for rhetoric was over, and that the focus should be on each candidate's record. Meanwhile, he got away with never having to explain one of the zaniest, most corporatist, empty, and hateful performances in the US Senate.

The monetized minds running our elections also make sure that our civic culture and its many intelligent civic advocacy groups are sidelined when it comes to informing the voters about important issues. This is just about the most amazing exclusion of them all. Nonpartisan civic leaders and specialists, people who know the most about energy, the environment, the health industry, militarism abroad and public budget abuses at home, about taxation and electoral reforms, and about corporate crime and the prison-industrial complex, were rarely given a voice by the media, including PBS and NPR.

Look at the Sunday morning network news shows. Pundits and politicians fill the screens. The real experts don't get interviewed; they have trouble getting into the op-ed pages of the print media and are rarely contacted by the candidates, who are too busy dialing for commercial dollars to seek out those who work with facts for truth and justice.

Consequently, shorn of any participatory civic culture, the political culture is ready for hijacking by the commercial interests and the corporate state.

As we saw in this election, the politicians ride merrily on a torrent of words and opinions without having to explain their record, which is so often at odds with what they are bloviating.

The 2016 presidential candidates were not asked whom they would consider for their White House advisers and cabinet secretaries. Given Trump's mostly underqualified corporate cabinet, this information would have given voters an idea of the likelihood of broken promises "draining the swamp."

In 2008 Barack Obama campaigned repeatedly for "hope and change." Then after his election he gathered for a surprise photo opportunity with Clinton retreads like the Wall Street bailout advocate and self-enrichment banker Robert Rubin, and others known for anything but "hope and change."

Now is the time for voters to change all this rancid defilement of our republic and its democratic norms and dreams. Voters, do your homework on the parties and the candidates, form informal groups to demand debates and agendas that you preside over, push for more choices on the ballot, and make votes count more than money. The Internet can help speed up such efforts. Nobody can stop you from making these moves but yourselves.

If just 1 percent of voters were actively involved in this way, you would far outnumber the politicos and their entourages everywhere. While the mainstream media remains more concerned with a horse race than with the human race, the American people are the ones who keep paying the price for letting politics remain a deadly form of distracting entertainment.

19.

The Primaries, Structurally Warped: The Democrats

Before announcing his run for president in the Democratic primaries, Bernie Sanders had started out telling people he would not run as an independent and "be like Nader"—invoking the politically bigoted word "spoiler." Well, the spoiled corporate Democrats in Congress and their consultants began mounting a "stop Bernie campaign" once his campaign started gathering steam, because they believed he'd "spoil" their preordained election selections.

It didn't matter to them how many of Bernie's positions are representative of what a majority of the American people want for their country.

What comes around goes around. The unfortunate truth Bernie discovered was that anybody who challenges the positions of the corporatist, militaristic, Wall Street–funded Democrats, led by Hillary Clinton, in the House and Senate is, by their twisted definition, a "spoiler." Despite running a clean campaign, funded by small donors averaging twenty-seven dollars per donation, with no scandals in his past and with consistency throughout his decades of standing up for the working and unemployed people of this country, in January 2016 Sanders was about to be Hillaried. The shunning and sabotage of Bernie Sanders was under way. He stood alone during the crowded State of the Union address.

Many of the large unions that Bernie has championed for decades endorsed Hillary, known for her job-destroying support for NAFTA and the World Trade Organization and her very late involvement in working toward a modest minimum wage increase. National Nurses United, one of the few national unions endorsing Bernie, was not fooled by Hillary's sudden anti-Wall-Street rhetoric in Iowa. They viewed Hillary Clinton, the Wall Street servant (who delivers speeches to big business groups at a rate of nearly $5,000 a minute), with disgust.

Candidate Clinton preposterously pledged to "crack down" on the "greed" of corporations, declaring that Wall Street bosses were opposing her because they realized she would "come right after them."

Because Sanders is not prone to self-congratulation, few people knew that he received the highest senatorial approval rating and the lowest disapproval rating from his Vermonters than any other US senator received from his or her constituents. This peak support for a self-avowed "democratic socialist" came from a state once known for its rock-ribbed conservative Republican traditions.

Ganging up with Hillary, Minority House Leader Nancy Pelosi unleashed her supine followers to start wounding and depreciating Sanders. Pelosi acolyte Adam Schiff (D-CA) told the media he doubted Sanders's electability, speculating that Sanders could have "very significant downstream consequences in House and Senate races."

Mr. Schiff somehow ignored that the House and Senate Democratic leadership repeatedly could not defend the country from the worst Republican Party in history, whose dozens of anti-human, pro-big-business votes should have toppled many GOP candidates. Instead, Nancy Pelosi led the House Democrats to four straight calamitous losses (in 2010, 2012, 2014, and 2016) to the Republicans. A four-time loser!

Pelosi threw her own poisoned darts at Sanders, attempting to debunk his far more life-saving, efficient, and comprehensive full Medicare for All plan (with free choice of doctor and hospital) with the knowingly misleading comment, "We're not running on any platform of raising taxes." Presumably that included continuing the Democratic Party's practice of letting Wall Street, the global companies, and the super-wealthy continue to get away with their very profitable tax escapes.

The plutocracy and the oligarchy running this country into the ground have no worries. The genders of the actors may change, but the moneyed interests maintain their corporate state and hand out their campaign cash—business as usual.

Bernie Sanders, however, did present a moral risk for the corrupt Democratic Party and the Democratic National Committee: his years in politics so cleanly contrasted with the sordid, scandalized, cashing-in behavior of the Clintons.

Moreover, there was the conflicted interest–maneuvering of donors to the Clinton Foundation, shady deals involving global corporations and dictators, and huge speaking fees, with the Clinton Foundation and the State Department used to benefit the Clintons and their corporate political intrigues.

Now that Bernie Sanders has been brought down by the very party he was championing, the millions of disaffected voters on the left and right, especially younger voters, should *consider* breaking off into a new, clean electoral party that will make American history. The mere news of such an effort may provide a civic jolt to the smug, corporate-indentured major parties. For a viable third party on the ballots means a three-way election race that gives people more choices and agendas and can bring out more new voters. That means dissolving the dictatorial party duopoly and its ruinous, unpatriotic, democracy-destroying corporate paymasters.

Bernie Sanders was far too easy on Hillary Clinton in their debates. Clinton inflated and flaunted her record and experience in ways that Sanders could have used to emphasize the serious vulnerabilities that disqualified her from becoming president. Sanders did respond to Clinton's points, but without the precision that could expose her arrogance.

For example, Clinton repeatedly said that Sanders has not leveled with people about the cost of *full* Medicare for All or single-payer. Really? In other countries, single-payer is far simpler and more efficient than our present profiteering, wasteful, corporatized health care industry. Canada covers all of its citizens, with free choice of doctors and hospitals, for about $4,500 for each person per capita, compared to the over $9,500 per capita cost in the US system (which still leaves tens of millions of people uninsured or underinsured).

Detailed studies in the *New England Journal of Medicine* show big savings would result from a single-payer system in our country.

It was Hillary Clinton who was not leveling with the people about the cost of maintaining the current health care system, with its spiraling drug prices, enormous fees for hospital stays, and insurance premiums that are the highest in the world. The costs include: 1) the waste of well over $1 trillion a year; 2) daily denials of coverage by the Aetnas of the corporate world; 3) about forty-five thousand Americans unnecessarily dying each year, according to a peer-reviewed Harvard Medical School study (thirty-five thousand after Obamacare), because they cannot afford health insurance to get diagnosed and treated in time; and 4) daily agonizing negotiations over insurance coverage denials, exclusions, deductions and bureaucratic paperwork that drive physicians up the wall.

Clinton never explained why she was once for single-payer, and why she changed her mind, merely commenting that she was currently "being practical"—evidently defining "practical" as refusing to take on, with the people, Big Pharma, commercial hospital chains, and the giant insurance companies. She has been very "practical" about taking political contributions and speaking fees from Wall Street and the health care industry.

As one eighteen-year-old student told the *New York Times* in February 2016, "With Hillary, sometimes you get this feeling that all of her sentences are owned by someone."

Hillary Clinton was not "leveling with the American people" when she refused to release the transcripts (which she herself had ordered) of her secret speeches (at nearly $5,000 a minute!) before large Wall Street and trade association conventions.

And yet she had the gall to accuse Bernie Sanders of not being transparent. Sanders was a presidential candidate who didn't deliver big-fee speeches or take big donations from fat-cat influence peddlers, and his record was as clean as the Clintons' political entanglements are unsavory.

But it was in the area of foreign and military affairs that Hillary the Hawk was most vulnerable. Her aggressiveness and poor judgment while secretary of state led her to sweep aside the strong objections of Secretary of Defense Robert Gates and push President Obama to bomb Libya and topple its dictatorial regime into explosive anarchy.

Gates had warned about this aftermath. He was right. Libya has descended into a ghastly state of chaotic violence that has spilled into neighboring African nations and opened the way for ISIS to establish an expanding base in central Libya.

Whether as senator on the Armed Services Committee or as secretary of state, Mrs. Clinton was the darling of the military-industrial complex regarding unaudited budgets and weapon systems. Hillary Clinton as president would mean more wars, more raids, more blowbacks, more military spending, and more profits for the large corporate contractors.

So in the debates when Bernie Sanders properly chided her for having as an adviser, Henry Kissinger, secretary of state under Richard Nixon, she bridled and tried to escape by asking Sanders to name his foreign policy advisers.

In fact, Kissinger and Clinton have much in common when it comes to projecting the American empire to brutal levels. Kissinger was the "butcher of Cambodia," launching an illegal assault that destabilized that peaceful country and led to Pol Pot's slaughter of millions of innocents. Clinton was the illegal "butcher of Libya," an ongoing, unfolding tragedy whose so-called unintended consequences are building by the week.

In a devastating recounting of Hillary Clinton's disastrous war making, Jeffrey D. Sachs, professor of sustainable development at Columbia University, concludes that Clinton "is the Candidate of the War Machine." In a widely noted article on the *Huffington Post*, Professor Sachs, an adviser to the United Nations on millennium development goals, called Clinton's record a "disaster," adding, "Perhaps more than any other person, Hillary can lay claim to having stoked the violence that stretches from West Africa to Central Asia and that threatens US security."

Sachs gave exactly the type of critique that Sanders should have been unleashing upon his rival. Sanders supporters saw the way the hard-bitten, corporatist Democrats moved Hillary Clinton through the presidential primaries. They used "Republican speak" to beat down Bernie Sanders, claiming he favored Big Government and more taxes, while ignoring his sound, popular positions.

What emerged, then, was the reaction of millions of Sanders supporters who felt repudiated. The political experience gained by the Sanders workers, many of them young, helped Sanders register primary victories over Hillary in Colorado, Oklahoma, Minnesota, Vermont, and New Hampshire. They came very close in Nevada and Massachusetts, and probably won in Iowa.

Hillary's rhetoric outraged Sanders's supporters. She berated Sanders regularly for not being practical or realistic in his proposals for Medicare for All, breaking up big banks, a $15 minimum wage over a few years, a tax on Wall Street speculation and carbon, and reforms for getting big money out of politics. Clinton's put-downs exemplified why so many people who backed Sanders wanted to defeat her. Clinton was the candidate of the status quo, favored over all other candidates from both parties by the Wall Street crowd and quietly adored by the military-industrial complex, which correctly saw Clinton as a militarist who would maintain the warfare state.

In February 2016, Democrat Robert Reich, former secretary of labor under Bill Clinton, derided this "We Shouldn't Even Try" attitude common among many frightened Democrats. These are, in Reich's words, the "establishment Democrats—Washington lobbyists, editorial writers, inside-the-Beltway operatives, party leaders and big contributors—[who] have grown comfortable with the way things are." These hereditary Democratic opinion shapers told their audiences that Hillary personified experience and elect- ability. They argued it was either Clinton or Trump or some other crazed Republican.

Every four years, the Democratic leaders define the Democratic candidate only in contradistinction to how bad the Republicans are. This strategy is designed to panic and mute their followers. Every four years, both parties become more corporatist. If things don't change radically, the same playbook will pit another bland corporate Democrat against Trump in 2020.

Sanders's voters wanted to define the Democratic Party by how good it could be for the people. These Sanders voters may not stay in the Democratic Party fold.

Voter turnout for the Democratic primaries was being compared to a somewhat higher turnout for the Republican primaries. Noticing that, some predicted that a low turnout in November would dim Hillary's chances in the Electoral College's winner-take-all system.

Once crowned as the party's presidential candidate, Hillary could not credibly adopt any of Bernie's agenda, considering where her campaign money was coming from and how unwilling she was to alienate her circle of advisers, including the Hillary-favored stagnant Democratic National Committee.

Sanders scrutinized Clinton's speaking fees and supposed pragmatism with regard to higher education and health care, but he should have pressed her on her militarism as well. Her policies as secretary of state drew the US further into ill-considered, unwinnable wars. Her belligerent, scripted speech in March 2016 to the American Israel Public Affairs Committee (AIPAC), should have given him more incriminating material with which to highlight her constant warmongering.

It is well known to Washington political observers that politicians invited to speak at the annual, giant AIPAC convention ask for suggested talking points from this powerful pro-Israeli government lobby. Hillary Clinton's pandering, anti-Palestinian, anti-Iranian speech must have registered close to 100 percent on AIPAC's checklist.

Of course, both parties pander to AIPAC to such obeisant depths that reporters have little to report as news. But giving big-time coverage to sheer political power is automatic. Compare it to the sparse attention given to the conference a few days earlier at the National Press Club that questioned the benefits of Israeli lobbying, featuring scholars, authors, and the well-known Israeli dissenter Gideon Levy of the respected *Haaretz* newspaper.

But Mrs. Clinton's speech was noteworthy for its moral obtuseness and the way in which it promised unilateral White House above-the-law armed support should she become president. An attentive audience might have noticed that her condemnation of Palestinian terrorism omitted any reference to the fact that Israel is the daily military occupier of what is left of Palestinian lands, colonizing them, seizing their water and property, and terrorizing the native population. She continued to overlook the institutional terror caused by the selective illegal blockade of Gaza, the world's largest gulag ever since the Israeli army's so-called "disengagement" from the area in 2005.

Clinton emphasized her condemnation of Palestinian schools where children were "taught to hate" their Israeli oppressors, and she decried the deplorable attacks against Israeli soldiers and civilians. But she neglected to point to the far greater violence perpetrated by Israel and backed up by US-supplied deadly weapons that over the last decade has caused four hundred more civilian Palestinian fatalities and serious injuries than the defenseless Palestinians have caused their Israeli civilian counterparts. For example, one of Prime Minister Netanyahu's coalition partners from the Jewish Home Party had recently called for the slaughter of all Palestinians, specifically singling out the mothers of Palestinian combatants. "They should go, as should the physical homes in which they raised the snakes. Otherwise more little snakes will be raised there."

Clinton did not mention any of these brutalities, though they are components of an occupation that is illegal under international law and the United Nations Charter. The Yale Law graduate simply chose not to know better. Instead, she told her wildly applauding audience of her support for increasing the amount of US taxpayer spending for the latest military equipment and technology, even as prosperous Israel already receives nearly $4 billion from US taxpayers each year.

In an obvious slap at President Obama, whose name she never mentioned (though even Netanyahu thanked Obama in his address to AIPAC), Clinton almost shouted out, "One of the first things I'll do in office is invite the Israeli prime minister to visit the White House." This was a thinly veiled reference to Netanyahu's trip to a joint session of Congress in 2015, in which he tried to undermine President Obama's negotiations with Iran. Not surprisingly, Obama did not ask Netanyahu over to visit the White House for a drink before he headed back to Israel.

High on AIPAC's checklist is insisting that all speakers condemn what Clinton called the "alarming boycott, divestment and sanctions movement known as BDS." She twice slanderously associated this modest effort (in which brave Jews are active participants) to get Israel to de-escalate its oppression of occupied Palestinian territories, with anti-Semitism. However, by totally erasing any nod, any mention, any compassion toward the Palestinian children, women, and men slaughtered in their homes, schools, and hospitals, Hillary Clinton made a bitter mockery of her touted Methodist upbringing and her declared concern for children everywhere.

For repeated applause at AIPAC's convention and for support from its associated campaign contributors, she lost all credibility with the peoples of the Arab world. Moreover, her hostile words signaled ugly support for "the other anti-Semitism," to echo the title of an address by author James Zogby before an Israeli university in 1994—that is, racism against Semitic Arabs.

With all her self-proclaimed experience in foreign affairs, Mrs. Clinton didn't pause to ponder why she was backing state terrorism against millions of Arab Palestinians trapped in two diminishing enclaves, surrounded by walls and military outposts and suffering from deep poverty, widespread diseases, and severe childhood anemia.

From the speech, it appeared that her militant animosity toward Iran was unlimited, as she bragged about "crippling sanctions" that she had spearheaded (which caused untold harm to the health of millions of families). She threatened military force "for even the smallest violations of this [nuclear] agreement." Yet for decades Israel has violated UN resolutions to withdraw its soldiers occupying Palestine, and Secretary of State Clinton didn't raise so much as a murmur. As a presidential candidate, Clinton mindlessly opposed a role for the UN Security Council (over which the US has often-used veto power) in the Israeli-Palestinian peace process.

In her AIPAC speech, there were a few times she did exhibit some restraint. She reiterated her support for a Palestinian state but wondered whether the Palestinian leadership was up to the negotiations. Also, she resisted going along with recognizing the shift of Israel's capital from Tel Aviv to Jerusalem (though she had supported such a shift when she was running for senator of New York in 1999).

Her very oblique reference to illegal, expanding Israeli settlements did not amount to anything more than a wink, suggesting there would be no action on her part to stop the expansion of colonies in the occupied territories should she reach the White House.

Near the conclusion of her deferential remarks, she stated, "If you see bigotry, oppose it. If you see violence, condemn it. If you see a bully, stand up to him." Some courageous Israeli human rights groups, such as B'Tselem, that defend Palestinian human rights might view her words as applicable daily to how they perform their noble work.

And yet Sanders never pointed out his opponent's hypocrisy on foreign policy, or how she was posturing as an advocate for children everywhere while apparently making exceptions for those little ones in Iran and other countries she didn't like. She even went so far as to say that if Iran were to "foolishly consider launching an attack on Israel, we would be able to totally obliterate them."

Sanders faced another hurdle when the labor movement betrayed him. Labor almost exclusively tied its boats to Clinton, no matter how weak (except rhetorically) she was on labor issues and no matter how little she promised to support any pro-labor agendas. While Sanders had always been an engaged champion of workers' rights, the labor barons made little note of this; they alienated themselves from their own constituents and rank-and-file union members, as the Democrats did from theirs.

This came out around a private conference table inside the large Washington headquarters of the AFL-CIO. A furious exchange occurred between labor union presidents. It was late February 2016 and up for decision by the executive council was whether the country's principal labor federation was going to make an early primary season endorsement for Hillary Clinton.

According to insiders, tempers flared when smaller unions challenged such Hillary-endorsing big unions as the American Federation of State, County and Municipal Employees (AFSCME), the American Federation of Teachers, the National Education Association, the Service Employees International Union (SEIU), and the United Food and Commercial Workers (UFCW). These large unions came out for Clinton in late 2015 and early 2016 before they sensed the growing rank-and-file workers' preference for the lifetime advocate for workers and unions, Bernie Sanders.

Listening to the nurses' union head, RoseAnn DeMoro, speak out for Sanders's strong pro-labor history, Lee Saunders, president of AFSCME, interrupted her, exclaiming, "I will not allow you to do a commercial for Sanders." DeMoro retorted, "You mean for the only candidate who has a one hundred percent labor record?"

A postal workers' union leader charged the unions backing

Hillary with being "completely out of touch with their workers." AFL-CIO president Richard Trumka then cut off the microphones.

All over the country, the observation by the postal workers' leader rang true. Even as Lee Saunders read the names of the Democratic presidential contenders at a large Washington state AFSCME membership meeting in October 2015, "Sanders' name was the only one to draw loud, sustained applause," according to the *Washington Examiner*.

Few union leaders allowed a worker referendum to make the endorsement decisions. The six-hundred-thousand-member Communications Workers of America (CWA) did, and the result was a "decisive endorsement" of Sanders, reported Rafael Navar, the union's political director. Whether enthusiastically campaigning to get out the vote or talking up their candidate's record on such issues as minimum wage increases, abolition of public university and college tuition, full Medicare for All (in a single-payer system), and standing up to Wall Street, Bernie's tenacious supporters knew how to put up a fight. And for Hillary supporters, it certainly didn't help that Hillary's votes and statements did little to respect the working families of America compared to Bernie's consistent thirty-year record.

This unaffiliated labor awakening bears remembering today, especially by the long-entrenched, affluent big union leaders. The Labor for Bernie campaign fomented defections by local unions in defiance of their Hillary-endorsing national organizations. Over eighty local unions ultimately endorsed Bernie Sanders.

Typical of this exodus was United Food and Commercial Workers Local 5, whose executive board voted 30 to 2 for Sanders, reflecting the views of most of its twenty-eight thousand members. Local 5's Mike Henneberry said, "For us, it was not a very difficult decision. Compare an individual who's been supporting workers since he was mayor of Burlington [Vermont] with someone who's been on the board of Walmart."

The Service Employees International Union Local 1984, New Hampshire's largest public sector union, disagreed with its national union and came out for Sanders in November 2015. The big union leaders didn't smell revolt yet, but they must have been worried.

It is the AFL-CIO's practice to endorse Democrats without demanding before and insisting after the election that candidates champion "card check" for union-seeking workers, revisions of trade treaties, the repeal of anti-union labor laws, and stronger job safety regulations. The Democratic Party continues to treat the mostly shrinking labor unions as having nowhere else to go. And most union leaders meekly oblige by their chronic submissiveness. However, the mini-revolt in favor of Sanders is a sign that such rubber-stamping practices are in peril. Corporate candidates are endorsed at the top, but far less popular among members.

Despite a lot of tricky Democratic Party machinery hampering his course, by April 2016 the progressive lone ranger was leading in the polls nationally as the preferred candidate to defeat Donald Trump—ahead of Hillary in that matchup.

One structural element that hindered Sanders from receiving his just deserts was the policy of closed primaries, which in many states barred independent voters from voting for any of the Democratic or Republican candidates. Pointedly, Senator Sanders won only one of the five states with primaries on April 26, 2016: Rhode Island. Why? Because that state has an open primary, which allowed independent voters, heavily pro-Sanders, to carry him to victory.

Had some of the closed primary states—Pennsylvania, Maryland, Delaware, Connecticut, and New York—held open primaries, Sanders would likely have defeated Hillary Clinton as Obama defeated Hillary in 2008. That could have given Sanders a chance to change the minds of many permanent superdelegates.

Chalk up another blockage of the people's will to those state laws obstructing the rights of voters and insurgent candidates. Twenty states have open primaries, presumably to increase voter choice and turnout, and to justify having taxpayers pay for the primaries of private political parties.

Another structural obstacle Sanders faced was the influence of unelected superdelegates, such as members of Congress and party leaders, who wield 15 percent of the voting power in the primaries. The superdelegates scheme was cooked up to avoid "weak candidates" or any bottom-up "revolts" against the party establishment and its ever-present consultants. This also tilted the convention in Hillary's favor.

At the convention, Clinton did expediently accept a few Sanders demands, including calls for a higher minimum wage, an expansion of Social Security, making public colleges tuition-free for lower-income students, and setting a price on greenhouse gas emissions. Other demands—for breaking up the big banks, and for universal health insurance (in a single-payer system)—were scuttled.

Thus, the Sanders movement was confronted with disappointment at the convention, where the victorious vanquish the runners-up with arms locked and hands raised high on the convention stage. Following this display of party unity, the vanquished are expected to retire to the shadows and take their orders to launch their full-throated campaigning for the nominee.

If you still remember it, the 2016 Democratic National Convention in Philadelphia was a multilayered, raucous display of political theater. A host of delegates loyal to Senator Bernie Sanders were inside in large numbers, exclaiming "No more war" during former secretary of defense Leon Panetta's speech and raising all kinds of progressive, rebellious signs and banners against the Hillary crowd. Although Hillary addressed them directly in her acceptance speech—"Your cause is my cause"—those dissatisfied delegates in the hall saw her rhetoric for what it was: insincere and opportunistic.

She said she'd tax the wealthy for public necessities, but notably declined to mention a sales tax on Wall Street speculation. She opposed "unfair trade deals," but remarkably omitted saying she was against the TPP.

She paid lip service to a "living wage" but avoided endorsing a staggered $15-an-hour minimum wage, which would help single moms and their children in our country. For Hillary, giving "kids the opportunities they deserve" didn't extend to encircled Gaza's defenseless children, thousands of whom have been killed by American-made weapons wielded by the all-powerful Israeli military. On the stage in Philadelphia, Hillary again spoke of backing Israel's security without any mention of Palestinian human rights, supported by most of the world's nations, including US allies.

Numerous speakers repeated that Clinton was the "most qualified and experienced," but her record shows those qualities have led to belligerent, unlawful military actions that are now boomeranging against US interests, among other noted derelictions.

The media coverage of political conventions tends to sink to the level of the circus. Even the PBS/NPR coverage, with nearly a dozen reporters and commentators, proved to be thin, soft, and superficial. Otherwise smart media communicators were reduced to very heavy focus on exactly what the party's manipulators wanted. "What is Hillary really like?" Of course the stage was filled with frothy admiration, awe, and acclamation. But why didn't the media point out some of the factual omissions, the contradictions to the endless sugarcoating of the nominee?

To her credit, NPR/PBS reporter Susan Davis did blurt out that the convention program was mostly about personality and character with little policy. Other reporters pointed out that, unlike all other candidates, Hillary Clinton had not held a news conference since the previous December to showcase her supposed experience, qualifications, and knowledge!

Why didn't Hillary Clinton, in her attack on Donald Trump, demand the release of his tax returns? Hillary and Bill have regularly released their tax returns. Maybe Hillary demurred because Trump would have demanded in response that Hillary release the transcripts of her nearly-$5,000-a-minute paid speeches to big bankers and other businesses. Only she really knows why.

To her credit, Hillary Clinton raised the charge against too many (though not all, she added) US corporations' lack of patriotism when it comes to our country. Born in the USA, grown to profit on the backs of American workers, and bailed out by American taxpayers, these giant companies have no allegiance to country or community. They are, with trade agreements and other inducements, abandoning America's workers and escaping America's laws and taxes.

Hearing the word "unpatriotic" applied to those companies, I could imagine their executives and PR flacks shuddering for the only time during her fifty-five-minute address. The stigma of being "unpatriotic" to their enabling native country could have consequential legs, perhaps turning public opinion even more deeply against these monetized corporate goliaths.

Stung by her consistently high "untrustworthy" ratings in the polls (with only Trump exceeding her in that description), Hillary declared again that no one achieves greatness alone, that it takes us working together—that "It Takes a Village," alluding to her earlier book. For that to be true, those who are *together* must have more power than the *few*. "Together" must include workers, consumers, small taxpayers, voters, and communities who have been excluded from power, wielding the tools of democracy. Did she have an agenda for a devolution of power from the few to the many so that we can be "stronger together" (her slogan for 2016)? No way. Mum's the word!

Maintaining this immense gap between the powerful and the people has been the Clinton duo's con job on America for many years. Sugarcoating phrases, spouting populist flattery, getting the election over with, and jumping back into the fold of the plutocracy is their customary MO.

One anti-Hillary campaign button sums it up: imagine a nice picture of Hillary with the words "More Wall Street" printed above her head and the words "More War" printed below.

The best thing Hillary Clinton had going for her, but it obviously wasn't enough, was the self-destructive, unstable, unorganized, fact- and truth-starved, egomaniacal, bigoted, cheating, plutocratic Donald Trump.

That's where our nation's two-party political leadership is today.

20.

The Primaries, Glitter Trumps Substance: The Republicans

Trump's egotistical bombast—false statements, displays of shocking factual ignorance on policy issues, and planned, staccato insults of the other Republican contenders—got him lots of media attention. But when an elastic band is stretched to its limit, there comes a time when the band must snap.

At one point in the campaign, while engaging in petty retaliation against Senator Cruz after one of Cruz's super PACs distributed a semi-nude pin-up picture of Trump's wife, the casino baron stopped campaigning for a week before the crucial Wisconsin primary to spend some time in Washington, DC. He continued to be barraged by reporters asking about his campaign manager's facing a potential criminal charge in Florida for having vigorously pulled a reporter's arm. He then stumbled badly in an interview with MSNBC's Chris Matthews (a fervid Democrat). In the interview, The Donald said that women who have abortions should receive "some form of punishment." His recanting of that statement hours later didn't catch up with the immediate uproar.

At that juncture, things didn't look good for Trump. National polls of all voters had never been good for Trump; now they spilled over into disasterland. He had the highest unfavorability ratings of any candidate, followed by Hillary Clinton. Nationally, only 26 percent of American women supported him, and almost three out of four American women opposed him.

When Trump left his lavish Florida vacation mansion for Wisconsin that April, he found a maelstrom of opposition from the Republican Party, the Republican governor, and the Republican legislators controlling the state government. What's more, the state's influential conservative talk radio bloviators—most of whom backed the madcap Ted Cruz at the time—were bashing Trump daily for being juvenile and not a conservative.

Trump, weakening at that point, warned that if the party treated him unfairly, he could always go independent. I don't think that was a serious proposition. Trump's trap was that by the time he had to admit his quest had failed, it would have been too late for him to meet many state ballot access deadlines for an independent candidacy. Moreover, he would learn what the resounding cry of "sore loser" means to voters.

Another fallback he proffered at the time was that even if he did not get the majority magic number of 1,237 delegates, "you'd have riots" from his supporters if he wasn't simply *given* the nomination.

The trouble with Trump's scenario is what is called "backfire." Riots in the streets for a sore loser? Riots because he couldn't survive the succeeding rounds of voting inside the Republican National Convention in Cleveland? Riots wouldn't sit well with most Republicans, not to mention the local police and the voters who would see the televised images.

Although neither of these scenarios came into play—neither Trump running independently, nor riots in the street—what happened was much worse: Trump in the driver's seat.

Unfortunately, in the final stretch of the primaries, Trump ended up matched against a fellow bloviator, Ted Cruz. Neither of them had much to offer voters. Here is a column I wrote at the time that, in retrospect, reveals some of the crucial topics of that moment:

> To avoid a historic tumble in the November elections, what should the Republican Party do at its July 18–21 nominating convention if "Doubtful Donald" Trump and "Terrible Ted" Cruz cancel each other out?
>
> Their best chance is to nominate the remaining man in the race—Ohio governor John Kasich, who polls better than Hillary Clinton, who, in turn, polls better than both Trump and Cruz. (Bernie Sanders polls better than all the Republicans.)
>
> Many of the convention delegates may be in high heat and playing with the irresistible, venomous, masochistic fervor. This would be okay with the Democratic Party, which would enjoy the televised spectacle of the GOP imploding. But if cool heads are bent on rescuing the Republican Party from the brink, here is the case they can make for Kasich:
>
> The son of a postal worker, Kasich is a candidate who thinks, as well as being a wily politician. He spent years in the House of Representatives as a close confidante of the insurgent Newt Gingrich, who overthrew the Democrats and defeated then-speaker of the House Tom Foley in that memorable election of 1994.
>
> I remember seeing Kasich huddling around a lunch table at a nearby Washington restaurant strategizing with Speaker Gingrich. Yet he was not a sycophant. He even publicly suggested that the Pentagon budget may be more than a little bloated.
>
> Kasich became chairman of the influential House Budget Committee. In that capacity, he responded well

to my request for the first congressional hearing in history on corporate welfare, or so-called crony capitalism. The day-long hearing, being of pioneering consequence, received very little press, because the reporters knew that Kasich was not going to seriously follow through with legislation. See, he is a politician.

As Ohio governor, he swung into attacking the deficit, neglecting the fact that cuts to corporate welfare payments and tax abatements are an important way to reduce the deficit. Three letters from me reminding him of his House Budget Committee hearing went unanswered. But he did often reveal his compassion, most notably applying his religious principles by going with Obamacare's Medicaid program, unlike other Republican governors, who ideologically rejected health insurance for poor families.

During the presidential debates, Governor Kasich, a decided underdog, became a contrasting voice to the crazed, belligerent, insult-soaked waves of false statements and braggadocios from Trump, Cruz, Christie, Rubio, and other early dropouts.

Kasich won only one state primary—defeating Trump—in his state of Ohio. But Kasich was on the modest upswing about midway through the primaries and received more press for being a comparatively sane voice amid the shouting and overtalking of his fellow candidates.

I saw three versions of Kasich on the debate stage. Kasich, the advocate for reason, negotiation, and compromise. Kasich, the presentation of himself—experienced, knowledgeable, and steady. And Kasich, pulled down by the madness of the stage to say some "wild and crazy" things, especially about his proposed military policies.

He seems relatively scandal-free, has a fine family, and can talk folksy because he is folksy. The biggest operating problem in his campaign is an inability to raise enough money to match his major competitors.

If things hadn't gone as Trump hoped, at least we might have had a dignified race. Unfortunately, that sane course was not the way of today's political environment.

The reality turned out to be much more bizarre. Donald Trump bragged about "branding" his political opponents. He called Marco Rubio "Little Marco," Ted Cruz "Lyin' Ted," and Hillary Clinton "Crooked Hillary." A ratings-frenzied media bullhorning Trump and his own repetitiveness made these epithets stick—a lesson Trump drew from the advertising world and his own fragile ego.

Astonishingly, his opponents did not even try to brand him—choosing instead to first ignore and then argue with Trump, who is a chronic overtalker, shouter, and prevaricator. The mass media, delighted with its ratings, rarely chose to challenge his rapid-fire false assertions, preferring instead to let him perpetuate his mendacities.

There were exceptions—two of the leading ones being Glenn Kessler, the *Washington Post* fact checker, who in July 2016 handed Trump a record thirty-three "Four-Pinocchio" awards, and David Cay Johnston, a Pulitzer Prize–winning reporter, who wrote "21 Questions for Donald Trump." Based on these and other solid published sources, I think the new moniker for Trump should have been "Cheating Donald" (including on his wives).

The name has added resonance today, but even during the primaries anyone looking into it would have seen that Donald cheated his workers, including undocumented laborers. Through his numerous tactical company bankruptcies, he has cheated his creditors and employees who were thrown out of their jobs. *Fortune*'s 1999 list of the most admired companies ranked his hotel and casino resort company near the bottom—worst or almost worst in management, use of assets, employee talent, long-term investment value, and social responsibility. And that was still a few years before Cheating Donald's company went bankrupt.

He cheated consumers—most recently the students at Trump "University," which New York State attorney general Eric T. Schneiderman called an "illegal educational institution."

Trump has cheated taxpayers—using political influence to get tax abatements for his properties, while admittedly paying little or no taxes (which, of course, would be proven by the tax returns he refuses to disclose). His first major tax escape was on a New York City hotel worth at least $400 million over forty years, according to David Cay Johnston. As the highly regarded director of Citizens for Tax Justice, Robert McIntyre, has often said, tax breaks for the corporations and super-rich mean other taxpayers have to pay more, receive fewer services, or experience larger public deficits.

Trump has cheated voter beliefs by inflating his wealth and business prowess as credentials for running the federal government, thereby concealing his many business limitations, failures, and his true net worth.

He has cheated in matrimony and boasted about his many past infidelities with, in his words, "seemingly very happily married and important women."

Finally, he has cheated the truth, producing a veritable Trump Tower of false statements, twisting facts into webs of deception while vaingloriously shouting to rallies, "We're going to win so much, you're going to be so sick and tired of winning" (without ever once answering the question of "how?").

Trump's campaign trail was strewn with illusory promises, and a staggering number of self-glorifications suggesting deep personal instabilities. These childish displays of hubris confirmed day after day that it is all about him and not the American people.

Yet the Republican Party leaders and their corporate funders were unable to stop his rampage, which was aided and abetted by a profit-seeking commercial media (including the likes of Leslie Moonves, CEO of CBS, who said of the rise of Trump, "It may not be good for America, but it's damn good for CBS").

Cheating Donald is the latest manifestation of what happens when commercialized elections separate from the discipline of a democratic society and its civic communities. This is turning our land into a plutocratic-oligarchic domain, where the rich rule the many by entrenching the corporate state so dreaded by our founding fathers.

It is not only the supine media and the Republicans, hungry for a win at any cost, that engineered The Donald's rise. The Democrats—by blocking Sanders, the only candidate in the field who had a populist message that resonated with the workers—turned off their younger voters, and suggested yet again that they would not mobilize enough of the voting public to fight against the worst Republicans in that party's history.

When the media was reporting on Trump, they were long on posturing on his latest outrageous statements and short on digging into his background. I've been denouncing those with political and corporate power throughout these reflections, but the average voter who doesn't do a little homework assumes considerable responsibility.

Notwithstanding that Trump was certainly speaking (in a veiled manner) for many racists, sexists, immigrant bashers, and other bigots in the electorate—and those I'm not talking about—there were still many ethical voters who believed Trump's blatantly false claims about being a great businessman, a success on TV, and a patriot.

Samuel Johnson famously considered patriotism "the last refuge of a scoundrel." His biographer James Boswell, who passed along that judgment, clarified that Johnson "did not mean a real and generous love of our country, but that pretended patriotism which so many, in all ages and countries, have made a cloak for self-interest."

The Wall Street Journal's Peggy Noonan theorized in an April 2016 column that Trump's major appeal to Republican voters came not from his adherence to any political ideology, but rather from his radiant patriotism, which, in her view, has been absent from the political status quo. "What Trump supporters believe, what they perceive as they watch him," she wrote, "is that he is on America's side."

Yet there was little in Trump's rambling, off-the-cuff speeches and media interviews, or in his reactionary stream-of-consciousness tweets, that demonstrated his understanding of patriotism. Trump is a snake oil salesman. Smart political consumers should have done their research to find out the truth about the "product" they were being sold by Mr. Trump.

He is still using that branding as president, but consider the following examples of where the real estate plutocrat has come up short on patriotism:

- Peeved by the *Washington Post's* coverage of his presidential campaign and their investigation of the details surrounding his grand claims, Trump revoked the paper's press credentials for attending his rallies and political events. He also banned reporters from *Politico, Univision, Mother Jones*, the *Daily Beast*, the *Huffington Post*, and others. What's patriotic about muffling the free press when you are running for the highest office in the land?

- Despite lofty rhetoric about "bringing jobs home," Trump used cheap foreign production in China and Bangladesh for his signature clothing brands. "They don't even make this stuff here," the ever-defensive Trump told *ABC News*'s George Stephanopoulos when questioned about it. Stephanopoulos informed Trump that Brooks Brothers clothing does, in fact, "make this stuff" here. What's patriotic about making profits on the backs of poorly paid foreign workers who are often suffering under dictatorial rule?
- Big talker Trump claimed to have given millions of dollars to many different charities over the years. According to an October 2016 *Washington Post* investigation, he's given far, far less than he's boasted—and far less than other billionaires of his (alleged) comparable wealth. Most of his donations have come through the Trump Foundation, to which he has donated little of his own fortune. All in all, over the past eight years, the *Post* reports that Trump personally gave less than $10,000 to charities. What's patriotic about lying about your own philanthropy?
- One of Trump's more preposterous statements has been calling for a "total and complete shutdown of Muslims entering the United States." Drawing much justified criticism, Trump was pressured into clarifying and restating his position. He then claimed that only immigration from "terrorist countries" would fall under his proposed ban, and went on to push three different versions of a travel ban against five majority-Muslim nations (though not, of course, the ones he does business with). He also stated that he was "open" to the idea of creating an Orwellian database of all Muslims living in the United States. Is the accusatory language of ethnic stereotyping reflective of our patriotic traditions? The inscription on the Statue of Liberty reads "Give me your tired, your poor, Your huddled masses yearning to breathe free." Is repudiating Lady Liberty patriotic?

- Donald Trump's bid for the presidency was based upon the supposed strength of his talent and judgment as a businessman and dealmaker. These skills, however, are not verifiable, since Trump to this day refuses to release his tax returns. Trump has managed to avoid any severe blows to his personal wealth by strategically insulating himself from failed corporate business endeavors. He has bragged that he "used, brilliantly," corporate bankruptcy as a competitive advantage. When Trump fails, only the little guys suffer—not exactly reflecting the last words of the Pledge of Allegiance—"with liberty and justice for all."

- In 2015, Donald Trump shamefully criticized Senator John McCain for having spent over five years as a prisoner of war in North Vietnam. The ever-brash Trump dismissed McCain's extraordinary ordeal, claiming, "He's not a war hero." Trump continued, "He was a war hero because he was captured. I like people who weren't captured." Is degrading the suffering of an American veteran patriotic? Unlike McCain, Trump chose not to serve during the Vietnam War. Not a pacifist, he has gone on the record as making a different kind of sacrifice. Trump described his romantic escapades in the 1980s as his "personal Vietnam" due to how he put himself at risk of sexually transmitted diseases. He told Howard Stern that this made him feel "like a great and very brave soldier."

- "I believe that Trump University was a fraudulent scheme," Ronald Schnackenberg, a former employee of the unaccredited Trump University, stated in testimony, "and that it preyed upon the elderly and uneducated to separate them from their money." Indeed, much of the information that has come to light about Donald Trump's "university" reveals that it was little more than a scam meant to drain people of their money while promising them success. Cornered by the allegations, Trump resorted to accusing Judge Gonzalo P. Curiel, who was in charge of trying the case, of being "a hater of Donald Trump" due to his Mexican ethnicity. Are these the words of man who loves America or those of a con man caught with his hand in the cookie jar? Trump settled the case for $125 million.

■ Since starting his bid for the presidency, tall-tale Donald Trump has produced a an avalanche of outrageously false statements. According to the nonpartisan PolitiFact, nearly 70 percent of the statements made by Donald Trump fall under the categories of "Mostly False," "False," or "Pants on Fire." His campaign won the distinction of being PolitiFact's 2015 Lie of the Year for its entire spider web of deceptions. What's patriotic about chronically lying when you're running for the presidency of the United States?

So what does it truly mean to be patriotic? My parents defined it quite simply. They taught my siblings and me that loving one's country meant working hard to make it more lovable. This means working to reduce poverty, discrimination, corruption, greed, cheating, crime, harms to health and safety, and other injustices that weaken the promise and potential of America.

PART III

THE CAMPAIGN FOR
PRESIDENT UNDER WAY

Were it not for the antiquated, atavistic Electoral College, there would have been no Trump presidency. He was selected by the members of the Electoral College. Since 1787, no citizen in the US has ever voted for a presidential candidate. Absurdly enough, we vote for the electors, who then select our presidents. Six times in our history, the loser of the national popular vote won the election because of the Electoral College—most recently George W. Bush over Al Gore in 2000 and Trump over Clinton in 2016. The trillions of words written and spoken about Trump are owed to this Electoral College and not the majority of voters in 2016. That neither party strives to abolish it is evidence of the decay of formal politics in our country. That task is being undertaken by a tiny group of citizens.

Trump, however, has taught America sobering lessons. *First*, the mass media as a safeguard for our democracy has collapsed into frenzied short-term profiteering. The independent media doesn't have the reach to counterbalance the failures of mainstream media. *Second*, enough voters fail to do their homework, thereby rendering themselves easily flattered, fooled, and flummoxed by both the devious Donald and the party duopoly tied to big business. *Third*, if as few as 1 percent of voters mobilize majority opinion in each congressional district in ways suggested in this book, informed popular sovereignty can control the 535 lawmakers in Congress to put people first. If not, say goodbye to the prospects for democracy. Say hello to mass decline and despair on the road to accelerating serfdom.

21.

Duking It Out

Once the race for president got under way, the Democrats were hit with a double whammy. It was not just that the voters were ignoring Trump's obvious duplicity, it was that Hillary Clinton had her own tendency toward mendacity.

This was a climate in which *the only candidates were both secretive and averse to scrutiny*. Such candidates give politicians in general a bad name and make the public feel that Washington is a "swamp," as Trump labeled it. Little in Hillary's campaign dispelled this notion; rather, many things stoked it.

In August 2016 there was a growing asymmetry between the mounting demands for Donald Trump to release his tax returns (Hillary did) and the diminishing demands that Hillary release the secret transcripts of her very lucrative speeches before closed-door banking conferences and other business conventions.

The Washington Post, an endorser of Clinton, devoted a section of its August 18, 2016, issue to questioning why Trump didn't want to release his tax returns—speculating that he isn't as rich as he brags he is, that he pays little or no taxes, and that he gives little to charity. Other media outlets endorsing Hillary were less than vociferous in demanding that she release the transcripts of just what she told business leaders in these pay-to-play venues.

When asked earlier that year about her transcripts during the fifth Democratic primary debate, Hillary said she would "look into it." When the questions persisted in subsequent months, she said she would release the transcripts only if all the other candidates released theirs. Not exactly a sign of a leader. Bernie Sanders replied that he had no transcripts because he didn't give paid speeches to business audiences. Nonetheless, Hillary continued to be evasive.

We know she had such transcripts. Her contract with numerous business groups, prepared by the Harry Walker Agency, stipulated that the sponsor pay $1,000 for a stenographer to take down a verbatim record, exclusively for her possession and use.

At that point, many of us wondered: Why wouldn't Hillary tell the American people, whose votes she wanted, what she had told corporations in private for almost two years? Was it that she didn't want to be accused of doubletalk, of being "gushy" (as one insider told the *Wall Street Journal*) when addressing bankers, stock traders, and corporate bosses? On the campaign trail Hillary mimicked Bernie Sanders's tough, populist challenges to Wall Street. But Hillary was the clear choice for president for the Wall Street crowd and the champions of the military-industrial complex.

If Hillary had been elected, her White House would have been utterly predictable: more Wall Street, more military adventures. Many of us said at the time that it was bad enough that monetized politicians and the mass media reduced voters to the status of spectators, excluded from injecting their issues and their perceived injustices into the electoral campaigns. Now people were being told to stop complaining when candidates such as Hillary Clinton told the gilded few what she and they don't want many of us to hear.

The lesser-of-two-evils sickness once again had begun to plague the media establishment. Meanwhile, I wrote an editorial warning voters who might be considering Trump as a good alternative to Clinton, bringing out his off-the-charts level of mendacity. Here's what I wrote in October 2016:

> Let's say you're inclined to vote for Donald Trump largely because you dislike Hillary Clinton and are fed up with government messing up and serving Wall Street over Main Street. You've heard all the things said about Trump and it doesn't make any difference because he says with absolute confidence that he is going to shake up Washington and "make America great again."
>
> Why not try this experiment to bring matters down to earth where you live, work, and raise your family? Suppose you're souring on your friend, who has been increasingly disrespectful. Along comes a person who wants to be your friend and protector and make your life great again. He reassures you because he says he's quite well-to-do and always tells you how smart he is in all ways.
>
> Day after day, he tells you about his successful life, his determination to address many of your concerns about health care, safety, uppity newcomers, and he promises to lower your taxes and get your neighborhood roads fixed. He emphasizes that he'll prevent the factory where you work from closing and fleeing to China, and he says he'll make sure no more jobs in your community move to low-wage countries. He never says how, but that's okay because you believe him. He's like a father figure ready to make life better and more secure.
>
> All this sounds just great to you. But then you start hearing people cautioning you about the man. He bankrupted his gambling business while taking government subsidies. He doesn't pay taxes. He regularly says things

that are not true—about himself and about the country, about safety regulations in your factory, and about immigrants.

He harshly goes after anyone who takes him to task for his behavior, his false statements, and his sneering descriptions of other people, especially if they are overweight (like he is), or if they have fallen on hard times, or if they want a living minimum wage.

Worse still, you start noticing that he is a freeloader—cheating his own employees, not paying his small business suppliers, gouging customers, and not paying any taxes, unlike you. After a few drinks, he even brags about his "competitive advantage" over the people he's stiffed.

Sometimes he's even made vicious comments about people you like and even about you, as if he thinks he is better than you. Although your neighbors have pointed out these rough edges, you keep forgiving him because of the many ways he's promised to make your life better. But after a while, you see that he never apologizes for his falsehoods and never takes responsibility for any of his failings, always blaming someone or something else. He especially bullies weaker or poorer people in his business dealings.

Like a schoolyard bully, he knows how to dish it out but can't take it himself. You'd better not give him a taste of his own medicine because he'd lash out at you with uncontrollable rage. You admire people who can control their temper and ego, but he seems unable to control his own explosive impulses.

Other remarks he's made bother you. He is too rough on women and minorities. He jeers about people's physical features and thinks he's perfect. For all his assurances about what he'd do for you, he doesn't know very much about anything or how he might get anything done. You've never seen him pick up a check. He takes everything personally, and goes berserk when criticized or corrected.

But somehow, he talks your language, thinks your thoughts, and, oh, how he can describe your resentments about "other people." What you might be thinking to yourself, he says out loud, afraid of nobody.

Over the years, your friend has moved away, built and lost bigger gambling casinos, and gotten into lots of debt (though he's always managed to personally escape his creditors). He anchored big-time television shows as the hero-decider, then ran for president against all odds, and stunned the country by getting people like you to make him the Republican Party's nominee.

If he wins, he'll still be the same person, except he'll have huge power over everyone. Unfortunately, his disturbing characteristics and temperament will only get worse if he is elected.

At that point, he could impose his will on you with all the power of the White House. Already, you've noticed he's siding with the big oil, gas, and coal interests, asking for campaign money from the very fat cats he vigorously denounced for a year to get your primary vote.

As president, he could dictate, start wars, and make life very unpleasant for people like you, and he could respond to little protests with big-time retaliation from Big Brother in Washington.

You know, a wise philosopher two thousand years ago said, "Character is destiny." I would add, "Personality is decisive."

We all confront these traits in our neighbors, coworkers, and others. Do you really want your friend, whose traits you yourself have noticed and worried about, lodged in a secretive presidency with the greatest power to betray his supporters and lashing out in all directions?

A lot of voters purchased snake oil in the 2016 election. And by that time, the Democrats had gotten used to losing. Why else did they replicate the same strategies that brought them down in the midterms?

In 2014, when Obama was in charge, the ruffian Republicans, who barely gave lip service to anything but serving the rich and powerful, usurped the national legislature from the Democrats. It's not that the Republicans won, exactly; *they were handed the seats by the Democrats*, who refused to stand tall for the majority of the American populace, aiding them with labor, health, and environmental protections, the prosecution of big-buck malefactors, a better social safety net, and other necessities.

The same road was taken in 2016 by Hillary Clinton and other Democrats running for office. They should have been damning the Republicans for their record of the last two years, when they controlled the national legislature. Republicans voted more than a dozen times for measures attacking women's health; they blocked all votes on comprehensive immigration reform; they offered only the back of their hand for the cause of children's well-being; they blocked a vote to raise the frozen federal minimum wage of $7.25 an hour; they twice voted *against* affirming that climate change is real and caused by humans; and they passed tax cuts of which 99.6 percent go to the richest 1 percent of Americans. Furthermore, they voted unanimously *against* even considering a constitutional amendment to overturn the Supreme Court's 5–4 *Citizen's United* decision that opened the floodgates for big corporate money in elections. They continued to protect secret money in elections and twice voted against even allowing a vote on the Paycheck Fairness Act to give women new tools for winning equal pay for equal work.

One hundred percent of the House Republicans voted against allowing a vote to let American workers earn just seven job-protected paid sick days each year—far less than has been given for decades in all Western European countries.

Republicans are so in hock to the student loan industry that they have repeatedly voted against even bringing up for a vote the student loan refinancing bill. *One hundred percent* of House Republicans voted against even bringing up a bill to stop unpatriotic big companies from dumping their US charter and fleeing abroad to avoid paying their fair share of taxes. And lead-poisoned children in Flint, Michigan, got the straight-arm by 233 House Republicans.

House Republicans in recent years have stupidly cut the IRS budget, assuring the non-collection of some $450 billion in taxes each year, and thereby swelling the federal deficit that the GOP is supposed to care about. The Republicans were knowingly complicit in protecting this massive tax evasion.

Worse, these Republicans were complicit in shielding the health care industry's computerized billing fraud, amounting to about $350 billion in 2018 alone. This corporate crime wave estimate comes from the leading expert on billing fraud, Harvard professor Malcolm Sparrow (the author of *License to Steal*), and previous estimates by the Government Accountability Office (GAO) of the Congress. The Republicans feel there is simply too little money in the federal budget for adequate investigators and criminal prosecutors, even when *every dollar* in enforcement brings more than seven dollars in recoveries and fines!

So, here is where the Democrats running in 2016 should have been concentrating their fire. Instead, the Democratic Party declined to give us a competitive election process that focused on substantive matters uppermost in the minds of the American people. So the party went into further decline. It took strenuous demands by some civic leaders in Washington, DC, just to get the House Democrats to compile these aforementioned Republican votes and passively release them in a concise form to the public, and then only two months before the November 2016 elections! But in order not to offend their donors, the Democrats didn't take the Republicans to task on their own ugly and cruel voting records, with dire results for the people.

22.

The Lessons of Trump's Ascent

Charlatan that he was, Trump at least had ears. He heard the people's cry for justice. So, while there are many negative lessons about the weakness of our democracy shown by his election—such as the media's chase after sensation, not substance—one might also find positive pointers. One important lesson is that voters are attuned to someone who talks about their issues. In fact, here's a run-down of the lessons Trump taught us in his rise. Let's call them his inadvertent silver linings.

1. *New York Times* star columnist James B. Stewart may be right when he claims that bipartisan outrage over Donald Trump's not paying income tax for perhaps several decades may lead to stronger support for "a comprehensive overhaul of the nation's loophole-riddled revenue gathering system." The brazen Trumpeteer may be just the jolt that Congress needs. *Maybe.*

2. By raising the trade agreements issue (NAFTA, TPP, etc.), Trump startled many complacent Republicans into an awareness long dimmed by the empirically starved, obsolete nineteenth-century "win-win" "free-trade" dogmas. Unknowingly, of course, Trump missed the deeper insidiousness beneath these corporate-managed trade agreements that are

driving American industries to Asia and Mexico. I'm referring to the loss of our freedom to improve consumer, worker, and environmental protections in our country embodied in these agreements. Instead they bypass our legislatures and courts to allow unimpeded the overriding imperatives of commercial international trade.

3. On November 2, 2016, the *New York Times* ran the headline "Veterans, Feeling Abandoned, Stand by Donald Trump." Veterans' spreading disdain for both major parties is about more than how they have been neglected regarding consumer protections, jobs, and health care. Once Trump was in office, he did nothing about this, but he did raise the issue.

4. Trump inadvertently further revealed the consequences of our educational system's deliberate decision not to expose students to critical thinking *about power* in all its forms. To those millions of fed-up Americans who, while disliking Trump's behavior and foul mouth, nevertheless support him because "he tells it like it is": please pause for a moment to consider the facts. How does "telling it like it is" equate to "being willing and able to do something about it," and just what is "it"? Trump is inordinately vague here.

   These same Americans, so knowledgeable about their own daily occupations and hobbies, somehow forsake any responsibility to face the facts by doing some political homework and demanding that they be *participants* in the electoral process, not mere *spectators* of an electoral circus and its chief carnival barker.

5. More openly, by his performance Trump has shown us how the mass media can degrade election coverage so long as the prospect of greater profits outshines the impetus to offer varied and well-informed reporting. This is especially true for mass TV and radio. Indeed, Trump's ability to attract the media's greed for profits continues to pull the mass media closer to his gutter.

In addition, so addicted was the media to scouring speeches and Twitter feeds for the latest Trumpisms and provocations that it slammed the door on any participation by those civic groups that actually have been improving our country, know what they're talking about, and are able to inject broader topics and accuracy into candidates' campaigns. Some of the major topics civic groups can discuss that are closer to the peoples' concerns include looted pensions, corporate crimes against consumers and workers, crony taxpayer bailouts, and bureaucratic waste and anxiety-producing unresponsiveness by vendors and bureaucrats day after day.

6. Further, Trump cast some doubt on the invincibility of entrenched plutocracy and oligarchy over popular sovereignty. Consider this improbable dynamic: supporting Hillary Clinton were those on Wall Street, the bulk of the military-industrial complex, Silicon Valley, and, of course, the Democratic Party machinery. Yet she lost the Electoral College despite winning the popular vote.

 And lost to Trump, who, by contrast, had largely been abandoned by his party's elite; had less than half of Hillary's television advertising budget, had little get-out-the-vote ground game to speak of, and was being blasted by the mass media day after day.

7. Lastly, Trump has raised the peril of what South Americans have called "the politics of personalismo." By making his ego, his persona, his personal boasts, his personal insults and escapades, and his business conquests the core of 2016's campaign, he forced the media to reap what they have sown with their cynical mantra for the daytime and evening news, "If it bleeds, it leads" (meaning not only street crime but other sordid stories that are graphic, violent, or in otherwise poor taste, which are guaranteed to make the headlines). Trump's campaign is the embodiment of such misguided priorities.

These are all rather rough reminders of how much our society has departed from a people's government, with a dispirited public attracted to a pompous buffoon simply because he made big promises not shored up with any specifics. Those who voted for him were in for a rude awakening.

PART IV

TRUMP IN THE
DRIVER'S SEAT

Loving one's country without loving the people and their children is a contradiction in terms. In the first year and a half of President Trump's term, rhetoric and deeds embraced this contradiction almost across the board, as his appointed political oligarchy served the greed and power of the corporate plutocracy. Impervious to advice and critical feedback, Trump lunged into tweets and treachery that betrayed his presentations to the public in 2016 both substantively and personally.

Commuting between the White House and his ornate escape that is Mar-a-Largo, Trump daily tests the mettle, the stamina, the reserves of our democratic institutions—all of them at all levels of law, politics, media, nonprofit civic associations, academic centers, the professional and religious domains. He is probing the durability of our separation of powers between the legislative, executive, and judicial branches and the balance between our federal system of government and the states. So far he is getting away with his reckless maraudings, his flaunting of the rule of law and the abuses of his oath to enforce the law under our Constitution. His immediate predecessors in office made it easier for him to escape the accountabilities of his office. The burden shifts heavily onto the Constitution's preamble. "We the People"—in whom is vested the sovereign authority in our Republic—what we do with that awesome but eminently realizable responsibility will be the next challenge, a future chapter in our nation's history that will be written by all of you.

23.

Electoral Shenanigans

Trump slipped through into the presidency. "Slipped through" in the sense that he lost the popular vote by a lot, but still got the prize because he won the Electoral College. The Electoral College can deny the popular vote and has cost the Democrats two recent presidential elections (in 2000 and 2016), but the Democratic Party still hasn't joined an existing dynamic civic movement to override this ridiculous, antiquated, undemocratic institution with state compacts. Here is something I penned a year before Trump's surprise Electoral College selection:

> In the history of the United States, four presidential candidates who came in second in the popular vote were "elected" president (John Quincy Adams in 1824, Rutherford B. Hayes in 1876, Benjamin Harrison in 1888, and George W. Bush in 2000). This inversion of democratic elections was due to the fifty states' winner-take-all laws and the absurdity of the Electoral College. To political observers in other democratic countries, the US is a laughingstock for its failure to change this system that rejects the expressed popular will.
>
> Change is in the wind. A remarkable civic movement is

taking on this overlooked issue. The National Popular Vote organization (www.nationalpopularvote.com) is successfully pressing for an interstate compact, whereby states pass laws declaring that they will give all their electoral votes to the winner of the national popular vote for president. Presto! Therefore, there is no need for a constitutional amendment to repeal the Electoral College. What the compact does is align the electoral vote with the popular vote, since the Constitution exclusively accords the states the authority to select the manner of choosing its presidential electors.

Remember, from your history book, American voters do not vote for presidential candidates directly; they vote for a slate of presidential electors, who then vote for the candidates.

So far, led by philanthropist Steve Silberstein and his colleagues, ten states (and the District of Columbia) possessing 165 electoral votes altogether—or 61 percent of the 270 electoral votes necessary for a candidate to win—have enacted laws for this interstate compact. They are Rhode Island, Vermont, Hawaii, Maryland (the first to do so), Massachusetts, Washington, New Jersey, Illinois, New York, and California.

There are numerous other benefits of this long-overdue reform that has been backed by public opinion polls in the past few decades. (See www.gallup.com/poll/2140/americans-support-proposal-eliminate-electoral-college-system.aspx). With such a reform, presidential candidates will become more likely to campaign in more states, regardless of whether they are "blue" states, "red" states, or closely divided states. Presidential elections will no longer be focused in a tiny number of "battleground states," such as Florida, Ohio, Virginia, and Iowa.

In 2012, a majority of the general election presidential campaign events were just in those four states. That means most Americans never saw the presidential candidates to meet, question, support, or oppose them. Mitt Romney hardly campaigned in California or New York, apart from attending private fund-raisers; while Barack Obama did not campaign in Texas, Alabama, Michigan, or Minnesota.

As a presidential candidate, I always thought ignoring states was disrespectful to the Americans whose states were visited less frequently or not at all. Each time I ran for president, I campaigned in all fifty states, though there was no need for me to be concerned about the winner-take-all rule.

The National Popular Vote interstate compact, once it reflects a majority of the electoral votes—enough to elect a president (270 of 538)—assures that, in Mr. Silberstein's words, "*every* vote, in *every* state, will matter in *every* presidential election." When people know that their vote matters, they are going to be more motivated to turn out to vote.

Beyond the aforementioned four [now five] instances in which the popular vote's second-place winner became president, there were also many close calls. Mr. Silberstein explains that "a shift of 59,393 votes in Ohio in 2004 would have elected John Kerry despite President Bush's nationwide lead of over 3,000,000 votes. A shift of 214,393 votes in 2012 would have elected Mitt Romney despite President Obama's nationwide lead of almost 5,000,000 votes."

By shifting the power in presidential elections from the electoral vote to the popular vote, the National Popular Vote compacts will make voter suppression and intentional miscounting of the votes in specific swing states (as likely occurred, for instance, in Florida in 2000 and possibly in Ohio in 2004) much less likely.

The present skewed system gives more importance to a tiny number of "battleground" states that tip the election. Politicians favor these states with more visits and more tangible benefits once the candidate is in office. Perhaps it is a coincidence, but, as pointed out by the National Popular Vote organization, "'Battleground' states receive 7 percent more federal grants than 'spectator' states, twice as many presidential disaster declarations, more Superfund enforcement exemptions, and more No Child Left Behind law exemptions."

Applying my theory that it takes 1 percent or less of the citizenry to make major changes in American government (so long as they reflect majoritarian opinion), this tiny group, the National Popular Vote, could be moving toward a historic triumph with their educational and advocacy efforts at the state legislative level.

There is a lot of talk these days about growing inequality in the country. That inequality is exacerbated by the lack of direct influence in elections that a popular vote–led election process would give to currently underrepresented groups. This nationwide citizen drive working to reduce inequality among voters could be an important step toward closing the inequality gap.

To join the effort for the national popular election of the president, go to www.nationalpopularvote.com for clear and crisp guides toward becoming a participant in your state.

Needless to say, this effort to create a work-around that would have eliminated the power of the Electoral College to control the presidential vote was not achieved by 2016. If it had been, Trump would not be sitting where he is now.

24.

Trump's Big Reveal

As the elected Trump prepared to take power, he engaged in what might be called a *"big reveal."* All the false populist trappings of being against Wall Street and foreign military adventures, and of being pro–working class, were, one by one, stripped off.

When Trump geared up to take the reins of power, optimists were hoping for a Trump makeover. They clung to his brief victory remarks that suggested he wanted to be the "president for all Americans." In his *60 Minutes* interview following the election, Trump said that the protestors were out in the streets "because they don't know me."

Character and personality are not prone to change in most people. Especially in the case of Trump, who saw his campaign tactics as reasons for his "successes." However, the assumption was that exalted, higher offices of public trust and power could sometimes bring out the better angels.

Still, even in November 2016, the signs were foreboding. Trump knew very little about the awesome job given to him by that dead hand from the past—the Electoral College. Lack of know-how caused Trump to rely heavily on these old hands behind the worsening corporate state and military.

His transition appointments delighted the corporatists. The

man chosen to oversee changes in the Environmental Protection Agency, Scott Pruitt, denies that climate change is manmade and scowls at regulation of harmful pollutants. Trump opened the door for big oil and gas lobbyists to control the Department of Energy and the Department of the Interior. Wall Streeters are smacking their lips over Trump appointees who oppose regulating their gambling with other people's money.

His military advisers do not come from the ranks of prudent retired officials who see perpetual war for what it is—a mechanism for national *in*security, authoritarianism, and profits for the military-industrial complex. To the contrary, Trump's military advisers have been quick to embrace an imperial mentality and its warfare state.

One can imagine how a major stateless terrorist attack on the United States during this administration would provoke Trump into a heavy-handed retaliation, with dangerous and unforeseen consequences. This is exactly what these adversaries abroad want him to do, as it would help them spread their propaganda campaign against the US. Meanwhile, our civil liberties, and the domestic necessities of the people, will be further shoved aside.

In past Republican Party electoral victories, there was always a modicum of checks and balances to slow the party's plutocratic greed and power grabs. But as of January 2018, the Republican Party controls the executive branch, the Congress, the Supreme Court, thirty-three governorships, and thirty-two state legislatures. The incompetence of Trump and the implosion of some of the congressional Republicans has somewhat reduced this administration's momentum, but the only real relief for our democracy must come from the redeeming power of the people, through the grass roots and the ballot box.

Our country is in an extraordinarily high-risk condition, given who possesses the reins of power. Authentic conservatives and liberals can curb that power if they form alliances back in the congressional districts around the major initiatives on which they agree. (See my book *Unstoppable: The Emerging Left-Right Alliance to Dismantle the Corporate State.*)

With the power brokers employing their divide-and-conquer tactics, such potent political alliances will require citizen action and adequate funding in all congressional districts, with focused and sustained personal intensity on senators and representatives. Congress, with only 535 lawmakers, is the most accessible of the checks and balances reachable by the people back home.

How many enlightened billionaires, serious citizen-patriots, and advocates for transforming elections and governance are willing to step up?

By mid-November 2016, Trump had already cast off everything but the most bare-bones fundamentals of populist rhetoric. His appointments indicated that his remarks about curbing Wall Street and the military-industrial complex were empty gestures, and not indications of his true intentions. But by early December, as the appointments continued, he dropped even the slightest pretense (except verbally) of having any interest in helping the vast majority of citizens. For instance, he put forward an education czar, Betsy DeVos, who wants to replace public schools with for-profit educational enterprises.

You can often see where a president-elect's forthcoming administration is going by the people he nominates to high positions. Across over a dozen crucial posts, Mr. Trump chose war hawks, Wall Streeters (with a former Goldman Sachs partner, Steven Mnuchin, as his pick for Treasury secretary), and clenched-teeth corporatists determined to jettison life-saving, injury-and disease-preventing regulations and to leave bigger holes in consumers' pocketbooks.

It's almost embarrassingly transparent. When running for election, Trump's last big TV ad blasted "a global power structure" that has "robbed our working class," with images of Goldman Sachs's CEO flashing across the screen. Fast-forward several weeks, and he selected cabinet secretaries who want to dismantle the public school system, fund private schools with tax dollars, reduce regulation of banks, roll back protections against air, water, and soil pollutants, cut consumer protections, and weaken labor laws and job safety standards. Other appointees say they want to privatize Medicare, which has led health insurance company stocks to soar, and some want to transfer Medicaid to even more hostile state manipulations.

Regarding national security, Trump's White House advisers are advocates of imperial intervention and bombing Iran. Trump's calls for reneging on the Iran nuclear agreements the US made with two dozen leading nations risk escalating hostilities.

As an accomplished sleight-of-hand specialist—a failed gambling CEO who always jumped ship with his gold and left his workers, creditors, and shareholders stranded—in December 2016 Trump traveled to Indiana to brag about the decision by Carrier Corp. and its parent company, United Technologies (UT), to retain about half of the two thousand jobs they planned to ship to Mexico. Trump had made Carrier his poster child for showing how the US loses jobs under NAFTA.

Indiana taxpayers will have to pay $7 million for Carrier to agree to only a partial retention of jobs, with, presumably, additional goodies for UT coming later. UT and Carrier had already long been loaded up with tax and other "incentives," subsidies, and all the complex corporate welfare that defense companies receive from the Pentagon.

Being a longtime recipient of crony capitalism himself, Trump hopes that his working-class supporters will never catch on to this kind of backroom "dealmaking."

It was getting hard to find policies for the people themselves in Trump's victory, but it was also certain that such double-dealing as seen in the Carrier episode must have enlightened some to Trump's two faces. Trump doesn't like to be accused of disloyalty by workers who supported him. Therein lies some leverage. Laborers, who were crucial to the Boaster's Electoral College victory, will have many opportunities to laser-focus on Trump's betrayals in very personal ways (see Public Citizen's report on Trump's 101 betrayals of his voters at https://www.citizen.org/sites/default/files/pc_news_issues/2018/mar-apl/files/assets/basic-html/index.html#1). They should make the most of them.

What must combat Trumpism now is an angry, informed, progressive, battling public. It's not Democratic Party hacks who offer any hope, but the Sanders wing of the party, backed by energetic voters, who get involved in the political process and—as in Sanders' campaign—force the Democrats, or even some third party, to start standing tall for the people's rights.

Month after month, as Trump approached his occupation of the White House, his lies got bigger and his appointments got worse. This continuing hiring of *swamp dwellers* signaled to any voters who were not yet disabused where Trump's true sympathies lay.

Even for a failed gambling executive, Donald Trump was surprisingly quick to show his hand as he set the course of his forthcoming presidency. With a reactionary fervor, he burst backward into the future. He accomplished this feat, as I've been documenting, through the first wave of nominations to his cabinet and White House staff.

Only if there is a superlative added to the word "nightmare" can the dictionary provide an apt description of Trump's bizarre selection of men and women marinated either in corporatism or militarism, with strains of racism, class cruelty, and ideological rigidity. Many of Mr. Trump's nominees lack any appreciation of the awesome responsibilities of public office.

Let's run through Trump's "picks":

First there are the selections who will make it easier to co-opt the Republicans in Congress. He appointed Elaine Chao, the wife of Senate Majority Leader Mitch McConnell, for secretary of transportation. Ms. Chao does not like regulation of big business, as in the auto, aviation, railroad, and oil industries. Next was Congressman Tom Price (R-GA) (since resigned) to lead the Department of Health and Human Services. Price wanted to dump Obamacare, deny adequate court awards to wrongfully injured people, turn over control of Medicaid to the states—and to plenty of governors who dislike Medicaid—and even wanted to privatize (i.e., corporatize) Medicare itself, dropping it into the hands of a business sector that already defrauds that very program of about $60 billion a year.

Trump selected Congressman Mike Pompeo (R-KS) to be the director of the Central Intelligence Agency (CIA). Pompeo is a Cold War warrior who believes in a militaristic, interventionist CIA, especially in the case of Iran, taking that agency even further away from its original mission of gathering intelligence.

Then came the generals. Notwithstanding the constitutional imperative for civilian control over the military, Trump has placed two generals in charge of foreign and domestic military theaters. For secretary of defense, Trump chose recently retired Marine general James Mattis. Nicknamed "Mad Dog" Mattis, he believes Barack Obama was too weak, indecisive, and nonstrategic in his dealings with the Middle East. He looks very much like he is a believer, however with some restraint, in the American empire.

The next general in line was recently retired Marine general John Kelly, chosen to run the Department of Homeland Security and since moved around to White House chief of staff. He is seen as a modern believer in the Monroe Doctrine over the Hispanic world south of Florida and the Rio Grande. He shares General Mattis's dangerous views on Iran and Islam.

Then there are the Trump nominees selected to run the departments whose numerous missions under existing law they want to dismantle. For instance, Trump appointed climate change denier Scott Pruitt to head the EPA, the same agency he, as Oklahoma attorney general, fought tirelessly to undermine.

Those who made big donations to Trump's campaign are another magnet for his nominations. For Linda McMahon's $7 million to pro-Trump super PACs, she gets to head the Small Business Administration (an agency she had previously campaigned to have eliminated). As a highly controversial CEO of professional wrestling, she worked to monopolize the professional wrestling market and stifle competition.

For the Department of Education, schoolchildren and their teachers are forced to face Betsy DeVos. From a billionaire family, she is a ferocious advocate of using taxpayer money in the form of vouchers for private schools. She makes no bones about her hatred of public schools and her desire to have commercial managers of school systems.

To lead the Justice Department, Trump selected Senator Jeff Sessions (R-AL), who is big on police surveillance, weak on civil rights enforcement, a hard-liner on immigration, and very mixed on corporate crime.

Add these strong-willed ideologues to Trump's easily bruised ego, his Twitter tantrums on trivial matters, and his penchant for always being the decision-making strongman, and you've got the makings of an explosive regime with almost daily eruptions.

Whatever the media makes of the inevitable intrigue, infighting, and likely resistance by civil service officers trying to adhere to their lawful missions, it is the people who will be paying the price.

As the profiteers of Wall Street and the war hawks blend with the corporate statists, the super-confident Trump tells us what their products will be like and that he'll be their salesman. It is time to mobilize as citizens in the Paul Revere mode.

While on the downside we have Trump and the plutocrat and military comrades he is putting in power, on the upside, we have seen a rising tide of civil resistance, with continual marches and speak-outs denouncing Trump before he even got behind his desk in the Oval Office. Principled resistance, including Veterans for Peace, came quickly on the heels of Trump's dismal appointments.

Moreover, Trump's appointments and priorities showed that he is vulnerable on many fronts. Take just these:

First, the Trumpsters vowed to dismantle various government programs. They are determined to severely limit the protection of labor, replace public schools with taxpayer-funded vouchers for private schools, and drop regulatory protections in the health, safety, and environmental fields, among others. If they are acting without the requisite legal authority, that's of little concern to Mr. Trump.

Second, as we've seen, the Trumpsters have established a more secretive government, led by their very secretive boss (note Trump's refusal to reveal his potentially incriminating tax returns). Heavily staffed with militarists and corporatists, the Trump regime has proven hostile to open democratic processes and vulnerable to governing by cover-ups, which have a way of getting revealed.

Third, since most of Trump's top nominees are wealthy with many financial interests, they stand accused of conflicts of interest, even as they divest assets and place them in so-called blind trusts. For more information, see Public Citizen's report on conflicts of interest under Trump at https://www.citizen.org/watchdog-ging-conflicts-of-interest.

People were asking early on: How can the restaurateur and

fast-food chain magnate Andrew Puzder escape being seen as conflicted in his role as secretary of labor when he has opposed labor unions and increases to the stagnant $7.25-per-hour federal minimum wage? These pertinent questions led to Puzder withdrawing his nomination, as he couldn't take the grilling he got in the Senate. Similar conflicts exist with the former secretary of state—former ExxonMobil CEO Rex Tillerson—considering that company's far-flung concessions and investments around the world.

Fourth, Trump's nominees are for the most part confirmed role players in radical corporate statism. They can talk a good game against crony capitalism or corporate welfare, but they show Trump's promises to be full of hot air, particularly as they call for a bigger military budget, corporate tax cuts, and fewer regulatory health and safety protections for consumers, workers, and the environment. With a Republican-dominated Congress Trump's administration may achieve all or some of these objectives, but they will be accompanied by rising deficits, more inflation, preventable human casualties, and scandals.

Fifth, the maximum peril of Trump's administration may come from the extreme hubris of its military aggressiveness overseas. Trump has picked three retired generals suited to advancing empire's constantly boomeranging attacks in whichever Asian or African country they choose. The Trump military and national security team, as of April 2018 led by super–war hawk John Bolton, is not looking for peace treaties or strategies that avoid the spread of stateless terrorism around the world.

One major terror attack on the US and Trump will become a warring, civil-liberties-destroying monster of overreaction, forsaking and crowding out other priorities and necessities that a mature society must address.

Trump is leaving himself open to principled attack on all sides.

Citizens from all walks of life—left and right—need to defend our democracy, our civil liberties, and the health and safety protections that at their best made our country a model for so many others.

25.

Trump in Power, Night Falls in America

Donald Trump, from his first days in office, proved himself a jaw-boning president without equal in American history—jawboning, that is, by exerting rhetorical bombast against people, corporations, and institutions, with massive media propulsion behind his very personal presidency. The media has, in a sense, become a natural daily extension of his boundless, easily bruisable ego.

Trump has embraced these tactics as both a candidate and president. He went after Boeing for charging too much for the new Air Force One, and after Lockheed Martin for overpricing its F-35 fighter planes.

Previous presidents, knowing they have the "bully pulpit," have generally been averse to the sort of jawboning that singles out specific firms and persons. President Harry Truman did take on a newspaper columnist who criticized his daughter Margaret's singing skills. And President John F. Kennedy went after US Steel, referring to price hikes from the industry as "a wholly unjustifiable and irresponsible defiance of the public interest."

But generally presidents do not want to be seen as bullies, preferring one competitor over another or frittering away their presidential authority by getting into petty squabbles. In the midst of more serious matters of state, jawboning can be a serious distraction that alienates large numbers of people who may side with the assailed.

With Trump, none of this seems to matter. He has said repeatedly that he always slams back a hundred times harder than anyone who slams him. He revels in his thirty or forty million Twitter followers and delights in how his tweets are reported by the mass media. That gives him a personal "mass media" that he controls, unfiltered by his antagonists in the press.

Rather than playing the "going-through-channels" game in Washington, he throws his opponents off balance through personal attacks, focusing on human frailties, vanities, and occupational vulnerabilities. He knows that jawboning one person, firm, or politician puts others on the defensive, wondering whether they will be next, and he may even think he is putting foreign powers off balance because of his furious unpredictability.

The downside for Trump is that he is so absorbed in jawboning and rebutting critics that he doesn't pay attention to what his underlings are doing until the trouble rises to his level. Jawboning can lead to complex consequences when it comes from the most powerful office in the country.

Trump is known to dislike detailed immersion into issues and detailed briefings by civil servants. He likes to set the pace, establish the new focus of the day, and, above all, get even with anyone who stands up to or embarrasses him. He seems to believe rules and norms do not apply to him.

Trump's strange personality can radiate in many directions. He may worsen a bad situation because of impulsive and violent overreaction, leading to a worsening situation overseas and damage to the national interests, civil liberties, and other constitutional rights of the American people.

Now more than ever we have to remain alert, keep up with our fellow citizens at the congressional grass roots, stay informed on current events, and always be ready to foresee and forestall initiatives by politicians and corporatists that recklessly or greedily gobble up our tax dollars and undercut our health, safety, and civil rights. Applied patriotism, you might say. Focus heavily on the 535 members of Congress.

26.

His Appointments Were Bad, His Governing Worse

Here is the advice I gave to Trump upon his inauguration in January 2017:

> Judging by your remarkably low approval rating for an incoming president-elect according to national polls, it is not just Meryl Streep and Rep. John Lewis who think that your transition to becoming "presidential" has not yet materialized. In the hope that you might actually make such a transition, here are some challenges you will need to overcome in order to avoid embroiling your administration (and the nation) in a self-initiated avalanche of charges, disputes, and scandals.
>
> 1. Your Achilles' heel has thus far proven to be your easily bruised ego, which is put on display with every one of your furious, sometimes bullying, tweets. When you are president, however, you have more ways to retaliate and more ways to get both yourself and our country in trouble if you react in such a spasmodic manner. This is the big leagues. Adversaries abroad are keenly aware of how easily they can provoke you into impulsive missteps that play

into their hands. You would benefit from reading the 2004 book by Richard Clarke, *Against All Enemies: Inside America's War on Terror*, penned after Clarke left his position as counter-terrorism adviser to President George W. Bush.

In it, Mr. Clarke writes, "It was as if Osama bin Laden, hidden in some high mountain redoubt, were engaging in long-range mind control of George Bush, chanting 'invade Iraq, you must invade Iraq.'"

As for the American people's widespread dissent, if you take this personally instead of presidentially, you're going to give way to your worst traits and end up stereotyping whole groups in bigoted ways. There are reasons past presidents did not personalize their presidency—though some went to extremes and ignored any responsibility to acknowledge or answer serious letters. (See my book, *Return to Sender: Unanswered Letters to the President, 2001–2015*).

2. Your Twitter account can get you into twenty-four-seven disputes that are unbecoming of our nation's highest office. Thus far, you have managed to distract media attention from other negative stories about you with personal Twitter attacks. This may have worked during your campaign, but when you are president your customary aggressive tweets will distract focus and attention *from your own agenda* and turn off even your crucial Republican friends on Capitol Hill. A continuing lack of impulse control will erode your presidency quickly during the hundred-day honeymoon period. Best to restrain yourself. There are other, more important matters waiting on your desk.

3. Early on you'll have to decide to what extent you'll delegate to your nominees at the cabinet and agency levels,

and to what extent you will make these significant decisions yourself. Since you are known for your aversion to detailed briefings, memos, and studies, your subordinates will take advantage of your de-management style and go on their own, undoubtedly clashing with each other. In that case, decisions will end up in the White House after lots of press about chaos and tumult in your administration and low morale within the critical civil service.

The most immediate manifestation of the foregoing is the phenomenon widely known as "Terror Tuesday," the weekly meeting during which national security advisers briefed President Obama about "signature strikes" on suspects in faraway places like Yemen, Somalia, Afghanistan, Iraq, and Syria, carried out by drone operators in Virginia or Nevada with the push of a button. President Obama wanted to make many of these decisions directly as prosecutor, judge, jury, and executioner. Do you wish to continue such extra-judicial slayings (inside sovereign nations), in violation of international law, that have taken the lives of thousands of innocent women, children, and men?

4. Your well-publicized business ownerships are to be transferred to family members. Leading constitutional scholars, including Harvard Law professor Larry Tribe, and ethics experts, both Republican and Democratic, are not at all persuaded that this move complies with the emoluments clause of the Constitution (Article I, Section 9, Clause 8). They believe that your assets must be sold to nonfamily members, with the proceeds, liquid or otherwise, being held in a "blind trust."

Once again, whether to curry favor with you by patronizing your hotels and other properties and brandishing your surname here and abroad, or to subject you to an extortion attempt or provocative attacks on these properties, business and even government leaders could take advantage of your financial vulnerabilities. Change your transfer plan or you put the entire country and its future at risk for your personal convenience and gain. Address these concerns or this could spell early constitutional trouble for you, including lawsuits by businesses claiming loss of business due to others currying favor with you. A Supreme Court case gives such businesses standing to sue, under the Emoluments Clause of the Constitution.

5. Lastly, some various suggestions. Please meet early on with a leading delegation of top scientists and engineers and their groups, such as the National Academy of Sciences. They can prevent your administration from getting into lots of unsound, ill-advised, and costly science/technology trouble.

If you wish to squeeze out hundreds of billions of dollars in waste, you should reach out to the legendary presidential and gubernatorial consultant and manager of four large public utilities (including the TVA), S. David Freeman, the leading expert on reducing energy waste. To help cut over $350 billion in annual billing fraud in the health care industry—including $60 billion in yearly rip-offs of Medicare alone—contact the pioneer researcher on the topic, Professor Malcolm Sparrow of Harvard. And for advice on reducing soaring drug prices and other bilks and harms from the "politically protected" (your words) drug giants, look no further than Dr. Marcia Angell, former editor of the *New England Journal of Medicine*. These are just three of the many experts in cutting wasteful spending who are unlikely to be recommended to you by corporatists in your administration.

Trump, for all his wild rants, is, in some ways, actually eminently predictable.

Within a couple of weeks of assuming office, the Trump Gang was giving strong, petulant signals that it was hijacking the checks and balances of our democratic institutions. Coupling the Boss's easily bruisable ego, marinated in infinite megalomania, with ideologues harboring corporatist objectives that would have frightened Nixonites and Reaganites alike, the beginning of Trump's reign was a runaway train leaving the station.

Looking at the Trump regime critically, there is a method to their madness. Striving to govern early with a stream of poorly written executive orders (dictates), their basic message to all was "get with the program or get out." Building on precedents of presidential lawlessness, Trump planned to rule by directives and tweeted dictates against any challengers. Temperamentally, he has little patience for governing in a democracy and thinks he can rely on showmanship, bluster, and bullying.

Those traits, however, harbor dangerous vulnerabilities to outside provocations—foreign and domestic—which in turn could unleash furious, reckless, impulsive lashing out by Trump himself.

Start with stateless adversaries abroad engaged in long and violent struggles in their backyards with the US. They will capitalize on the perception that the Trump administration's travel ban is an attack against all Muslims. These dangerous actors will use Trump's executive orders as the ultimate recruitment tool. This will lead to a more dangerous world for Americans and refugees alike, and could provoke a vicious cycle without discernible restraints.

As noted earlier, one major terrorist attack in this country and Trump could become a bellowing monster, throwing to the winds rules of law, free speech, and other serious protections of health and safety for the people.

It is questionable whether Donald Trump, so self-obsessed and devoid of impulse control, realizes that our militarily powerful country has much more to lose than our suicidal opponents and that we should not be trapped and embroiled in such an escalating vortex of destruction. As a friend of mine said, "He's playing into their hands."

The big question is, where will the restraints on him come from? Here is what can be expected from establishment forces:

Presumably some caution will be advised by his secretaries of defense, state, and homeland security, backed by a vocal professional civil service with no ax to grind. Already a thousand US diplomats at embassies abroad have signed a petition pointing to the dangers of his executive order barring travelers from seven Muslim-majority countries.

Trump constantly attacks the media—sometimes as a general institution, other times naming reporters in his disfavor. The mass media made him viable as a candidate by devoting staggering amounts of free airtime and print space to his campaign. He then turned on them, because, for The Donald, "Enough is never enough." Bruised, some of the media will cower. But some have been asserting themselves with penetrating coverage.

What of the Congress—a place driven by fear, insecurity, constitutional abdication, and suddenly rising protests? Trump has given high-level positions in his government to five major Republicans from the Congress. Those members of Congress each have their own circles on Capitol Hill.

Even so, should Trump's already historically low approval rating in the polls start sticking to the Republicans headed into the 2018 elections, expect pushback from members of the GOP looking to save their own skins.

Can we expect action on Trump from the unions? The labor union leaders have gotten themselves into a quandary. Having supported either Hillary (mostly) or Bernie (far less), they're not getting tickets to the White House to watch the Super Bowl.

Trump knows how to game unions through his real estate and gambling businesses. He has been reminding them that 30 to 40 percent of their rank-and-file members voted for him, and he's not reluctant to call out the leadership on this sensitive point.

Trump has the unions in the cross fire for the time being. For their part, organized labor chiefs know that he has nominated or appointed the most anti-labor cabinet in modern times. That included Andrew Puzder, Trump's original nominee for secretary of labor, who is blatantly anti-union and against a higher minimum wage and fair labor standards. Puzder never made it out of the gate, but that wasn't for lack of support from Trump. Trump did get billionaire Betsy DeVos as education secretary, and she is bent on breaking the teachers' unions.

Lunging from one eruption and outrage to the next, it seems that the Trumpsters are grabbing the country and racing together toward the cliff. The question is, who goes over the cliff first? And will any establishment forces be able to stop him and his acolytes?

What probably worried Trump more than the possibility of Washington elites blocking him was that some business executives were beginning to turn against him. Some were marching in the streets, a bad sign for Trump; business executives were questioning his piratical policies, an even worse sign.

The obvious problem was that, contrary to appearances, he was not a man of his word.

He made many conflicting promises throughout his presidential campaign. He was going to be the "voice of the people." He was going to make their safety and their job expansion his number-one priority. He was going to make sure that everybody had health insurance under his then-unannounced plan. He was going to deregulate businesses, cut taxes, increase the military budget, build and repair the country's public infrastructure, and not surge the deficit. He was going to scrap NAFTA and the WTO.

Once in the White House, he proceeded to push programs and policies that reneged on many of his promises. He ballooned an already massive, bloated military budget, vastly increasing the deficit in the process despite harmfully cutting the small health and safety budgets of consumer, environmental, and labor regulatory agencies, as well as housing and energy assistance.

There is more to this emerging betrayal. As we know, Trump supported Republican speaker of the House Paul Ryan's "you're on your own, folks" devastating health insurance plan. Slash-and-burn Ryan, who was himself fully insured by the taxpayers, publicly admitted he didn't know how many people would lose their health insurance should one of his attempts to repeal Obamacare succeed.

Meanwhile, Trump proposed increasing the budget of the sprawling Department of Homeland Security but cut the budget of the US Coast Guard (which is part of the department), whose budget is already strapped in safeguarding our coastlines. (See David Helvarg's engrossing book, *Rescue Warriors*, which describes the Coast Guard's important but often unsung missions.)

Trump is unwilling to oppose the more extreme "mad dogs" among the congressional Republicans who want to erase the budgets for public broadcasting, the National Endowments for the Arts and Humanities, and legal services for the poor (even as 150 *corporate* law firms signed a letter saying they support maintaining the budget for legal services for the poor). The total number of dollars for all these programs is about $1 billion annually, or one-thirteenth the cost of another redundant giant aircraft carrier.

As the opposition coalesces in its resistance to various measures pushed by Trump's tantrums, it is interesting to note the surprising diversity of those challenging President Trump. More than a few corporate leaders are appalled by extreme Trumpism.

Sure, corporate CEOs are tempted by the tax cuts and the jettisoning of some regulations. But they know they are making record after-tax profits and record corporate after-tax pay for themselves, and the stock market is soaring. As they watch the growing rumble from the people in street demonstrations and at congressional town hall meetings, a little foreboding is building.

They're thinking, why rock the boat (or yacht)? Trump is ready and willing to take away what people already have—their health insurance and their health and safety protections. When a society, blocked from advancing justice, unravels the meager fair play that remains, the corporate bosses, who see beyond tomorrow, get worried—and for good reason.

In terms of health care, the spectacular resistance to Trump and the Republicans' agenda actually exposed another potential silver lining.

In fact, you can thank House Speaker Ryan and President Trump for pushing their cruel health insurance boondoggle. This debacle created a big opening to put a single-payer system, with full Medicare for All, front and center. Single-payer means everybody in, nobody out, with free choice of physician and hospital.

The single-payer system that has been in place in Canada for decades comes in at about half the cost per capita of America's dysfunctional system. All Canadians are covered at a cost of about \$4,500 per capita, while in the US the cost is about \$9,500 per capita, with nearly thirty million people without coverage and many millions more underinsured.

By October 2017, 120 members of the House of Representatives cosigned Congressman Conyers's bill, H.R. 676, which proposes a health care system similar to that of Canada. These lawmakers like H.R. 676 because it has no copays, nasty deductibles, or massive, inscrutable computerized billing fraud, while giving people free choice of their doctor and hospital and far lower government administrative costs.

Often Canadians never even see a bill for major operations

or procedures. Dr. Steffie Woolhandler, who teaches at Harvard Medical School, estimated recently that a single-payer system in the US could save as much as $500 billion, just in administrative costs, out of the nearly $3.5 trillion in annual health care expenditures.

Already federal, state, and local governments pay for about half of this gigantic sum through Medicare, Medicaid, the Children's Health Insurance Program, the Veterans Health Administration, and insurance plans for public employees. But the system is corrupted in complex ways by the greed, oft-documented waste, and overselling of the immensely profitable and bureaucratic insurance, drug, and medical industries.

To those self-described conservatives out there, consider that major conservative philosophers such as Friedrich Hayek, a leader of the Austrian school of economics that is so revered by Ron Paul, supported "a comprehensive system of social insurance" to protect the people from the "common hazards of life," including "sickness and accident." He wanted a *publicly* funded system for everyone, not just Medicare and Medicaid patients, with a *private* delivery of medical/health services. That is what H.R. 676 would establish.

Maybe some of this conservative tradition is beginning to seep into the minds of the corporatist editorial writers of the *Wall Street Journal*. Seeing the writing on the wall, so to speak, the writer of a recent editorial, before the Ryan/Trump health care plans fell apart, concluded with these remarkable words:

> The health-care market is at a crossroads. Either it heads in a more market-based direction step by step, or it moves toward single-payer step by step. If Republicans blow this chance and default to Democrats, they might as well endorse single-payer because that is where the politics will end up.

Maybe such commentary, repeated by some of the *Journal*'s other columnists, will prod more Democrats to come out of the closet and openly push for a single-payer system. At a recent Baltimore news conference, House Minority Leader Nancy Pelosi blurted, "I've been for single-payer for thirty years."

Even without any media, or any major party calling for it, a poll by the *Economist*/YouGov showed 60 percent of the public supporting full Medicare for All, including 46 percent of Republicans, 58 percent of independents, and 75 percent of Democrats. Ever since President Harry S. Truman sent Congress his proposal for universal health insurance legislation in the 1940s, public opinion, left and right, has been supportive.

Think of all the positive traits of single-payer one finds in Canada. Canadians, for example, don't have to worry about pay-or-die prices, don't take or decline jobs based on health insurance considerations, aren't driven into bankruptcy or deep debt from medical expenses, and experience no anxiety over the possibility of being denied payment or struck with reams of confusing, trap-door computerized bills and fine print.

People in Canada do not die because they cannot afford health insurance to get diagnoses or treatments in time. Americans—as many as thirty-five thousand—die each year from that entirely preventable cause.

Canadians can choose their doctors and hospitals without being trapped, like many in the US, into small, narrow service networks.

In Canada the administration of the system is simple. You get a health care card when you are born or when you become a permanent resident. You swipe it when you visit a physician or hospital.

All universal health insurance systems in all Western countries have their problems, but Americans are extraordinarily jammed with worry, anxiety, and fear over how or if their care will be covered, not to mention all the perverse incentives for waste, gouging, and profiteering.

For more information on health care in the US, what's being done to combat vicious commercial assaults on our country's most vulnerable people, and to find out how you can help fight back, visit www.singlepayeraction.org.

To go back to what I just mentioned, while there were some checks and balances against Trump's plans for legislation, as in the case of his bungled health care scheme, he could still go to town on changing regulations over which he has sole control. With this license, Trump has gone on a rampage, destroying consumer and workers' protections.

The background to this rampage has been the long-running corporatist campaign to besmirch the word "regulation" (i.e., law and order for corporations) and to glorify the word "deregulation," to help bring about their dream state of dismantled or weakened laws for corporations.

One striking example of the ongoing disaster of non-regulation costing our country is on display in the airline industry. The patsy Federal Aviation Administration (FAA), for decades after a string of hijackings of planes to Castro's Cuba, refused to require the airlines to install toughened cockpit doors and stronger locks to prevent entry by terrorists bent on making the aircraft a destructive weapon. Why? Because the airlines objected to an increased cost of a mere $3,000 per aircraft. The FAA, by its very nature, acquiesced.

Then came the reports of 9/11 hijackers breaking through unreinforced cockpit doors. All because the airlines weren't required to protect their cockpits and pilots. Sure, the hijackers could still have hijacked the planes, but they could not have piloted them into the World Trade Center and the Pentagon with all the consequences that have followed to this day.

In an industrialized economy with corporations, hospitals, and other commercial entities producing old and new hazards, regulations are needed to foresee and forestall human casualties and damage to the natural world.

The role of sensible regulations has been all but ignored by Donald J. Trump. Day by day, the Trump administration continues to take away basic protections that save both money and lives. Proudly, Trump, House Speaker Paul Ryan, and Senate Majority Leader Mitch McConnell have turned their backs on ensuring cleaner waterways, making coal-polluted air less toxic, enforcing workplace protections, and preserving our public lands. Disastrously for our country, Trump has joined forces with the Republicans in Congress to immobilize our government's research and action against accelerating climate change, and to diminish our government's efforts to detect early and head off calamitous pandemics.

The worst of Trump's egregious attacks on regulatory protections are coming out of his impulsive executive orders (EOs) to federal agencies. While many are of dubious legality—they would require congressional legislation to take effect—his intent is clear: roll back major protections for Americans wherever they eat, breathe, drink, work, drive, and receive health care.

One EO requires agencies to repeal two regulations for every one they issue. Such an empty but dangerous gesture is mindless, yet it's emblematic of the prevaricating, boasting, failed gambling czar. The Trump administration's rejection of essential roles for government is stunning.

Trump would weaken the laws protecting your savings, investments, and retirement security or pensions from what shredded them during the 2008–2009 Wall Street crash. No Wall Street bosses were ever jailed, so they're likely to keep speculating with your money with impunity and pocketing huge fees from your accounts in the process.

Trump even put off a Department of Labor rule requiring your investment advisers to put your interests ahead of their conflicting interests—the so-called fiduciary rule. Trump—who betrayed creditors, employees, investors, and consumers alike during his business career—readily knows what that accountability mechanism is all about.

The intentions and likely dire results of this swath of destruction to our regulatory agencies did not escape millions of lawyers, accountants, physicians, engineers, scientists, and teachers at all levels. Even those blue-collar workers who rolled the dice and voted for Trump will soon have to face consequences they never anticipated.

Some of the public is not taking this lying down. Rather, they are standing up for their rights. Let's hope the people continue to turn out in ever-greater numbers at marches, rallies, and congressional town hall meetings, including those set up by the citizenry itself.

Only you, the American people, one by one and by joining together, can answer these questions and keep these deregulating politicians in check.

Of course, one thing that has derailed so many of Trump's plans is that, as they say, he doesn't work well with others. He can't get his legislative agenda rolling because he isn't adept at the give-and-take of bargaining. You see, *Trump is a haunted man.* Years of cheating his allies and workers, escaping his misdeeds through bankruptcy, and the interventions of powerful friends now have to be covered up. Not releasing his tax returns was one strategy, and firing nosy prosecutors was another, but how long will his allies cover for him?

Firing FBI director Comey was a *temporary* dodge. The turmoil inside the Trump White House was much more intense than the media reported. The intrigue in a palace under perceived siege by political and law enforcement adversaries tends to turn inward before it bursts outward.

In the first half of 2017, Trump went on a purge. After assuring Preet Bharara, the influential New York City attorney, that he could keep his job, Trump decided to abruptly fire him in March. It seems Mr. Trump caught wind of an investigation pertaining to various ill-defined, at least publicly, inquiries, tried to contact Bharara to find out what was going on (in a clear breach of ethics), and, not receiving a response, dispatched him. In May Trump fired Comey, who then testified about it the following month before the Senate, flanked by several of his loyal FBI agents in the front seats of the hearing room.

Can you imagine, President Trump has even considered firing Robert S. Mueller III, the special counsel chosen by Deputy Attorney General Rod Rosenstein to lead the investigation into possible connections between Trump's electoral campaign and Russian operatives.

Who else will he sack? There is speculation within Republican ranks that Trump may fire dozens of inspectors general who investigate waste, fraud, and abuse committed by federal agencies to which they are attached. This would be unprecedented. Inspectors general (IGs) are nonpartisan, independent civil servants with traditional bipartisan support. They return around fourteen dollars to the taxpayer for every dollar they spend on their investigations.

Trump looks askance on such independence when it involves snooping around his cabinet and his agency appointees. Thus far, he is leaving open IG positions unfilled, and he intends to cut IG budgets. In another brazen move, the White House has begun to invoke executive privilege, insisting that executive branch agencies don't have to respond to congressional inquiries. A bizarre narcissism has taken over in the White House: get rid of anyone who can hold you to the rule of law, have cabinet members bow and scrape the floor with their obeisance at White House meetings as they surrender their independent judgment to a firing-prone president. What's next, statues and giant pictures of Trump looking down on his subjects around the country?

Trump would do well to study what happened when another president, Richard Nixon, hunkered down in 1973 and fired Archibald Cox, the special prosecutor appointed to investigate the Watergate scandal. Nixon's attorney general, Elliot Richardson, refused to fire Cox and resigned in protest, followed by the protest resignation of Deputy Attorney General William Ruckelshaus.

Nixon's firing of Cox generated a public firestorm of protests, with millions of telegrams and calls pouring into Congress from the American people. The momentum to impeach Nixon accelerated. He quit just before the House of Representatives was to vote in August 1974.

Firing a special counsel would not sit well with the American people, including increasing numbers of Republicans in Congress who would have preferred Mr. Pence by a large margin over Mr. Trump.

Fasten your seatbelts, the wild card in the White House is sure to get wilder as Donald Trump seriously tests our nation's rule of law and its checks and balances.

27.

Resist on the Barricades

Democratic Party loyalists are always complaining about the big-money fat cats behind the Republican Party's candidates and platform. Over the last few election cycles, the well-funded Democratic Party, as noted, has lost most state legislatures, governorships, the US Senate, the US House of Representatives, and the White House. Republican control of the Senate has led to control of the US Supreme Court. It is time for Democrats to up the ante big time!

Instead of complaining constantly about the Koch brothers' zillions pouring into the political system, the Democrats need to start asking what their own billionaire supporters are willing to do in the era of the authoritarian Trumpsters. Democrats have their fair share of affluent supporters, such as George Soros. Besides their routine campaign contributions, and expressing among themselves a sense of dread over the fate of our democracy, why aren't the pro-Democratic super-rich harnessing their resources to address the impending crisis they foresee, a crisis all the more likely to be provoked by the power-concentrating Trump regime?

It is not difficult to see what they could be doing besides backing an authentic agenda for the necessities of the people and society. The first step would be a strategy session to determine what civic and political resources could lead to the creation of new action institutions spurring thousands of energetic organizers at the grassroots level in preparation for the 2018 elections. A few billion dollars could be astutely distributed to achieve several long-overdue reforms and larger voter turnouts for Democratic challengers in areas currently beholden to unsavory corporate interests and rampant militarism—that could readily dispel the depression and discouragement that that is felt by liberal and conservative Americans alike. "Policy precedes message," says political writer Bill Curry. You have to have something to fight for before you begin organizing. As I've pointed out in my book *Unstoppable: The Emerging Left-Right Alliance to Dismantle the Corporate State*, many major policy reforms have long enjoyed substantial Left-Right support, and organizing such a consensus could spark an unstoppable political movement. Tens of millions of Americans of all political stripes back such causes as full Medicare for All, living wages, cracking down on corporate crime, eliminating crony capitalism, taking action on climate change and other critical environmental degradations, protecting the commons, civil liberties, civil rights, developing robust civic skills in primary and secondary education, rationalizing the tax systems, expanding people's access to justice, pulling back on costly militarism abroad, protecting consumers, and reforming criminal justice (to name just a few).

Civic leaders and the enlightened super-rich citizens who want to make change must come together at the national and community levels. Each has the critical assets to get things done. They know of each other but rarely gather to maximize their combined dedication. Financial support linked to know-how can produce needed action. My colleagues and I would be pleased to host such an initial gathering.

Making civil society stronger by expanding the good work of existing organizations and starting new ones to tackle unaddressed challenges is essential. From that heightened level of advocacy can spring forth a new politics with a fresh perspective and honest candidates for public office.

The progressive super-rich know each other. People like Nick Hanauer in Seattle, a champion for raising the minimum wage, and Michael Moritz in San Francisco, a generous patron of higher education, have shown the benefits of supporting important initiatives. Over 170 super-rich philanthropists have signed up for the Buffett-Gates pledge to give away at least half their wealth to "good works." Of the pledgers, there must be at least three dozen who grasp the difference between *charity* and *justice* and seek the latter both structurally and programmatically.

As for the leading civic action groups from Washington, DC, to the state and local level, it is not enough for them to see more money coming in after the November 2016 *selection* by the Electoral College. They must reach out and organize small gatherings of wealthy people who recoil at the thought of handing our burdened country to the next generation without trying to reverse course from the unraveling conditions domestically and the nation's destructive impact abroad. Financial support for larger and better civic infrastructure should be generous and ongoing.

The opportunities need not start from scratch. In April 2017, more than one hundred outdoor clothing and equipment businesses, such as Patagonia and REI, signed an open letter directed to the Trump regime's antagonism toward public lands. The message was very clear: hands off the federal lands and stop your efforts to sell them off to private companies. Taken together, these companies represent billions of dollars in annual sales. They could create a powerful lobbying organization, well beyond our present efforts, with majority public opinion support pushing for Congress to stop this sell-off of our commonwealth.

There is a group of high–net worth Americans, known as

Patriotic Millionaires (patrioticmillionaires.org), committed to building a more prosperous, stable, and inclusive nation. They can maximize their impact and enlarge their ranks by increasing funding for action groups all over the country.

Why all this hasn't yet scaled up to momentous proportions of resistance, recovery, and reform is more than a failure of imagination or a sign of collective defeatism and despair. It reflects the historical asymmetry between the forces of greed and tyranny, which, by definition, organize out of self-interest, and the forces of justice and democracy, which have to mobilize by *choice* for the public interest.

This difference in fervor can be overcome by an elevated sense of urgency, now and for posterity. Just reflect on the greatest advances in US history, when people organized to beat back and overcome the forces of darkness.

It has never been easier to challenge abuses of power than it is now, using modern technology and communication, with a pittance of available discretionary wealth on behalf of the great and crucial common good.

Not only should the progressive rich get in line behind the people who are organizing and marching, but Obama should join this resistance.

After eight grueling years in the White House, ex-president Barack Obama and his wife Michelle looked forward to a deserved, extended rest and vacation.

Since leaving office, the former self-styled community organizer has yachted with Tom Hanks and Hollywood mogul David Geffen, gone kitesurfing with billionaire Richard Branson at Necker Island in the British Virgin Islands, enjoyed the hospitality of designer Michael S. Smith in Southern California, turned up at the Mid-Pacific Country Club in Hawaii, and journeyed to Tetiaroa in French Polynesia, where, it is reported, he wants to write some of his memoir—part of a rumored $65 million book deal that includes Michelle's book.

In late April 2017, he enjoyed a $400,000 payday for an upcoming speech before a Wall Street firm, followed by an undisclosed fee for speaking in Milan, Italy, in May. The former first couple stayed at a "restored eight-hundred-year-old village" owned by John Phillips, a former public interest lawyer turned multimillionaire.

Meanwhile, back in Washington, DC, where the Obamas have purchased an $8 million home, Donald Trump was dismantling with cruel gusto as much of Obama's legacy as he could. Obama had spent his last months in office striving with his lawyers to Trump-proof his legacy.

There is a tradition that former presidents do not criticize their successors, just as new presidents do not go after their predecessors. There is an unwritten understanding that such behavior is beneath the dignity of the presidency and can lead to a barrage of destructive tit-for-tat accusations. But, with mad Donald Trump in the White House, the old rules of engagement are clearly no longer applicable.

Such traditions are going out the window with Trump's boorish, tweet-fueled mania putting the wrecking ball to just about every federal program and obligation serving the health, safety, and economic needs of the people. At the same time, Trump regularly attacks Obama for "the mess" he left him with and serves up other mostly fallacious jabs against his predecessor.

President Obama has spoken up very little, and needs to speak up more. Despite the tradition of former presidents passing the baton to the next generation of leaders in their party, today's Democratic Party is largely leaderless, leaving Obama still at center stage for much of the public. He understands that leadership gap, for, in addition to launching the Obama Foundation's presidential library in Chicago, he had his senior adviser Eric Schultz announce the major goal of "training and elevating a new generation of political leaders in America."

Still, while these new leaders are being located and trained, public figures like Obama need to step up and offer their support of all those people marching, rallying, and filling the usually empty seats at congressional town hall meetings around the country. After all, someone like Obama can get mass media coverage of such grassroots gatherings.

Barack Obama has always been very clever at telling us that he shares our sense of fair play. In his best-selling book, *The Audacity of Hope* (2006), then-senator Obama admitted, "I know that as a consequence of my fund-raising I became more like the wealthy donors I met, in the very particular sense that I spent more and more of my time above the fray, outside the world of immediate hunger, disappointment, fear, irrationality, and frequent hardship of the other 99 percent of the population—that is, the people that I'd entered public life to serve."

Well, it is never too late for Obama to translate these candid words into deeds. With his wealth and the wealth of a few other large donors he can assemble and organize watchdog groups in Washington, DC, to counter the corporate wish lists being presented to a very accommodating White House. Each group, with a modest $1 million annual budget, could fund ten determined public advocates dedicated to resisting what former Trump adviser Steve Bannon referred to as the "deconstruction of the administrative state." In real terms this of course means the dismantling of the Food and Drug Administration, the Federal Trade Commission, the Occupational Safety and Health Administration, the Environmental Protection Agency, sensible regulations for automobiles, railroads, and airlines, and so many other agencies and programs that protect Americans every day from reckless corporate violence.

With his resources and platform, Obama could spearhead additional organized civil actions against Trump's regime of corporatism, militarism, and racism. He could do that with ease, if he can resist the temptations of his plutocratic friends that he cautioned himself, and us, about in his book twelve years ago.

The resistance to Trump keeps growing. I talked earlier about the Occupy movement, how this earlier fight-back foundered, I believe, because it didn't translate its magnificent agenda of humane values, such as living wages, into proposed legislation and political power.

In the latter half of 2017 large marches in Washington, DC, and around the country called attention to the importance of focusing on the calamitous impacts of climate change and the need to take action to prevent environmental disaster. Those marches had impressive turnouts, but they would have been even more productive if they'd concentrated personally—in their slogans and signs—on the 535 politicians to whom we have given immense power to influence policies relating to those issues, for ill or for good.

I'm speaking of Congress.

Congress cannot be ignored or neglected simply because we know it to be a corporate Congress, or a gridlocked Congress, or a Congress that is so collectively delinquent, or perk and PAC addicted, or beholden to commercial interests, or self-serving through gerrymandered electoral districts where they, through their party's controlled state government, pick the voters to elect them.

There are probably one hundred good legislators on Capitol Hill. But many of these progressive elected officials fail to effectively network with citizen groups, or organize Left-Right coalitions back home into an unstoppable political force. Issues that invite such Left-Right consensus are numerous, and include raising the federal minimum wage, protecting civil liberties, tackling government waste and corruption, advancing solar energy, reforming the corporate tax system, initiating full Medicare for All (with free choice of doctor and hospital), reforming criminal justice, developing adequate housing, and cracking down on corporate crime and abuses against consumers, workers, and communities. Polls show big majorities behind these and other much-needed redirections and reforms.

All these improvements in the lives of all Americans have to go through Congress. Sure, some efforts can be partially achieved by self-help and state and local governments. But for a national, comprehensive change movement, Congress must be effectively and forcefully instructed to act in the public interest.

The big business lobbies haven't given up on Congress, have they? They're swarming over the senators and representatives to get the constitutional power we've given these lawmakers regularly deployed on behalf of the crassest, most avaricious and harmful demands of their business bosses.

The most successful "citizen lobbies" focused on Congress do not bother with major marches and demonstrations. Groups like the NRA and AIPAC focus, with laser-beam precision, on each member of Congress. They know their background, their strengths and weaknesses, their key advisers and friends back home, their physicians, their lawyers and accountants, the social clubs they belong to, even the kinds of hobbies and vacations they pursue. The NRA and AIPAC advocates get to personally know the lawmakers' staff, sources of their campaign contributions, their concerns about possible primary challengers, and what kinds of well-paid positions members of Congress seek after retirement or defeat.

With this face-to-face lobbying and ample campaign contributions, these groups have gotten their way in Congress to an amazing degree, given their relatively small numbers of ardent supporters.

Here is some advice to those on the march: get to know your state's senators and representatives personally and on your terms. Same for your state lawmakers, it's easier to do this with a comprehensive agenda of long-overdue reforms, which can give you broad-based Left-Right support in your state. Then issue a formal *Summons* (a template of which appears earlier in this book) for your senators and representatives to attend YOUR town hall meeting on YOUR agenda.

Every congressional district has about seven hundred thousand men, women, and children. Most districts have community colleges and/or universities. All have the necessary 1 percent of serious citizens working together to focus majority opinion directly on members of Congress. Often what is required is less than 1 percent—even, say, two thousand people per district, if they work collectively as volunteer congressional watchdogs for an average of five to ten hours a week and raise enough money for two full-time offices each with two or three staff members in each congressional district. Victories will soon emerge. The civic void will be replenished with civic energies. People with a sense of urgency and higher expectations of themselves can move knowledge to action.

The fruits of such efforts are numerous and immensely important to our country, our children, and their children, not to mention the rest of the world.

To expedite and increase the ratios of success, such congressional watchdog organizations require study, discussions, and some training sessions with easily available material in bookstores or on the Internet. Just consider how much serious time and effort millions of Americans put into hobbies all the time. Consider participating in this very important "civic hobby" to achieve a better life for the people with "liberty and justice for all." First the civic spirit and civic motivation must be gathered around these modest but critical citizen initiatives. Some would call this real patriotism—for justice and peace.

In late February 2017, cowed legislators came back to Congress following that month's recess, with its surprisingly raucous town hall meetings. Republicans in particular were shuddering. Instead of nearly empty auditoriums, where legislators' staff often outnumbers voters in attendance, meetings were packed with citizens determined to block the "take-away" agenda of the Trump Republicans.

It takes provocation for people to show up for face-to-face confrontations with their senators or representatives. So when out-of-touch politicians in safe electoral districts are seen attempting to take away people's health insurance, Social Security benefits, or other protections—watch out! As the *New York Times* reported at that time, "In the reddest of districts and the smallest of towns, a movement without a name has hurtled ahead of expectations."

Among those smug Republicans who escaped because they had not scheduled any town hall meetings, the response was dismissive, alleging the protestors were professional, paid disrupters. This charge only made the people—many of whom were attending their first political town hall meetings—angrier. In western New York, Susan and Tom Meara, both in their sixties, held a sign up for Republican congressman Tom Reed to see. It read, "I am not being paid to be here, but you are, Mr. Reed."

Once again, history repeats itself. As I describe in *Breaking Through Power: It's Easier Than We Think*, throughout American history it has taken at most 1 percent of the people becoming politically conscious and engaged to change conditions or policies, *so long as they represent a majority opinion.* My estimate is that, apart from the huge demonstrations on January 21, 2017—the day after Donald Trump's inauguration—less than two hundred thousand people, showing up at congressional town hall meetings or demonstrations, have changed the political atmosphere among 535 members of *your* Congress. It took just one week of a few riled-up voters expressing the "enough is enough" fury of many more voters, who for now are still a part of the "silent majority." Can it be sustained, enlarged, and reiterated daily? That is the question before us that only "We the People" can answer.

Listen to the easily reelected Republican senator from Iowa, Charles E. Grassley. After one spirited town-hall-style meeting, he said, "There's more of a consensus among Republicans now that you got to be more cautious what you're going to do." *You betcha!*

It was this uproar that stopped the repeal of Obamacare in its tracks. After supporting bills to repeal Obamacare dozens of times in the Republican-controlled House of Representatives during President Obama's two terms in office, Republican congressman Mo Brooks of Alabama told a local radio station, "I don't know if we're going to be able to repeal Obamacare now, because these folks who support Obamacare are very active. They're putting pressure on congressmen . . ." No kidding!

Every action prompts a reaction. Members of Congress, who do not like to face real people in real auditoriums between elections, responded by refusing to meet with those they represent or insisting on telephone "town hall meetings." Well, the response by the voters should be to announce their *own* town hall meetings with their *own* demands and reforms, at a publicly convenient location, formally summoning the congressional lawmakers to attend, listen, and respond.

Citizens need to expand and refine what they want from Congress, keep the focus very personally on each senator or representative, and strive to build a local Left-Right alliance on as many contemporary reforms as possible.

To better inform the politicians sent to Washington, citizens should tap the expertise of blue-collar and white-collar professionals alike in their communities. Remember, there is a vast reservoir of "We the People" who could join the efforts to press for a government of, by, and for the people.

We are a country that has far more problems than it deserves and far more solutions than it applies. This is largely due to the control of the many by the few, which creates a democracy gap filled by a plutocracy.

With President Trump displaying a revealing ignorance toward the role of governing, now is the time for the people to stand up and shape the future of their families and communities. We must demonstrate stamina and hold those in power accountable until they faithfully serve the interests of the people, and not a handful of corporate paymasters. All justice movements begin with a handful of people who multiply their numbers.

We must tell our lawmakers we are not going away, and that we will keep coming back with more and more of our fellow citizens, ever more informed and determined to achieve the good life with justice, peace, health, and opportunities. This kind of momentum really gets the attention and concern of members of Congress.

It's in *our* hands.